Financial Planning Foundations

Study Guide for 556

Revised February 2021

At the time of this printing, this publication contains the most accurate and complete information available. Due to the nature of licensing and credential examinations, subject matter may have been added to the actual examination that is not covered in this publication. Please contact help@bigdaddyu.com to ensure you are using the most current edition of this publication.

ISBN: 978-1-4951-1011-5

Printed by SAW Financial Group, L.L.C., in the United States of America.

www.bigdaddyu.com

Published in 2021 by SAW Financial Group, L.L.C. d.b.a. BigDaddy U.

Financial Planning Foundations
Study Guide For 556

Module 1

Overview of Financial Planning

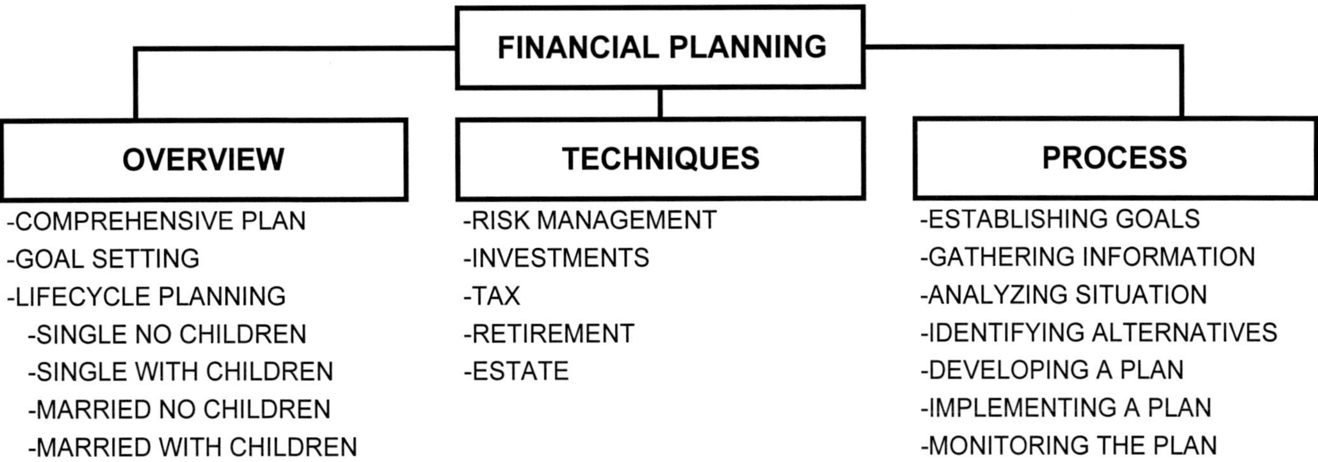
FINANCIAL PLANNING
OVERVIEW
TECHNIQUES
PROCESS
-COMPREHENSIVE PLAN
-GOAL SETTING
-LIFECYCLE PLANNING
-SINGLE NO CHILDREN
-SINGLE WITH CHILDREN
-MARRIED NO CHILDREN
-MARRIED WITH CHILDREN
-RISK MANAGEMENT
-INVESTMENTS
-TAX
-RETIREMENT
-ESTATE
-ESTABLISHING GOALS
-GATHERING INFORMATION
-ANALYZING SITUATION
-IDENTIFYING ALTERNATIVES
-DEVELOPING A PLAN
-IMPLEMENTING A PLAN
-MONITORING THE PLAN

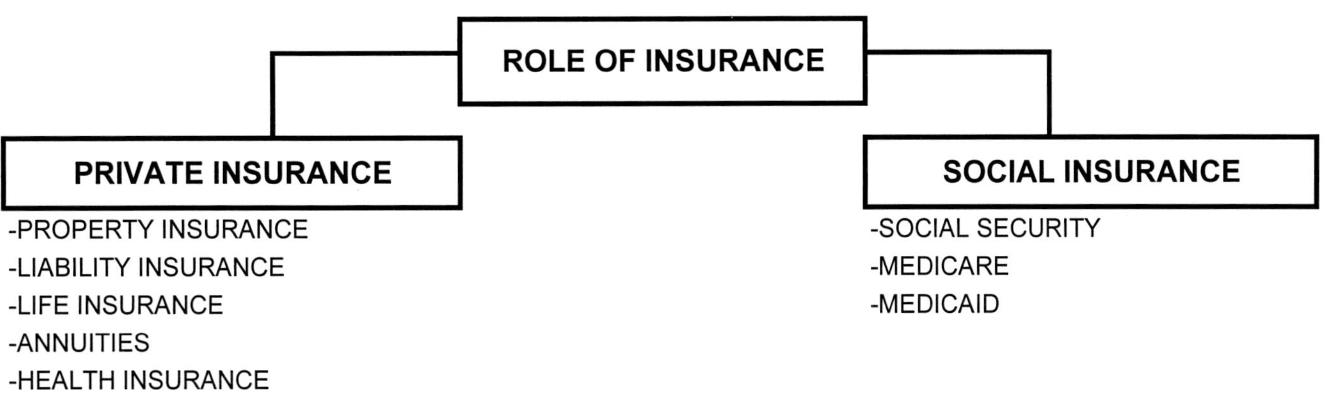
ROLE OF INSURANCE
PRIVATE INSURANCE
SOCIAL INSURANCE
-PROPERTY INSURANCE
-LIABILITY INSURANCE
-LIFE INSURANCE
-ANNUITIES
-HEALTH INSURANCE
-DISABILITY INSURANCE
-SOCIAL SECURITY
-MEDICARE
-MEDICAID

Overview of Financial Planning

Module 1
Chapter 1

1

1

Objectives

- Obj I: Financial Planning Overview
- Obj II: Financial Planning Techniques
- Obj III: Role of Insurance
- Obj IV: Financial Planning Process

2

2

Financial Planning Overview

Objective I

3

3

Financial Planning

- Financial planning is the process of developing a comprehensive financial plan to help achieve financial goals.
  - Laws and regulations may change impacting the timing of strategies.
- Many individuals attempt to satisfy their goals on an ad hoc basis.
  - Comprehensive financial plans attempt to avoid this problem.

4

4

Goals

- Financial goals are different among individuals and families and change over time.
  - Financial goals often create conflict because individuals have limited resources to satisfy their goals.
- Basic financial goals typically include:
  - Protecting against loss of income or wealth.
  - Providing for basic living expenses.
- Building wealth is a secondary goal.

5

5

Hierarchy of Financial Goals

Estate Planning

Building Wealth, Saving for Retirement, College

Protecting Against Loss of Income and Providing for Basic Living Expenses

6

6

Lifecycle Planning

Stage	Income/Wealth	Focus On
Single	Relatively low	Auto and health insurance
Single/Married no children	Increases; saving for major purchases	Auto, health, and property insurance
Single/Married with children	Wealth under pressure due to child care costs	Life, disability, emergency fund, and college funding

7

7

Lifecycle Planning

Stage	Income/Wealth	Focus On
Single/Married with children in college	Peak earning years; college costs offset wealth buildup	Retirement planning
Empty nester	Peak earning years continue; college costs finished	Retirement planning, long-term care insurance, and estate planning
Retired	Declines over time	Preserving wealth and estate planning

8

8

Practice

- Which one of the following is considered a basic financial goal that is generally satisfied by individuals before focusing on other financial goals?
  - A. Emergency fund establishment.
  - B. Creating an estate plan.
  - C. Saving for retirement.
  - ✓ D. Protecting against loss of income.

9

9

Practice

- Which one of the following represents characteristics of an empty nester?
  - A. Peak earnings, focus on retirement planning and estate planning.
  - B. Wealth declines, focus on long-term care insurance and wealth preservation.
  - C. Peak earnings, focus on college funding.
  - D. Income increases, focus on auto and health insurance.

10

10

Financial Planning Techniques

Objective II

11

11

Financial Planning Techniques

- A comprehensive plan includes the following planning techniques:
  - Risk management planning.
  - Investment planning.
  - Tax planning.
  - Retirement planning.
  - Estate planning.

12

12

Risk Management

- Risk management focuses on identifying and analyzing loss exposures.
  - Insurance is the primary method of risk management planning.
- Loss exposures that can be covered by insurance:
  - Loss of health.
  - Property and liability losses.
  - Death of the primary income source.

13

13

Risk Management

- Areas typically not handled by insurance:
  - Retirement loss exposure.
  - Unemployment loss exposure.
- Emergency savings plans may help mitigate these losses.
  - May not be sufficient to cover all losses.
  - Financial planner can review a client's cash flow statement to determine adequate emergency fund.

14

14

Savings and Investment Planning

- Savings and investment planning helps individuals determine appropriate types and amounts of investments.
  - Short-term investment horizons typically call for little or no risk of principal loss.
- Enormous variety of financial instruments and investment strategies.
  - Dollar cost averaging – investing the same amount every period, regardless of the movement of the stock market.

15

15

Tax Planning

- Tax planning focuses on minimizing federal, state, and local taxes.
  - Can ensure that more assets are available for retirement.
  - Can even reduce the cost of health insurance.
  - Can increase a family's standard of living.
- Investment decisions are often influenced by tax law.

16

16

Retirement Planning

- Retirement planning involves estimating resources necessary to meet retirement goals.
  - Most financial planners suggest individuals accumulate assets sufficient to replace 70-100% of preretirement income each year.
- Income can come from Social Security, retirement plans, and personal savings.
  - Social Security benefits were never designed to be the sole source of retirement income for retirees.

17

17

Estate Planning

- Estate planning assists with the transfer of property during a person's lifetime and at death.
  - Will – legal document outlining specifics of property distribution.
    - Does not eliminate need for formal estate planning.
  - Trust – legal document controlling property.
    - A special needs trust allows an individual to receive benefits from an inheritance without losing government assistance.

18

18

Practice

- Which one of the following statements is correct regarding personal financial planning techniques?
  - A. Social Security benefits were originally designed to be the sole source of income for retirees.
  - B. A formal Will eliminates the need for comprehensive estate planning.
  - C. For individuals, the number of investment strategies tends to be somewhat limited.
  - ✓ D. Short-term investment horizons typically call for little or no risk of principal loss.

19

19

Role of Insurance

Objective III

20

20

Types of Insurance

- Risk management uses a combination of private and social insurance.
- Private insurance:
  - Property and liability insurance.
  - Life insurance and annuities.
  - Health and disability insurance.
- Social insurance:
  - Social Security.
  - Medicare and Medicaid.
  - Unemployment insurance.

21

21

Property & Liability Insurance

- Provides protection for tangible assets.
  - An individual's home is typically the largest owned asset and largest loss exposure.
- Homeowners insurance protects the structure, as well as personal property.
  - Includes liability coverage in the package.
  - Flood exposures are not covered in the typical homeowners insurance policy.
- The state minimum limits of automobile liability coverage are usually not adequate for a family.

22

22

Life Insurance

- Life insurance is a cost-effective way to manage premature death.
  - Needs approach – estimate a family's financial needs to determine the appropriate amount of life insurance.
  - Human life value approach – estimates the present value of the income earner's financial contribution to the family.
    - Often used by courts to determine compensation for wage earner's family.

23

23

Life Insurance

- Insurance planning may involve the use of either temporary or permanent coverage.
  - Permanent insurance – provides for a cash surrender value.
  - Term insurance – temporary coverage with no cash value.
    - Provides greater death benefit per dollar of premium than permanent insurance.

24

24

Annuities

- Annuities provide income that an insured cannot outlive.
  - May be funded with annual premiums or a lump sum payment.
  - Offer tax-deferred growth.
  - May be immediate or deferred.

25

25

Health and Disability Insurance

- Employer-sponsored health plans are the major source of health insurance in the United States.
  - Include deductibles and co-insurance provisions.
- Disability insurance may be more important to a family than life insurance.
  - Disability policies don't cover most types of custodial care.
  - Custodial care is typically only covered by a long-term care policy.

26

26

Social Insurance

- Social Security provides benefits to retirees, as well as survivor and disability benefits.
  - Benefits are based on a worker's life-time earnings.
  - A retiree can begin collecting benefits as early as age 62.
  - By the year 2027, the full retirement age will be age 67.

27

27

Social Insurance

- Medicare provides medical coverage for eligible individuals.
  - Coverage generally begins at age 65.
- Medicaid provides state and federal funds to low-income persons for health and disability benefits.

28

28

Unemployment Insurance

- All state governments sponsor unemployment compensation programs.
  - Benefits are funded by a combination of employer-paid premiums, taxes, and government contributions.
  - Benefits are usually not paid for more than one year, unless poor economic conditions provide for additional benefits.
  - Benefits are limited and vary by state.

29

29

Practice

- Which one of the following statements is correct regarding the role of property and liability insurance in personal financial planning?
  - A. Homeowners insurance policies include liability exposure coverage as part of the package.
  - B. An individual's automobile is typically the largest asset and therefore the largest property expense.
  - C. Flood exposures are covered in the typical homeowners insurance policy.
  - D. Most families are able to adequately cover their auto liability exposures by purchasing the state limits of auto liability insurance.

30

30

Practice

- Which one of the following statements is correct regarding life insurance and annuity products?
  - A. One of the most effective ways a family can manage the premature death loss exposure is to purchase an annuity.
  - B. Term insurance provides a greater death benefit per dollar of premium than a cash value life insurance policy.
  - C. The human life value approach attempts to estimate a family's financial needs to determine the appropriate amount of life insurance.
  - D. Annuities are primarily designed to provide income in the case of a disability.

31

31

Practice

- Which one of the following statements is correct regarding health and disability insurance?
  - A. Most disability policies cover custodial care for older individuals.
  - B. Medicare is the major source of health insurance in the United States.
  - C. Disability insurance may be more important to a family than life insurance.
  - D. Employer-sponsored health plans usually waive any deductibles and coinsurance provisions.

32

32

Financial Planning Process

Objective IV

33

33

Financial Planning Process

- Steps of the financial planning process:
  - 1) Establishing and prioritizing goals.
  - 2) Gathering information.
  - 3) Analyzing the current situation.
  - 4) Identifying and evaluating alternatives.
  - 5) Developing a plan.
  - 6) Implementing the plan.
  - 7) Monitoring and revising the plan.

34

34

Financial Planning Process

- Establishing and Prioritizing Personal Financial Goals (Step 1):
  - Goals are identified.
  - Priorities for the goals are established.
- Gathering Information (Step 2):
  - Gathered information helps build the plan.
  - Financial statements are created.

35

35

Financial Planning Process

- Analyzing the Current Situation (Step 3):
  - Reviewing the current financial situation.
  - Determining how current status will impact desired goals.
- Identifying and Evaluating Alternatives (Step 4):
  - Determine appropriate insurance policies, investment vehicles, and retirement planning strategies.

36

36

Financial Planning Process

- Developing a Plan (Step 5):
  - Using the previous steps and information gathered, develop the plan.
- Implementing the Plan (Step 6):
  - To reach goals established by the client, the plan must be implemented.
  - Wills and other documents are created.

37

37

Financial Planning Process

- Monitoring and Revising the Plan (Step 7):
  - Plan must be monitored in order to ensure it stays on track to reach the client's goals.
  - Revise the plan as the client's goals change.

38

38

Practice

- Which one of the following occurs during the "Identify and Evaluate Alternatives" step of the financial planning process?
  - A. Creating a balance sheet and cash flow statement.
  - B. Drafting Wills and incapacity documents.
  - C. Revising the financial plan.
  - D. Determine appropriate insurance policies.

39

39

Practice

- Tom and Laura, a married couple, have a 2-year old daughter. They would like to begin saving for their daughter's education, so they had a financial plan created by a local personal financial planner. The plan indicated they need to save $10,000 per year to fund the education. Tom opened a Section 529 plan and deposited $10,000 yesterday. This is an example of which step of the financial planning process?
  - A. Establishing financial goals.
  - B. Monitoring the plan.
  - C. Analyzing the current situation.
  - D. Implementing the plan.

40

40

Module 2

Life Insurance and Annuities

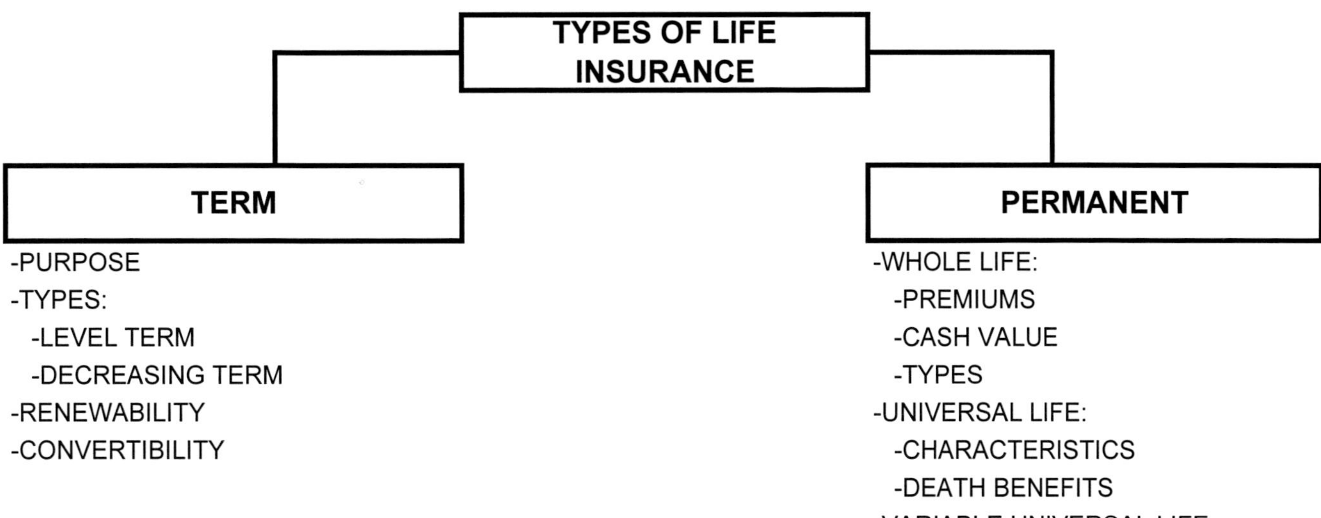

-PURPOSE
-TYPES:
  -LEVEL TERM
  -DECREASING TERM
-RENEWABILITY
-CONVERTIBILITY

-WHOLE LIFE:
  -PREMIUMS
  -CASH VALUE
  -TYPES
-UNIVERSAL LIFE:
  -CHARACTERISTICS
  -DEATH BENEFITS
-VARIABLE UNIVERSAL LIFE

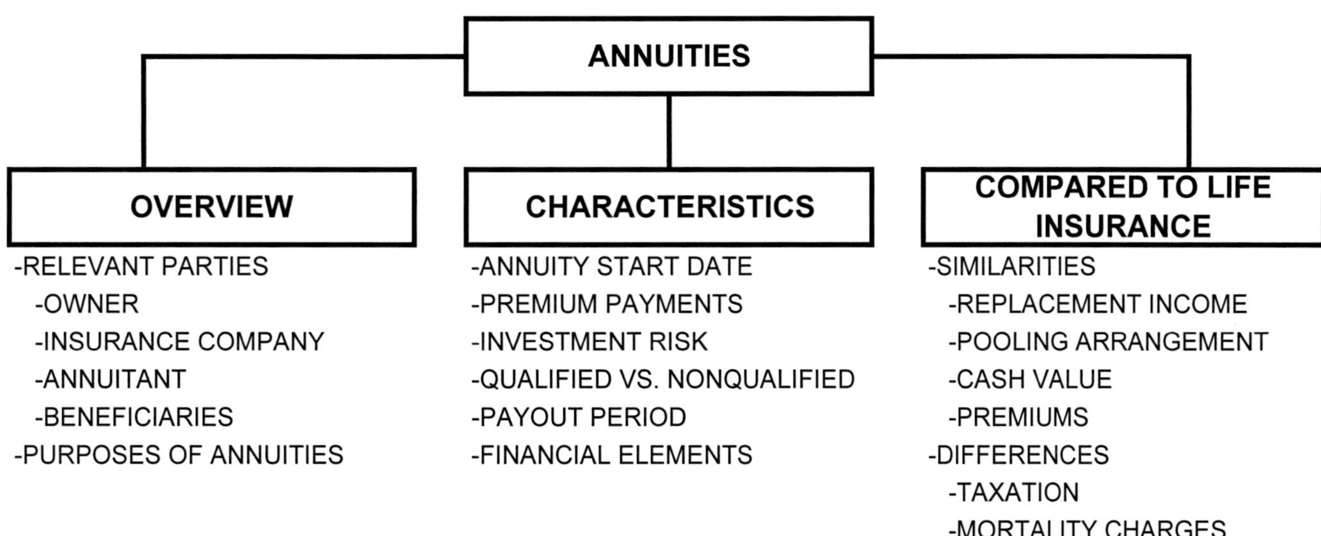

-RELEVANT PARTIES
  -OWNER
  -INSURANCE COMPANY
  -ANNUITANT
  -BENEFICIARIES
-PURPOSES OF ANNUITIES

-ANNUITY START DATE
-PREMIUM PAYMENTS
-INVESTMENT RISK
-QUALIFIED VS. NONQUALIFIED
-PAYOUT PERIOD
-FINANCIAL ELEMENTS

-SIMILARITIES
  -REPLACEMENT INCOME
  -POOLING ARRANGEMENT
  -CASH VALUE
  -PREMIUMS
-DIFFERENCES
  -TAXATION
  -MORTALITY CHARGES

Life Insurance and Annuities

Module 2
Chapter 2

1

1

Objectives

- Obj I: Term Insurance
- Obj II: Whole Life and Universal Life Insurance
- Obj III: Characteristics of Annuities
- Obj IV: Structured Settlements

2

2

Term Insurance

Objective I

3

3

Term Insurance

- Term insurance pays a death benefit only if the insured dies during the policy period.
  - Temporary protection.
  - No cash value.
- Period of coverage varies.
  - Coverage will end at a specific time or age.

4

4

Purpose of Term Life Insurance

- Term insurance meets temporary life insurance needs, including:
  - Term loan.
  - Mortgage.
  - College education costs.
  - Income replacement.
- Can also provide insurance coverage for younger individuals with insufficient cash flow to afford permanent protection.

5

5

Types of Term Life

- Types of term life insurance:
  - Level term – death benefit remains constant.
    - Term can run from 1-30 years.
  - Decreasing term – death benefit declines.
    - Mortgage protection or straight-line decreasing term life.
- The annual premium charged initially is higher for longer term rate guarantee periods than for shorter rate guarantee periods.

6

6

Renewability

- A renewability feature allows the insured to renew the policy without providing evidence of insurability.
  - Most level term insurance is guaranteed renewable for an additional period.
    - Insurance companies typically do not allow renewals beyond a certain age.
  - Premiums generally increase at renewal.
    - May be able to qualify for lower premium if successful in re-entry requirements.

7

7

Convertibility

- A convertibility provision allows the insured to convert the policy to a permanent policy without evidence of insurability.
  - Both level and decreasing term policies are typically convertible.
  - Allows insured to move into permanent policy when budget allows.

8

8

Practice

- Which one of the following statements is correct regarding level term life insurance?
  - A. If a convertibility provision is available, the policy can be converted to permanent insurance upon proof of insurability.
  - B. It offers a cash value from which a policyowner can make withdrawals or take a loan.
  - C. The annual premium charged initially is higher for longer term rate guarantee periods than for shorter rate guarantee periods.
  - D. The death benefit under the policy decreases by a level amount over the term of the policy.

9

9

Practice

- Which one of the following statements is correct regarding the renewability feature of a term policy?
  - A. This feature allows the insured to renew the policy for a period of time without providing evidence of insurability.
  - B. Renewable term insurance is satisfactory for an individual and the insurance company when coverage extends into higher ages.
  - C. The premiums will not increase if this feature is used to renew the policy.
  - D. The chief function of this feature is to protect the insurance company from adverse selection.

10

10

Whole Life and Universal Life Insurance

Objective II

11

11

Whole Life Insurance

- Whole life insurance offers permanent protection.
  - Assumes policy owner will pay premiums for the remainder of their life.
  - Premiums remain level throughout the premium-paying period.
  - Paid-up additions increase coverage.

12

12

Premiums

- Expenses, mortality, and interest are bundled.
  - Actuaries made assumptions on mortality, interest, and expenses.
- Premiums are fixed and level for policy duration.
  - Lowest level-premium rates for guaranteed permanent life insurance coverage.
- Excess premiums are charged in early years.
  - Excess is placed in a reserve, which is used to meet the death benefit obligation.

13

13

Cash Values

- Cash values in a whole life policy are guaranteed and increase as policy ages.
  - May be used as collateral.
  - Can be used for reduced, paid-up policy.
  - Typically not available for first two years of policy life.
  - Tax-deferred until distributed.
- Eventually cash value equals policy face value.
  - Policy terminates and cash value is distributed.

14

14

Amount at Risk

- Decreasing insurance costs.
  - The net amount at risk is constantly decreasing.
  - Cost of insurance decreases over time.
- Loan availability.
  - Cash value is available tax-free for loans.
  - Loans not required to be repaid.
  - Interest is charged.

15

15

Types of Whole Life Insurance

- Ordinary whole life – premiums assumed to be paid for whole life of insured.
  - Provides for the lowest level premium outlay of all whole life insurance policies.
- Limited pay – shorter duration of premiums.
  - Single premium policy – most expensive.
  - 10-pay – paid up over 10 years; various durations offered.
  - To age 65 – paid up at age 65; various ages offered.

16

16

Characteristics of Universal Life

- Universal life insurance is permanent insurance that offers flexible premiums and death benefits.
  - Death benefit may be reduced or even increased based on insurability.
  - Cash value must be sufficient to allow insurer to take monthly deductions.
- Universal life policies are well suited for those who need flexibility.

17

17

Characteristics of Universal Life

- Unlike whole life policies, universal life policies have unbundled mortality, expense, and interest charges.
  - Reported separately on annual statement.
- Expense charges include a monthly cost for maintaining and administering the policy.
  - Insurer may also deduct a premium expense charge, designed to enable insurer to recover premium taxes and business acquisition costs.

18

18

Characteristics of Universal Life

- Universal policies contain a cash value.
  - Grows tax-deferred.
  - Interest is credited regularly to the cash value.
  - Surrender charges are subtracted from the cash value if the policy is cashed in.
- Policy owners can withdraw funds from the cash value without incurring any indebtedness.
  - Withdrawals of the cash value are considered partial surrenders.

19

19

Characteristics of Universal Life

- An insurer may increase its cost of insurance rates and expense deductions from the current level to the amount specified in the contract.
  - Helps provide a safety net to insurer.
  - Mortality and expense risk is shifted to the policyholder.
- Insurers impose surrender charges on universal life policies.
  - Typically declines over time then disappears.

20

20

Death Benefits

- Universal life insurance policies usually offer three death benefit options:
  - Level death benefit (option A or option 1).
    - Amount at risk decreases each year.
  - Increasing death benefit (option B or option 2), based on increase in cash value.
    - Amount at risk remains constant.
  - Increasing death benefit (option C or option 3) based on premiums paid.

21

21

Variable Universal Life Insurance

- Variable universal life insurance policies contain sub-accounts that contain a portfolio of securities.
  - Incorporates premium flexibility of universal life coverage with the investment aspect of variable life coverage.
  - Accounts contain various asset classes, investment objectives, and risks.

22

22

Regulation

- VUL policies are subject to SEC regulation.
  - Agents selling VUL policies are required to hold a Series 6 or Series 7 securities registration.
  - Must also hold a license to sell life insurance.

23

23

Practice

- Gene applied for a universal life insurance policy and specified a death benefit equal to $200,000 plus the total premiums paid. Gene elected a death benefit option referred to as:
  - A. Option A.
  - B. Option B.
  - C. Option C.
  - D. Option D.

24

24

Practice

- Brittney is age 38 and a single mother with two teenage children. She is in good health and is concerned there will be insufficient funds to pay for their college education if she should die prematurely. Assuming she is insurable, she should purchase a(n):
  - A. Annual renewable term insurance policy.
  - B. 10-year term insurance policy.
  - C. Universal life insurance policy.
  - D. Variable life insurance policy.

25

25

Characteristics of Annuities

Objective III

26

26

Parties to the Contract

- Parties to an annuity contract:
  - Insurance company – issues annuity contract.
    - Has obligation to invest premium payments responsibly and credit earnings on interest to the funds placed in the annuity.
  - Owner – purchaser of the contract, who is responsible for premium payments.
  - Annuitant – person insured under the contract.
- The beneficiary is not a party to the contract.

27

27

Purposes of Annuities

- An annuity can provide for tax-efficient retirement savings.
  - During the accumulation period, an annuity accumulates a cash value.
  - If an annuity is owned by a person, the cash value growth is tax-deferred.
- A tax-deferred account can produce substantial additional accumulation.

28

28

Purposes of Annuities

- Annuities can provide income that cannot be outlived.
  - Some annuities offer minimum guarantees.
- Annuity payouts:
  - Straight life annuity – payments made for life.
  - Life annuity with period certain – guarantees payments for at least specified certain period.
  - Refund annuity – payments equal at least the premiums paid.

29

29

Purposes of Annuities

- Annuities offer a guaranteed death benefit if the annuitant dies during the accumulation period.
  - General death benefit is the greater of the net premiums paid or the cash value.
  - Other death benefit options are offered for an additional premium.

30

30

Immediate vs. Deferred Annuities

- Annuities can be immediate or deferred:
  - Immediate – systematic payments are made to annuitant starting right away.
    - Funded by a single premium.
  - Deferred – features an accumulation period.
    - Payments begin on annuity starting date.
    - Payments continue through the end of the annuitization period.

31

31

Single vs. Installment Premium Annuities

- Annuities can be funded with a single premium or installment premiums:
  - Single premium – only one premium payment.
  - Installment premiums – fixed or flexible.
    - Fixed premium – equal premium payments made in monthly or annual installments.
    - Flexible premium – owner may make premium payments at times other than premium billing dates.

32

32

Fixed vs. Variable Annuities

- Annuities can be fixed or variable:
  - Fixed annuity – insurer guarantees.
    - Insurer bears the investment risk.
    - Interest depends on whether annuity is a declared-rate annuity or an indexed annuity.
  - Variable annuity – lack of guarantees.
    - Considered to be securities.
    - Contract owner bears investment risk.
    - Regulated by the SEC.

33

33

Qualified vs. Nonqualified Annuities

- Annuities can be qualified or nonqualified.
  - Qualified annuities – used as funding vehicles in qualified plans.
    - If contributions to the plan are pre-tax, the annuity premiums are paid with pre-tax dollars.
  - Nonqualified annuities – not used in conjunction with qualified plan.
    - Premiums are nondeductible.
    - Distributions generally taxed LIFO basis.

34

34

Temporary vs. Life Annuities

- Annuities can be temporary or life.
  - Temporary – fixed period or fixed amount.
    - Fixed period – annuitant chooses period and insurer determines amount.
  - Life – payments for annuitant's life.
    - Straight life annuity.
    - Life annuity with period certain guarantee.
    - Refund annuity.
    - Joint and survivor annuity.

35

35

Practice

- Which one of the following statements is correct regarding the differences between a qualified and nonqualified annuity?
  - A. Qualified annuities can only be purchased by individuals age 55 and older, while nonqualified annuities can be purchased by individuals at any age.
  - B. Premiums for a nonqualified annuity may or may not be deductible, while premiums for a qualified annuity are always deductible.
  - C. Individuals who sell qualified annuities must register with the SEC, while individuals selling nonqualified annuities need not register.
  - D. Qualified annuities are typically subject to the required minimum distribution rules, while distributions from nonqualified annuities are not.

36

36

Practice

- Which one of the following statements is correct regarding types of annuities?
  - A. Indexed annuities are the most regulated of the three types of deferred annuities.
  - B. A variable annuity allows the annuity purchaser to participate in the investment of the annuity funds.
  - C. Immediate annuities typically accept additional premiums after the first premium has been paid.
  - D. A deferred annuity is an annuity that accepts pre-tax dollars from an employer-sponsored retirement program or IRA.

37

37

Structured Settlements

Objective IV

38

38

Overview

- Individuals who are seriously injured in an accident may receive a structured settlement.
  - Settlement may be large if punitive damages are included.
- Structured settlement annuities typically present low risk to the annuitant.
  - Issued by life insurance companies with solid ratings.

39

39

Tax Benefits

- Both lump-sum and structured settlements in compensation for personal physical injury or illness are not taxable.
  - Structured settlements also offer the benefit of nontaxable interest income.
  - Interest or investment income earned on a lump-sum settlement is taxable.

40

40

Advantages of Structured Settlements

- Advantages of a structured settlement:
  - Courts can require a structured settlement to guarantee regular income.
    - As opposed to large lump-sum award.
  - Insured receives the security of a regular stream of nontaxable benefits.
  - Victim is less likely to become ward of state.
  - Insurers may provide a larger overall settlement through the purchase of an annuity than through a lump-sum settlement.

41

41

Advantages of Structured Settlements

- Advantages of a structured settlement:
  - Attorneys who fail to recommend a structured settlement have been sued when their clients wasted lump-sum settlements.
  - If claimants are eligible for Medicare/Medicaid benefits, settlement may need to be reviewed and approved by the Centers for Medicare and Medicaid Services (CMS).

42

42

Substandard Annuity

- Substandard annuities are sometimes used with structured settlements.
  - Amount of premium required is based on the annuitant's age and individual life expectancy.
  - Applicant whose medical history indicated a reduced life expectancy would be charged a lower premium.
- Structured settlement broker provides the annuitant's medical history and other relevant data to various life insurers.

43

43

Practice

- Which one of the following statements is correct regarding structured settlements?
  - A. Because of a structured settlement, an injured party is more likely to become a ward of the state.
  - B. Courts cannot influence the method by which the structured settlement payment will be made.
  - C. The settlement places the claimant at risk because the payments are typically discontinued after 10-15 years have elapsed.
  - D. The settlement may need to be approved by the Centers for Medicare and Medicaid Services (CMS).

44

44

Module 3

Health and Disability Insurance

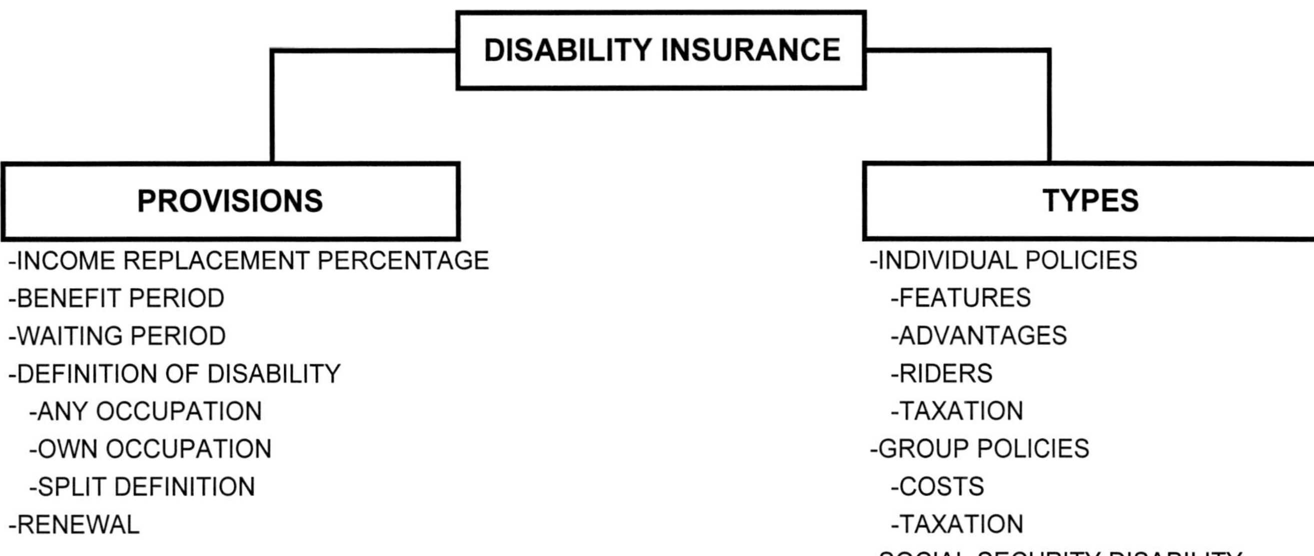
DISABILITY INSURANCE
PROVISIONS
-INCOME REPLACEMENT PERCENTAGE
-BENEFIT PERIOD
-WAITING PERIOD
-DEFINITION OF DISABILITY
-ANY OCCUPATION
-OWN OCCUPATION
-SPLIT DEFINITION
-RENEWAL
TYPES
-INDIVIDUAL POLICIES
-FEATURES
-ADVANTAGES
-RIDERS
-TAXATION
-GROUP POLICIES
-COSTS
-TAXATION
-SOCIAL SECURITY DISABILITY

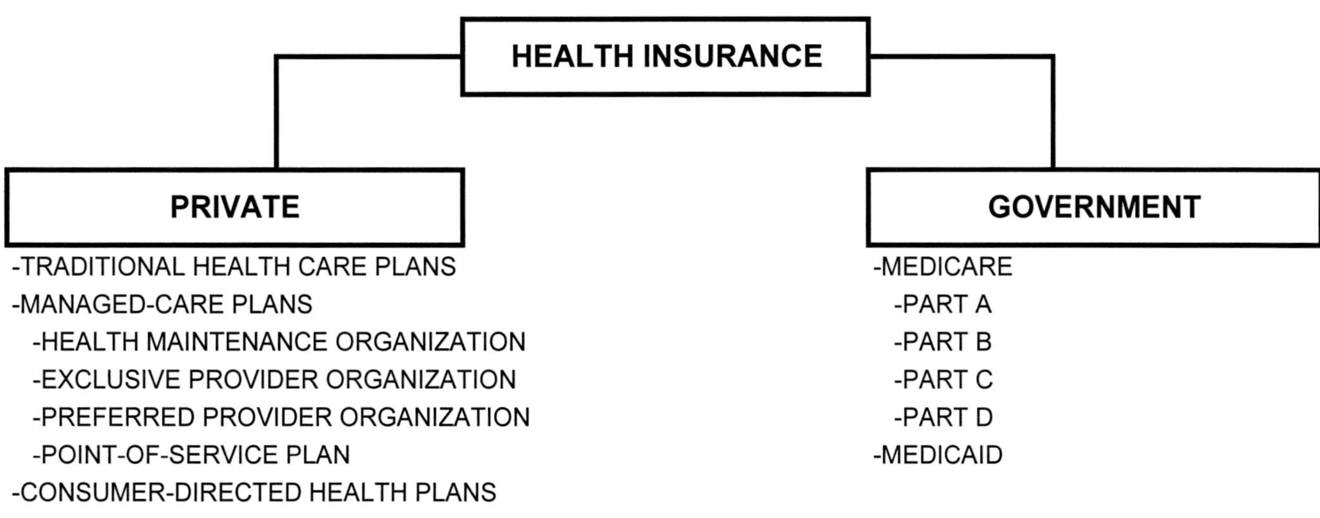
HEALTH INSURANCE
PRIVATE
-TRADITIONAL HEALTH CARE PLANS
-MANAGED-CARE PLANS
-HEALTH MAINTENANCE ORGANIZATION
-EXCLUSIVE PROVIDER ORGANIZATION
-PREFERRED PROVIDER ORGANIZATION
-POINT-OF-SERVICE PLAN
-CONSUMER-DIRECTED HEALTH PLANS
-HIGH DEDUCTIBLE PLAN
-HEALTH SAVINGS ACCOUNT
GOVERNMENT
-MEDICARE
-PART A
-PART B
-PART C
-PART D
-MEDICAID

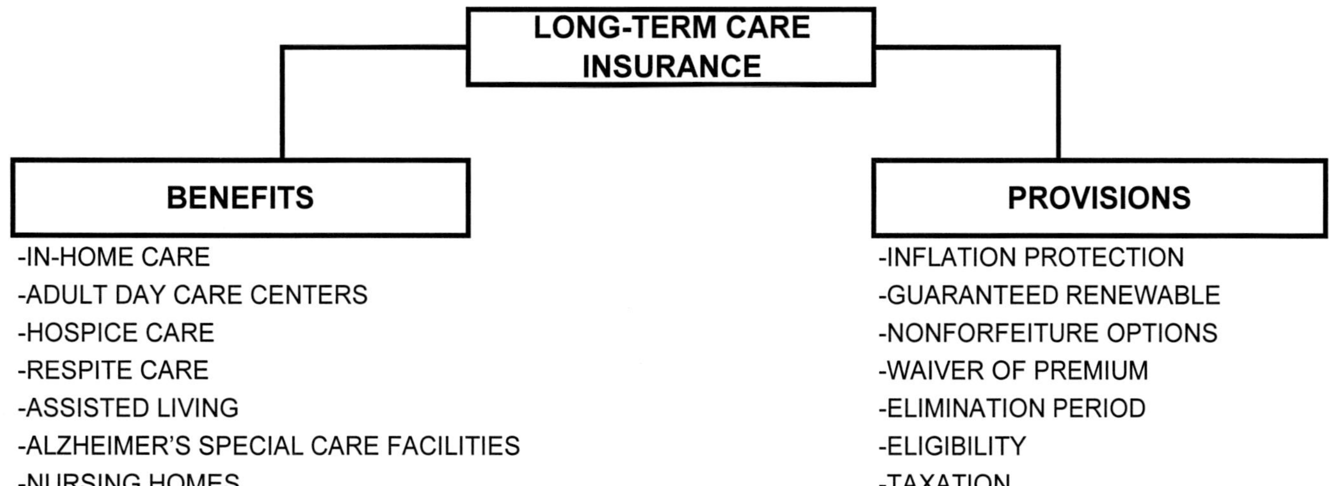
LONG-TERM CARE INSURANCE
BENEFITS
-IN-HOME CARE
-ADULT DAY CARE CENTERS
-HOSPICE CARE
-RESPITE CARE
-ASSISTED LIVING
-ALZHEIMER'S SPECIAL CARE FACILITIES
-NURSING HOMES
PROVISIONS
-INFLATION PROTECTION
-GUARANTEED RENEWABLE
-NONFORFEITURE OPTIONS
-WAIVER OF PREMIUM
-ELIMINATION PERIOD
-ELIGIBILITY
-TAXATION

Health and Disability Insurance

Module 3
Chapter 3

1

1

Objectives

- Obj I: Disability Insurance
- Obj II: Health Insurance
- Obj III: Medicare and Medicaid
- Obj IV: Long-Term Care Insurance

2

2

Disability Insurance

Objective I

3

3

Disability Loss Exposures

- Individuals may be injured outside the workplace or become seriously ill.
  - Although many families are concerned about premature death, disability may be more costly.
  - The probability of becoming disabled is higher than the chance of dying prematurely at all ages.
  - Most families have insufficient savings to sustain them for lengthy time periods.

4

4

Disability Loss Exposures

- Disability can lead to:
  - Loss of wages.
  - Medical expenses to be paid.
  - Costs for rehabilitation.
  - Education so a disabled person could qualify for another type of job.

5

5

Disability Loss Exposures

- Disability facts:
  - Roughly 25% of 20-year olds will experience a disability before they retire.
  - Fewer than 50% of Americans have savings to cover 3 months of living expenses.
  - It takes approximately 3-5 months for Social Security to review a disability application.
    - Only 34% of benefit claims are approved.
    - The average monthly disability benefit is slightly above the poverty line.

6

6

Disability Insurance Provisions

- Disability income insurance provides specified benefits in the event the insured suffers any illness causing the individual to lose income.
  - Some policies pay benefits for certain types of permanent injuries, such as blindness.
- The waiting period is the time that elapses after disability before benefits will be paid.
  - May be 7 days for short-term policy.
  - Shorter periods require higher premiums.

7

7

Disability Insurance Provisions

- A disability policy specifies a benefit period.
  - Ends when insured returns to work or reaches maximum benefit period.
  - Maximum benefit period is the longest period for which benefits will be paid to the insured.

8

8

Disability Insurance Provisions

- Definition of disability:
  - Any occupation – unable to perform the duties of any occupation.
    - Most restrictive (harsh) definition of disability for the insured.
  - Own occupation – unable to perform duties of specific occupation.
  - Split definition – "any" and "own" occupation concepts are combined.

9

9

Disability Insurance Provisions

- Renewal or continuance provisions:
  - Non-cancelable policy – cannot be canceled by the insurer, and the insurer cannot change benefits, rates, or other policy features.
  - Guaranteed renewable – cannot be canceled by insurer, but insurer can raise premiums.
  - Conditionally renewable – allows insurer to cancel policy if renewal conditions are not met.

10

10

Individual Disability Insurance

- Individual disability insurance generally provides monthly benefits to a disabled wage earner.
  - Reimburses wage earner's income during a period of total or partial disability.
  - Usually replaces up to 60%-80% of income.
  - Policies are available through insurance brokers and agents.

11

11

Individual Disability Insurance

- Advantages of individual policies over group:
  - No membership in a group is required.
  - Job change will not affect coverage.
  - Some individuals do not qualify for group coverage due to tenure requirements.
  - Group and Social Security benefits may not be adequate to cover income needs.
    - Individual policy may be used to supplement existing group coverage.

12

12

Individual Disability Insurance

- Riders (options) are available for purchase with an individual disability income insurance policy.
  - Premiums vary based on the payout.
- Individual disability income insurance is purchased using after-tax dollars.
  - Disability benefits received are not taxable to the insured.

13

13

Group Disability Insurance

- Group disability insurance is available through an employer or an association.
  - Economies of scale enable insurer to offer lower premiums to the insured.
  - Generally provides weekly or monthly benefits for a selected period.
- If premiums are paid by the employer, the premiums are deductible.
  - Benefits received are taxable to the insured.

14

14

Group Disability Insurance

- Employer may offer short- and long-term plans.
  - Short-term plans – usually offer weekly benefits, a short waiting period, and short maximum benefit period.
  - Long-term plan – may replace 60% of lost income and have longer waiting period.
    - Typically uses split definition of disability.

15

15

Group Disability Insurance

- Most long-term plans have coordination-of-benefits provision.
  - Defines how other plans' disability income benefits affect benefits paid by the LTD plan.
  - These provisions generally do not account for individual disability income insurance.
- Coverage terminates when employment ends, if employer fails to pay premiums, or if policy is terminated by employer or association.

16

16

Social Security Disability

- The requirements for Social Security disability are very strict.
  - Provides monthly cash benefits to disabled.
- Definition of disability – unable to engage in any substantial gainful activity because of a physical or mental impairment.
  - Similar to "any occupation" of disability.
  - Impairment must be expected to last for at least 12 months or result in death.

17

17

Social Security Disability

- Monthly benefit is generally equal to PIA.
  - Payment of benefits requires a five-month waiting period.
  - Additional benefits may be available for eligible dependents.
  - Benefits may be reduced by workers compensation benefits, or federal or state disability benefits.
- Benefits are subject to Family Maximum Benefit.

18

18

Practice

- Which one of the following statements is correct regarding individual disability insurance policies?
  - A. Membership in a group is required to purchase coverage.
  - B. Disability benefits received by the insured are income tax-free.
  - C. Benefits are typically inferior to those offered in group policies.
  - D. These policies typically replace 30-40% of an insured's income.

19

19

Practice

- David works for a package delivery company. He injured his leg, preventing him from performing his regular job duties. However, he can perform alternate duties for the company, such as entering delivery requests into the company's computer system. Under his disability insurance plan, David is eligible to receive full benefits for the first 9 months that he is performing the alternate duties. After the 9-month period, if David is not able to resume his regular job of delivering packages, the disability benefits cease. This policy uses which definition of disability?
  - A. Own occupation.
  - B. Any occupation.
  - C. Split definition.
  - D. Modified own occupation.

20

20

Health Insurance

Objective II

21

21

Health Insurance

- Most Americans participate in group healthcare plans.
- Types of health insurance plans offered:
  - Employer self-insured plans.
  - Traditional health insurance plans.
  - Managed-care plans.
  - Consumer-directed health plans.

22

22

Traditional Health Insurance Plans

- Traditional health insurance plans insure families through indemnity coverage.
  - Allows patients to choose their own healthcare provider.
  - Reimburses the patient or provider at a certain percentage for services, after the deductible is paid.
- Blue Cross and Blue Shield plans provide basic coverage and major medical coverage.

23

23

Traditional Health Insurance Plans

- Basic medical expense coverage pays for routine healthcare expenses.
  - Hospital, surgical, physician.
- Major medical coverage provides broader coverage and catastrophe coverage.
  - Hospital, physician, drugs, medical equipment, diagnostic tests, X-rays.
  - Typically have deductibles.

24

24

Managed-Care Plans

- Managed-care plans manage the quality of their members' care and control healthcare costs.
  - Insured receives significant premium savings and reduced out-of-pocket costs.
  - Plans may have reduced flexibility.
- Managed-care plans differ from traditional plans by providing negotiated benefits and fees with a network of healthcare providers.

25

25

Managed-Care Plans

- Types of managed-care plans:
  - Health maintenance organization – contracts with providers to offer various services.
    - Features gatekeeper physician.
    - Providers are paid a monthly fee.
  - Exclusive provider organization – charges insurers an access fee for use of the network.
    - Negotiates with healthcare providers to set fees for guaranteed service levels.
    - Providers only paid for services rendered.

26

26

Managed-Care Plans

- Types of managed-care plans:
  - Preferred provider organization – members may choose any provider.
    - One of the most expensive forms of managed-care plans.
    - Network physicians are less expensive and have lower deductibles.
    - Gatekeeper physician not required.
  - Point-of-service plan – member must choose primary care physician within the network.

27

27

Consumer-Directed Health Plans

- Consumer-directed health plans provide consumers with access to care.
  - Premiums are generally lower due to high deductibles.
  - Deductibles are typically not required for preventive care.
  - Often incorporate a network of health care professionals.

28

28

Consumer-Directed Health Plans

- Consumer-directed plans typically include:
  - High-deductible medical coverage, with preventive care not charged against the deductible.
  - Health savings account (HSA) or a health reimbursement arrangement (HRA).
  - Access to informational tools for making informed healthcare decisions.

29

29

Affordable Care Act

- Affordable Care Act was intended to reform private health insurance industry.
  - Insurers cannot decline insurance for people with pre-existing conditions.
  - Children up to age 26 can remain on parent's health insurance plan.
  - Annual/lifetime dollar limits are not permitted on essential benefits.
  - Insurers may be required to pay for certain preventative services.

30

30

Practice

- Which one of the following statements is correct regarding PPOs?
  - A. PPOs are one of the most cost-effective forms of managed-care plans.
  - B. The majority of PPOs provide benefits for a wider selection of medical procedures if non-network providers are used.
  - C. Employees may see a specialist without a referral by a gatekeeper physician.
  - D. Members can choose any physician, but network physicians are more expensive and have higher deductibles.

31

31

Practice

- Which one of the following managed-care plans typically features a gatekeeper physician and provides all the care needed by its members in exchange for a fixed fee?
  - A. Health maintenance organization.
  - B. Point-of-service plan.
  - C. Exclusive provider organization.
  - D. Preferred provider organization.

32

32

Medicare and Medicaid

Objective III

33

33

Medicare

- Medicare is part of the Old Age and Survivors Disability Health Insurance (OASDHI) program.
  - Social insurance program covering medical expenses of most individuals 65 and older.
  - Medicare benefits can begin at age 65, even if Social Security benefits deferred to later age.
- Medicare benefit programs:
  - Parts A and B – Original Medicare.
  - Part C – Medicare Advantage.
  - Part D – Prescription Drug Coverage.

34

34

Medicare

- In order to be eligible for Medicare, individual:
  - Must work at least 10 years in Medicare-covered employment.
  - Can be either a U.S. citizen, or a non-citizen who is a permanent resident of the U.S.
  - Generally must be age 65 or older.

35

35

Medicare Part A

- Medicare Part A provides hospital insurance coverage.
  - Offers some skilled nursing care and hospice care.
  - Largely financed through payroll taxes.
  - Helps pay for in-hospital services.
  - Most people receive coverage at age 65.

36

36

Medicare Part B

- Medicare Part B provides medical insurance coverage.
  - Offers physical therapy and some home healthcare.
  - Largely financed through a monthly premium paid by beneficiaries.
  - Beneficiary can enroll in Part B any time during a 7-month period that begins 3 months before turning age 65.

37

37

Medicare Part C

- Medicare Advantage (Part C) plans provide benefits in addition to basic Medicare.
  - Beneficiaries can choose to be covered under a managed care plan.
  - Benefits offered must at least equal Medicare Part A and B benefits.
  - Financed by premiums paid by the insured.
  - Some plans limit members' annual out-of-pocket spending to protect against catastrophic medical costs.

38

38

Medicare Part D

- Medicare Part D is a program through which the government subsidizes prescription drugs.
  - Beneficiaries may sign up for Part D upon first becoming eligible for Medicare.
- Beneficiaries generally pay monthly premium and part of the prescription cost.
  - Beneficiaries with limited resources may be eligible for extra assistance and may not have to pay a premium.

39

39

Medicare Supplement Insurance

- Medicare Supplemental Insurance is designed to fill the gaps in coverage associated with Medicare Part A and Part B.
  - Medigap insurance.
  - Does not include coverage for costs under Parts C and D of Medicare.
- Individuals purchasing Medicare Part C do not need to purchase Medicare Supplemental Insurance.

40

40

Medicaid

- Medicaid is a means-tested federal-state program.
  - Covers medical expenses of low-income persons.
  - Benefits and eligibility vary by state.
  - Federal government pays almost 60% of all Medicaid expenses.
  - Each state administers its own program.
- Largest group of recipients is children.
  - Disabled children may be eligible, even if their parents are not.

41

41

Practice

- Which one of the following statements is correct regarding Medicare Part C plans?
  - A. They are financed through payroll taxes.
  - B. They allow a retiree to qualify for coverage prior to age 65.
  - C. They may offer more coverage than Part A and Part B, such as dental coverage.
  - D. They are typically less expensive than coverage under Part A and Part B combined.

42

42

Practice

- Which one of the following statements is correct regarding Medicaid?
  - A. The largest group of Medicaid recipients is persons with disabilities.
  - B. Disabled children may be eligible, even if their parents are not.
  - C. The program is funded exclusively by the various states.
  - D. Individuals with 10 years of work experience are automatically eligible upon attaining age 65.

43

43

Long-Term Care Insurance

Objective IV

44

44

Long-Term Care

- LTC insurance policies typically cover skilled nursing home care, intermediate nursing care, and custodial care.
  - Medicare limits skilled nursing care coverage to 100 days and doesn't cover custodial care.
- Under most policies, insured qualifies for benefits when:
  - Unable to perform a specified number of ADLs listed in the LTC policy.
  - Insured is cognitively impaired.

45

45

Coverage Basics

- Factors to consider when comparing policies:
  - Benefit period – length of time after filing a claim that the insurer will pay for care.
  - Daily benefit – maximum dollar or percentage amount the insurer will pay for care daily.
  - Elimination period or deductible – length of time and the amount of money an insured must pay.
  - Inflation protection – amount by which benefits will increase each year.

46

46

Benefits Provided

- Majority of policies sold today typically cover:
  - In-home care.
  - Adult day care centers.
  - Hospice care.
  - Respite care.
  - Assisted living.
  - Alzheimer's special care facilities.
  - Nursing homes.

47

47

Benefits Excluded

- LTC policies have these typical exclusions:
  - Services provided by a family member.
    - Some policies pay daily benefit regardless.
  - Services for which no charge is made.
  - Services provided outside the U.S.
    - Some policies have international benefits.
  - Services resulting from a suicide attempt.

48

48

Benefits Excluded

- LTC policies have these typical exclusions:
  - Services for alcoholism or drug addiction.
  - Treatment provided in a government facility.
  - Services for which benefits are available under Medicare.

49

49

Policy Provisions

- Policy provisions include:
  - Inflation protection – daily benefit is increased by a percentage each year.
  - Guaranteed Renewability – insurer cannot cancel the policy but can increase premiums.
  - Nonforfeiture options – if policy cancelled, premiums can be returned or used to:
    - Purchase same benefit for shorter period.
    - Reduce benefit for existing benefit period.

50

50

Policy Provisions

- Policy provisions include:
  - Waiver of Premium – disabled insured can stop paying premiums while receiving benefits.
  - Elimination Period – longer elimination period can substantially reduce the annual premium.
- Age is the primary factor in determining the cost of a long-term care policy.

51

51

Tax Treatment

- If the LTC policy is qualified:
  - Premiums are deductible.
    - Subject to age limit and AGI reduction.
  - LTC benefits received are tax-free.
- Some states allow premium deductions on state income tax returns, regardless of whether policy is qualified.
- Employees in group plans generally can pay premiums with pretax dollars.

52

52

Practice

- Which one of the following represents a common trigger that determines eligibility for benefits under a long-term care policy?
  - A. Substantial decline in standard of living due to excessive medical expenses.
  - B. Inability to perform two or more activities of daily living.
  - C. Inability to engage in any substantial gainful activity for at least one year.
  - D. Attainment of age 65 and completion of 10-years of work experience.

53

53

Module 4

Fundamentals of Investments

RETURN AND RISK

RETURN

- -CAPITAL APPRECIATION
  - -GOLD, SILVER
  - -ANTIQUES, ART
- -INVESTMENT INCOME
  - -CASH AND CASH EQUIVALENTS
- -APPRECIATION AND INCOME
  - -STOCKS
  - -BONDS
  - -RENTAL REAL ESTATE
- -MEASURING RATE OF RETURN

RISK

- -SYSTEMATIC RISK
  - -PURCHASING POWER
  - -INTEREST RATE
  - -MARKET
  - -EXCHANGE RATE
- -UNSYSTEMATIC RISK
  - -FINANCIAL
  - -BUSINESS
  - -LIQUIDITY

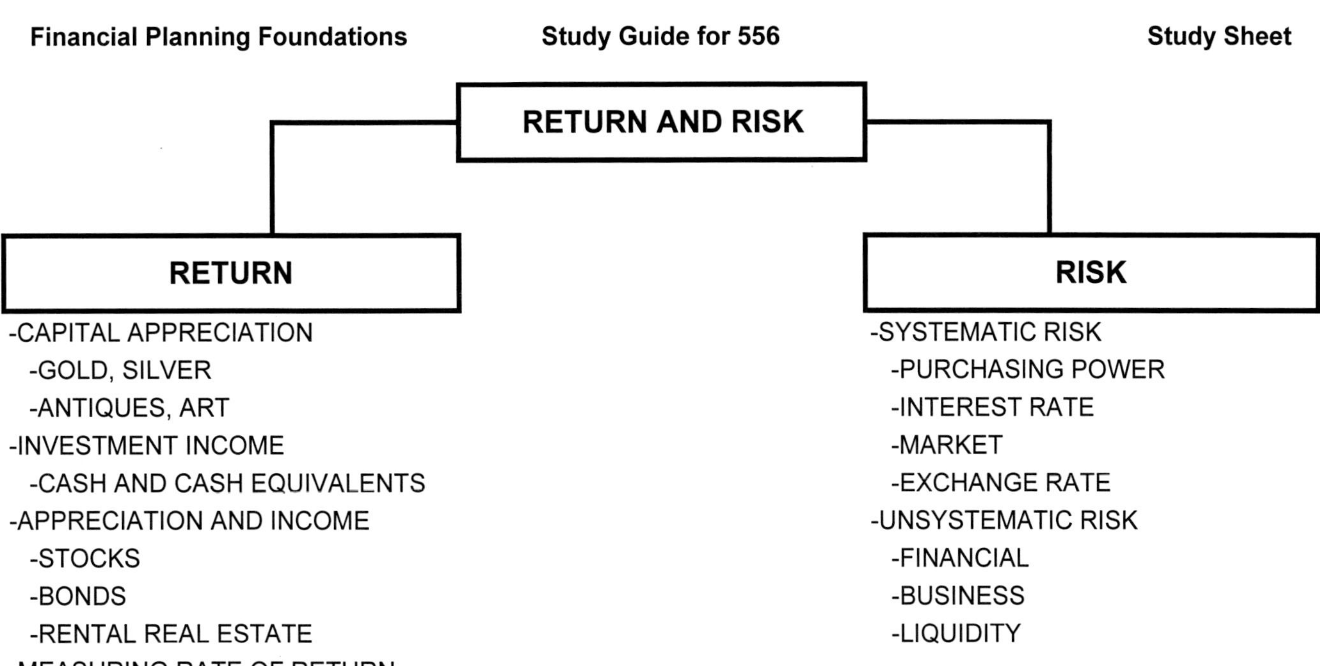

INVESTMENT STRATEGIES

DOLLAR COST AVERAGING

- -PERIODIC PURCHASE
- -MARKET DECLINES
- -LADDERING

REINVESTMENT

- -DIVIDEND REINVESTMENT
- -COMPOUND EARNINGS
- -MUTUAL FUNDS
- -CHARACTERISTICS OF DRIPs

ASSET ALLOCATION

- -REDUCES RISK
- -ASSET CATEGORIES
- -ADJUSTED BASED ON AGE

TYPES OF INVESTMENTS

BONDS

- -TREASURY SECURITIES
- -MUNICIPAL BONDS
- -CORPORATE BONDS
- -RISKS

STOCKS

- -COMMON STOCK
  - -GROWTH STOCK
  - -VALUE STOCK
  - -CYCLICAL STOCK
  - -DEFENSIVE STOCK
  - -INCOME STOCK
  - -PENNY STOCK
- -RISKS

MUTUAL FUNDS

- -OPEN END
- -CLOSED END
- -TYPES OF FUNDS
  - -MONEY MARKET
  - -BOND
  - -STOCK
  - -BLENDED

Fundamentals of Investments

Module 4
Chapter 4

1

1

Objectives

- Obj I: Risk and Return Concepts
- Obj II: Types of Investment Risk
- Obj III: Investment Strategies
- Obj IV: Types of Investments

2

2

Risk and Return Concepts

Objective I

3

3

Investment Return

- Investment return is the profit or loss earned on an investment.
  - Usually expressed as annual percentage rate.
- Two components of total return:
  - Capital appreciation – change in value of principal.
  - Investment income – interest, dividends, and rental income.

4

4

Capital Appreciation

- Capital appreciation is the amount an asset's selling price exceeds its purchase price.
  - Capital gain tax rate is typically lower than ordinary tax rate.
- Capital gain can be realized or unrealized.
  - Unrealized – when asset has experienced a gain but has not been sold.
  - Realized – when asset is sold at a gain.

5

5

Investment Income

- Investment income is periodic income paid to the investment owner.
  - Interest, dividends, or rental income.
  - Value stocks tend to pay high dividends, resulting in a large portion of the return being comprised of investment income.
- Investment income is typically taxed at ordinary rates.

6

6

Asset Selection

- Entire return based on capital appreciation:
  - Gold, silver.
  - Antiques, fine art.
- Entire return based on investment income:
  - Checking, savings accounts, CDs.
- Return based on appreciation and income:
  - Stocks – primarily offer capital appreciation.
  - Bonds – primarily offer investment income.
  - Rental real estate.

7

7

Measuring Rate of Return

- To compute an investment's rate of return, the total return is divided by the principal.
  - Rate of return is usually expressed as an annual percentage.
  - Average annual rate of return is calculated by dividing total return by the number of years investment is held.
- The compound annual rate of return is a better measure of total return than the rate of return.
  - Considers the return on invested income.

8

8

Trade-Off Between Risk and Return

- As the amount of risk increases, the return the average investor requires also increases.
  - The mix of high-risk and low-risk investments changes as goals change.
  - For long-term goals such as retirement or college, higher-risk investments are preferred.
  - As the time horizon shortens, investment risk can be reduced by shifting assets from high-risk assets into lower-risk assets.

9

9

Practice

- An investor wanting to purchase an investment that focuses on capital appreciation with minimal investment income should purchase:
  - A. Silver.
  - B. Common stock.
  - C. Government bond.
  - D. Fine art.

10

10

Practice

- Mildred purchased common stock for $1,000. She received the following dividends:
  - Year 1 - $50
  - Year 2 - $55
  - Year 3 - $60
- At the end of Year 3, she sold the stock for $1,100. What is her average annual rate of return on the stock?
  - A. 5.51%
  - B. 7.42%
  - C. 8.83%
  - D. 9.11%

11

265 x 100 / 1000   26.5 / 3   8.8

11

Types of Investment Risk

Objective II

12

12

Systematic Risk

- Systematic risk is a risk common to all securities, such as a downturn in the economy.
  - Systematic risk cannot be diversified.
- Systematic risk includes:
  - Purchasing power (inflation) risk.
  - Interest rate risk.
  - Market risk.
  - Exchange rate risk.

13

13

Inflation Risk

- Inflation risk is uncertainty caused by changes in the overall price level of goods and services.
  - CPI measures the rate of inflation.
  - What matters most to investors is what inflation will be over the life of the investment.
- Assets that emphasize capital appreciation are less susceptible to inflation risk but still possess some inflation risk.
  - Include stocks and real estate.

14

14

Interest Rate Risk

- Interest rate risk is the risk of loss caused by changes in the level of interest rates.
  - Risk is most associated with bonds.
  - Common stocks are less susceptible to interest rate risk than bonds.
- If interest rates rise, the price of older bonds will fall relative to the price of newer bonds.
  - Newly issued bonds will carry higher interest rates, but bonds issued in the past will still be paying the original, lower rate.

15

15

Market Risk

- Market risk is the uncertainty about an investment's future value because of potential changes in the market.
  - Most commonly applies to stocks.
- Market risk also applies to investments other than stocks and bonds.
  - Real estate market can experience a decline.

16

16

Exchange Rate Risk

- Exchange rate risk is uncertainty because of changes in the exchange rate between currencies.
  - Investors in one country can purchase securities issued by businesses in most other countries.
  - Exchange rate risk is most prevalent in an investment based on a currency other than that of the investor's home country.

17

17

Unsystematic Risk

- Unsystematic risk, or specific risk, is specific to a particular investment.
  - Can be reduced through diversification.
- Unsystematic risk includes:
  - Financial risk.
  - Business risk.
  - Liquidity risk.
- The goal of diversification is to achieve maximum investment return while minimizing investment risk.

18

18

Financial Risk

- Financial risk is the risk that a company has taken on too much debt.
  - Financial risk affects the value of an investment in a company's stocks and bonds.
- Higher levels of debt also increase bankruptcy risk for a company.

19

19

Business Risk

- Business risk is risk that is inherent in the operation of a particular organization.
  - Increases in overhead costs.
  - High operating expenses.
  - Changes in demand for products or services.
  - Inadequately financed liability and property losses.
  - Unfavorable changes in the economic, political, and social environments.

20

20

Liquidity Risk

- Liquidity is the ability to convert an investment into cash rapidly at an acceptable cost.
  - Cash is completely liquid and marketable.
- Investments having more liquidity risk generally have a lower market price than they otherwise would.
  - Reduced valuation compensates the investor for the liquidity risk by creating a higher expected return.

21

21

Practice

- Financial risk is uncertainty about the future investment returns of a given asset because of:
  - A. Changes in the level of interest rates.
  - B. The amount of debt of the organization on which the investment is based.
  - C. The lack of liquid assets owned by an organization.
  - D. Changes in demand for the company's product or services.

22

22

Practice

- Exchange rate risk is most prevalent in an investment:
  - A. Based on a currency other than that of the investor's home country.
  - B. That fluctuates wildly in conjunction with market fluctuations.
  - C. In which the organization cannot control outside factors.
  - D. Based on a company that is highly leveraged.

23

23

Investment Strategies

Objective III

24

24

Investment Strategies

- Investment strategies are long-term plans.
  - Investment tactics are short-term.
- Strategies include:
  - Dollar cost averaging.
  - Reinvestment.
  - Asset allocation.
- Most important factors in determining appropriate strategy are expected time horizon and anticipated need for funds.

25

25

Dollar Cost Averaging

- With dollar cost averaging, an investor makes small, periodic investment purchases.
  - Investors can reduce their risk of purchasing investments when prices are relatively high.
- Dollar cost averaging involves the purchase of more shares as market prices decline.

26

26

Dollar Cost Averaging

Month	Investment	Share Price	Shares
January	$1,000	$10	100
February	$1,000	$20	50
March	$1,000	$40	25
April	$1,000	$50	20
Total	**$4,000**	**$120**	**195**

- Average cost per share = $4,000 ÷ 195 = $20.51
- Average price per share = $120 ÷ 4 = $30

27

27

Dollar Cost Averaging

- Laddering is a dollar cost averaging strategy used for bonds.
  - Involves staggering the maturity dates and reinvesting the maturing investments at longer maturities.
- Since laddering involves the purchase of longer-term bonds, it increases the interest rate risk of a portfolio.

28

28

Reinvestment

- Reinvestment refers to using investment returns to make additional investments.
  - Investors can increase the returns from their investment portfolios.
  - Reinvested funds compound the earning by providing returns on the returns.
- Mutual funds usually offer an automatic dividend reinvestment option (DRIP).
  - Many publicly traded corporations offer DRIPs.

29

29

Reinvestment

- Characteristics of DRIPs:
  - Must own at least one share to participate.
  - Shares purchased are often provided without assessing any fees or commissions.
  - Account owners must pay federal income tax on the total amount of dividends reinvested.
  - Reduce investors' ability to increase portfolio diversification.

30

30

Asset Allocation

- Asset allocation allows an investor to tailor a portfolio to his or her own risk tolerance.
  - Enables investors to reduce investment risk substantially for a small sacrifice of return.
- Primary purpose is to ensure the risk of the portfolio is appropriate for the investor.
  - Typically, as an investor gets older, the allocation is changed to reduce the overall risk of the portfolio.

31

31

Practice

- Which one of the following statements is correct regarding the strategy of dollar cost averaging?
  - A. Laddering is a dollar cost averaging strategy that is appropriate for common stock.
  - B. Dollar cost averaging can reduce the risk of purchasing investments when prices are high.
  - C. Dollar cost averaging involves the purchase of fewer shares when market prices drop.
  - D. Laddering helps an investor reduce interest rate risk in a portfolio.

32

32

Practice

- Warren has decided that he would like to begin a monthly dollar cost averaging program. He purchased 10 shares of ABC Mutual Fund at a cost of $50 per share. What should Warren do in the second month, assuming the price of the mutual fund has increased to $100 per share?
  - A. Purchase 10 shares of ABC Mutual Fund.
  - B. Sell 5 shares of ABC Mutual Fund.
  - C. Purchase 10 shares of XYZ Mutual fund.
  - D. Purchase 5 shares of ABC Mutual Fund.

33

33

Types of Investments

Objective IV

34

34

Savings Accounts

- Commercial banks and other financial institutions offer a variety of different types of liquid, low-risk savings accounts.
  - Most accounts are insured by the FDIC.
- Savings accounts typically only offer an investor investment income.
  - Usually offer low interest rates.

35

35

Savings Accounts

- Types of savings accounts:
  - Regular – low interest rates that can change.
    - Liquid and safe investments.
  - Money market accounts – number of withdrawals per month is typically limited.
  - Money market mutual funds – do not have FDIC protection.
  - Certificates of deposits – substantial interest penalties may apply if redeemed before scheduled maturity.

36

36

Bonds

- Bonds are debt instruments issued by corporations or government entities.
  - Repay bond's par value at a specified maturity date and pay interest periodically.
- Most bonds pay a fixed rate of interest.
  - Coupon rate.
  - Floating rate bonds pay a rate of interest that is indexed.

37

37

Treasury Securities

- Treasury securities are backed by the full faith and credit of the U.S. government.
  - Subject to federal income tax.
  - Exempt from state and local taxes.
  - Considered free of default risk.

38

38

Treasury Securities

- Types of Treasury securities:
  - Series EE and Series I savings bonds.
    - Interest not paid until redeemed.
    - EE bonds – sold at a discount.
    - I bonds – sold at face value.
  - Treasury bills – maturities of less than 1 year.
    - Sold at a discount.
    - Redeemed at par.

39

39

Treasury Securities

- Types of Treasury securities:
  - Treasury notes and bonds – longer maturities.
    - Pay semi-annual interest.
    - Notes – maturities from 2-10 years.
    - Bonds – maturities over 10 years.
  - Treasury Inflation-Protected Securities – adjust par value to reflect inflation.

40

40

Municipal Bonds

- Municipal bonds are issued by state and local governments and represent government debt.
  - General obligation bonds – secured by full faith and taxing authority of the issuer.
  - Revenue bonds – payable entirely from revenue received from the projects financed.
  - Assessment bonds – payable from taxes on those who benefit from the improvements.
- Municipal bond interest is exempt from federal income tax and possibly state income tax.

41

41

Corporate Bonds

- Corporate bonds are evidence of debt issued by a corporation.
  - Typically have no collateral.
- Most bonds pay interest semiannually.
  - Interest payments are fully taxable at the federal, state, and local levels.
- Risks associated with corporate bonds:
  - Default risk.
  - Interest rate risk.
  - Purchasing power (inflation) risk.

42

42

Corporate Bonds

- Corporate bonds with collateral:
  - Mortgage bonds – collateralized by the issuer's land and buildings.
  - Collateral trust bonds – collateralized by specific securities, usually the bonds or common stock of other corporations.
  - Equipment trust bonds – collateralized by business personal property, such as equipment.

43

43

Corporate Bonds

- Corporate bonds that are not secured:
  - Debentures – only pay after collateralized debt has been satisfied.
  - Subordinated debentures – only pay after debentures have been satisfied.
  - Income bonds – lowest priority on payment.
    - Owners receive interest only if corporation has earnings from which interest can be paid.

44

44

Common Stock

- Shares of common stock represent proportional ownership of a corporation.
  - Return for stocks is a mixture of dividend payments and capital appreciation.
- A firm's stock price represents the discounted value of future earnings.
  - Returns of common stock are highly unpredictable in the short run.
  - Long term, stocks tend to outperform other investments.

45

45

Common Stock

- Types of common stock:
  - Growth stock – company earnings growing at a faster rate than general economy.
  - Value stock – considered undervalued since current price less than intrinsic value.
    - Have high potential for appreciation.
  - Cyclical stock – earnings are closely correlated with the economic cycle.
    - Auto companies.

46

46

Common Stock

- Types of common stock:
  - Defensive stock – earnings are less affected by the economic cycle.
    - Grocery stores, medical or drug companies, and tobacco companies.
  - Income stock – established record of stable dividend payments.
  - Penny stocks – stock price trading for less than $1.

47

47

Common Stock Risks

- Stocks are subject to systematic risks:
  - Purchasing power (inflation) risk.
  - Interest rate risk.
  - Market risk.
  - Exchange rate risk.
- Sensitivity to systematic risk is measured using the beta statistic.
  - Beta less than 1.0 indicates less sensitivity to systematic risk.

48

48

Mutual Funds

- Mutual funds pool investment dollars from many customers to purchase investments.
  - Investors receive proportional share of return.
- Open-end fund – new shares offered for sale.
  - Fund itself redeems any outstanding shares based on the current net asset value.
    - NAV is calculated by dividing the assets (net of liabilities) by total number of shares.
- Closed-end fund generally sells a fixed number of shares in the mutual fund.

49

49

Mutual Funds

- The key advantage of the mutual fund approach to investing is diversification.
  - Actively managed funds seek to earn higher-than-average rates of return for its investors through superior investment skill.
  - Index funds purchase the same set of assets that are included in the target index.
    - Aim to match performance of the index.
- Mutual funds charge management fees, and many charge a fee for marketing expenses.

50

50

Mutual Funds

- Types of mutual funds:
  - Money market – invest in safe liquid assets.
  - Bond – invest in municipal bonds, Treasury securities, corporate bonds, international bonds, or combinations.
  - Stock – invest in domestic and foreign stocks.
  - Blended funds – invest in a diversified portfolio that emphasize safety as well as performance.

51

51

Cash Value Life Insurance

- Permanent life insurance includes an investment component.
  - Should be evaluated against other investments using same risk/return criteria.
  - Offers minimum guaranteed rate of return.
  - Earnings are tax-deferred or tax-free.
  - Policy loans are available.
- Expenses may be difficult to measure, causing cost of investment to be difficult to measure.

52

52

Practice

- Which one of the following statements is correct regarding corporate bonds?
  - A. Debentures are corporate bonds that are backed by specific collateral.
  - B. Income bonds provide the lowest priority on payment of all corporate bonds.
  - C. Most bonds only pay interest at the time of maturity.
  - D. The capital appreciation on the bond is tax-free if held to maturity.

53

53

Practice

- Lori is considering an investment in a common stock. She is considering the following stocks:

Name	Share Price	Beta	Return
Stock A	\$13.50	1.2	12%
Stock B	\$25.00	1.0	9%
Stock C	\$22.36	0.9	14%
Stock D	\$20.25	1.3	11%

- If Lori's goal is to invest in a stock with the lowest systematic risk, what would be the best option for her?
  - A. Stock A.
  - B. Stock B.
  - C. Stock C.
  - D. Stock D.

54

54

Practice

- ABC Mutual Fund is an open-end mutual fund. The fund has $50,000,000 in assets and $8,000,000 in liabilities. If ABC Mutual Fund has 1,000,000 shares outstanding, the net asset value of the fund is:
  - A. $8.
  - B. $42.
  - C. $50.
  - D. $58.

55

55

Module 5

Education Planning

EDUCATION FUNDING

COSTS

-EDUCATION COSTS
- -TUITION, FEES, BOOKS
- -ROOM AND BOARD
- -TRANSPORTATION
- -PERSONAL EXPENSES

-ANNUAL SAVINGS REQUIRED

FINANCIAL AID

-FAFSA

-EXPECTED FAMILY CONTRIBUTION

-NEEDS BASED
- -FEDERAL PELL GRANTS
- -SEOG
- -PERKINS LOANS
- -SUBSIDIZED STAFFORD LOANS

-NOT NEEDS BASED
- -UNSUBSIDIZED STAFFORD LOANS
- -PLUS LOANS

-WORK/STUDY PROGRAMS

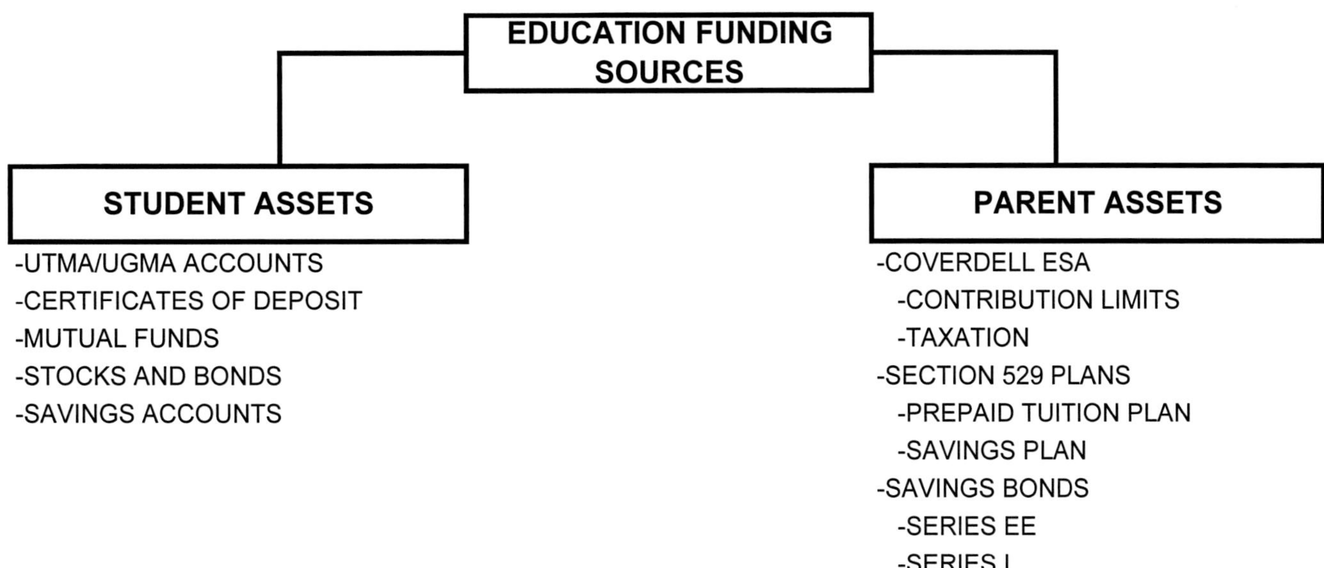

Education Planning

Module 5
Chapter 5

1

1

Objectives

- Obj I: Funding Postsecondary Education
- Obj II: Education Funding Calculation
- Obj III: Determining Needs-Based Financial Aid
- Obj IV: Sources of Funding for Education

2

2

Funding Postsecondary Education

Objective I

3

3

Funding Postsecondary Education

- The number of individuals in the U.S. pursuing postsecondary education has grown significantly in the last few years.
  - Data indicates a lower unemployment rate for the more highly educated.
  - There is a correlation between salary and level of education attained.
- Government funding for education has decreased.

4

4

Costs of Postsecondary Education

- The expenses associated with funding postsecondary education are high.
  - Increase each year at a rate exceeding CPI.
- Categories of postsecondary education expenses:
  - Tuition, fees, books and supplies.
  - Room and board, including utilities.
  - Transportation.
  - Entertainment, clothing, and other personal services and supplies.

5

5

Costs of Postsecondary Education

- Tuition and fees are the largest single cost category to consider.
  - All costs vary based on the duration, location, and type of educational program.
  - A university is more costly than a vocational trade school.
- Online schools do not offer much tuition savings over brick and mortar schools.
  - However, they do offer a substantially lower housing cost.

6

6

Investing for Education

- When estimating the cost of a college education, the following information is required:
  - Education inflation rate.
  - Number of years until enrollment.
  - Number of years of education.
- Using a financial calculator:
  - PV = Current Cost
  - i = Education Inflation Rate
  - n = Number of Year Until Enrollment

7

7

Investing for Education

- After estimating the costs of education, the annual savings amount must be determined.
- Accepted rule is to create a mix of investments in the education portfolio.
  - Anticipates student's age and number of years before the funds will be needed.
  - The closer the saver is to the funding need, the more conservative the allocation may be.

8

8

Conflicts With Other Goals

- Paying for the cost of a postsecondary education is a critical financial objective.
  - Must be balanced against other long-term financial goals and commitments.
  - Goals include caring for elderly family members, supporting dependents, saving for retirement.
- Additional factors affect the timing and amount of savings to put aside to meet future postsecondary education needs.

9

9

Practice

- Which one of the following is required information when estimating the cost of a four-year college education?
  - A. Rate of increase in the Consumer Price Index.
  - B. Number of years until enrollment.
  - C. Marginal income tax rate of the parents.
  - D. Rate of return on investments.

10

10

Practice

- Edward has a 3-year-old daughter that he hopes will attend college at the age of 18. When constructing an investment portfolio for the accumulated education savings, Edward would be wise to:
  - A. Invest the portfolio in equity investments and over time move some of the investments to short-term bonds and cash.
  - B. Purchase a single premium deferred annuity and begin taking distributions when the daughter starts college.
  - C. Buy a laddered portfolio of Treasury securities.
  - D. Invest the portfolio in cash and short-term bonds because education savings should always be invested conservatively.

11

11

Education Funding Calculation

Objective II

12

12

Determining Annual Savings Need

- Calculating the annual savings needed requires assumptions related to these factors:
  - Tuition and other costs in today's dollars.
  - Length of time until education begins.
  - Length of the education in years.
  - Education inflation rate.
  - Investment rate of return.

13

13

Determining Future Value of Tuition

- The first step in determining the education savings amount is to determine the future value of tuition.
  - $FV = PV * (1 + i)^n$
- Variables:
  - PV = tuition in today's dollars
  - i = tuition inflation rate
  - n = number of years until tuition must be paid
- This calculation would have to be performed for each year of college.

14

14

Determining Future Value of Tuition

- Example – tuition for a local university is $25,000 in today's dollars. The student will begin college in 15 years, and the education inflation rate is currently 5%.
- The amount of tuition in the first year will be:
  - $FV = PV * (1 + i)^n$
  - $FV = \$25{,}000 * (1 + .05)^{15}$
  - $FV = \$25{,}000 * (2.078928)$
  - FV = $51,973

15

15

Determining PV of Tuition

- The next step in determining the education savings amount is to determine the present value of tuition.
  - $PV = FV / (1 + i)^n$
- Variables:
  - FV = future value of tuition
  - i = investment rate of return
  - n = number of years until tuition must be paid
- This calculation would have to be performed for each year of college.

16

16

Determining PV of Tuition

- Example – tuition for a local university is $51,973 in 15 years. The rate of return on investments is 8%.
- The present value is:
  - $PV = FV / (1 + i)^n$
  - $PV = \$51,973 / (1 + .08)^{15}$
  - $PV = \$51,973 / (3.172)^{15}$
  - PV = $16,385

17

17

Determining Savings Amount

- The final step in the calculation is determining the annual savings amount.
  - A financial calculator can be used to determine this amount.
- Variables to be entered:
  - FV = lump sum education costs
  - n = number of years until education begins
  - i = rate of return on investments

18

18

Practice

- The Amits are calculating the amount needed to be saved for their son's education. He will begin his freshman year in 13 years, and the tuition inflation rate is 5%. Assuming tuition costs $20,000 per year in today's dollars, what is the future value of the son's tuition for his freshman year?
  - A. $21,000.
  - B. $29,263.
  - C. $35,917.
  - D. $37,713.

19

FV = PV (1+i)^n
20,000 (1.05)^13

19

Determining Needs-Based Financial Aid

Objective III

20

20

FAFSA

- The Free Application for Federal Student Aid is designed to identify a family's available resources to fund a postsecondary education.
  - Requires students and parents to report current assets and taxed and untaxed income.
  - Application process must be repeated each year student is enrolled in qualified postsecondary program.
  - Students completing a FAFSA receive a Student Aid Report containing official EFC.

21

21

Determining Financial Aid

- Family's financial need for postsecondary education is defined as the difference between:
  - Cost of attending the institution.
    - Includes tuition and fees, room and board, books and supplies, and transportation.
  - EFC and other financial resources.

22

22

EFC Formula

- EFC formula determines student's eligibility for grants, loans, and work-study programs.
  - EFC = Expected Parent Contribution + Expected Student Contribution.
  - Measures family's financial strength.
- EFC formula weighs a student's assets up to 6 times more heavily than those of the parents.
  - Family eligibility can be significantly improved by holding assets in parent's name.

23

23

EFC Formula

- Many postsecondary educational institutions use only the EFC formula.
  - Some institutions use EFC formula in conjunction with the College Scholarship Service (CSS) profile.
- CSS incorporates:
  - Equity in the family home.
  - Value of qualified retirement plans.
  - Income and assets of noncustodial parents.

24

24

Financial Aid

- Families can increase eligibility by managing both the parent and student assets and income.
  - If EFC + additional financial aid is less than COA, student qualifies for needs-based aid.
- The institution can adjust a student's status from dependent to independent.
  - Based on such factors as parents' divorce agreement or the student's marital status.
  - If student is independent, parent assets and income are not factored into EFC.

25

25

Financial Aid

- Financial aid is available for both needs-based and non-needs-based individuals.
- Grants are a type of financial aid for students with significant need.
  - Do not need to be repaid.
  - Award amounts are based on annual FAFSA, EFC calculation, institution's COA, and student's enrollment status.

26

26

Needs-Based Funds

- The following are needs-based funds:
  - Federal Pell Grants – primary grant program for undergraduate students.
    - Available to full-time and to part-time students (in lesser amounts).
    - Designed for low- & middle-income students.
  - Supplemental Education Opportunity Grants – administered by aid office at each school.
    - Extreme financial need.
    - Undergraduate students only.

27

27

Needs-Based Funds

- The following are needs-based funds:
  - Perkins Loans – both the school and the government contribute to the funding pool.
    - Payments begin and interest accrues after student leaves school.
  - Subsidized Stafford Loans – must be repaid within 10 years.
    - Stafford loans are the major source of education borrowing.

28

28

Not Needs-Based Funds

- The following funds are not needs-based:
  - Unsubsidized Stafford Student Loans – must be repaid within 10 years.
  - Parent Loans for Undergraduate Students – interest is charged beginning on the date the loan proceeds are received.
    - Can borrow entire cost of education.
  - Grad PLUS loans – allow graduate and professional degree students to borrow total cost of tuition, supplies, and room and board.

29

29

Financial Aid Packages

- Federal work-study (FWS) awards allow students to earn money while they are enrolled.
  - Pays an hourly wage in jobs that promote community service and relate to their study.
- Schools also provide grants, merit awards, and scholarships for academic achievement.
  - Options include tuition payment plans, and educational assistance for student-athletes, nontraditional students, and minorities.

30

30

Practice

- Which one of the following statements is correct regarding the Expected Family Contribution formula?
  - A. The formula weighs the parents' assets and student's assets equally.
  - B. The formula weighs the parents' assets up to 3 times more heavily than the student's assets.
  - C. The formula only incorporates assets owned by the student.
  - D. The formula weighs a student's assets up to 6 times more heavily than the parents' assets.

31

31

Practice

- Many postsecondary education institutions use only the Expected Family Contribution (EFC) formula, while others use the formula in conjunction with the College Scholarship Service (CSS) profile to determine a student's eligibility for private institutional financial aid. Which of the following represents a major difference between EFC and CSS?
  - A. CSS factors in the student's grades.
  - B. CSS considers all assets owned by the child.
  - C. CSS gives special consideration to the age of the parents.
  - D. CSS incorporates the equity in the family home.

32

32

Sources of Funding for Education

Objective IV

33

33

Sources of Funding

- A variety of savings options are available to fund postsecondary education.
  - Some vehicles offer tax advantages.
- When choosing vehicle, must determine if income is reported on the FAFSA as student or parental income.

34

34

Student Assets

- Most states have established UTMA and UGMA accounts to transfer funds to minors.
  - Irrevocable transfers to the minor that cannot be transferred to another child.
  - Parent or legal guardian serves as trustee.
  - Child obtains control of account upon reaching age of majority.
  - Anyone may contribute any amount to an UTMA or UGMA account.

35

35

Student Assets

- Students who have reached age of majority may save through regular savings plans.
  - Certificates of deposit.
  - Savings account.
  - Mutual funds.
  - Individual stocks and bonds.
- Savings accounts and CDs offer FDIC insurance, but usually have a low rate of return.

36

36

Parent Assets

- Coverdell Education Savings Accounts:
  - Savings vehicle that parents and other custodians may establish.
  - Owner controls investments and withdrawals.
  - Contribution is limited to $2,000 per year.
    - No restrictions as to whom can contribute.
    - Ability to make contributions phased out.

37

37

Parent Assets

- Coverdell Education Savings Accounts:
  - Contributions are not deductible for federal tax purposes.
  - Distributions are tax-free if made for qualified education expenses.
  - If beneficiary is an eligible family member, the beneficiary can be changed without incurring taxes or a penalty.
  - Funds must be distributed if beneficiary attains age 30.

38

38

Parent Assets

- A Section 529 plan is an education savings funding vehicle.
  - Every state sponsors and operates at least one Section 529 plan.
  - Prepaid tuition plans and savings plans.
- Owner controls timing and use of withdrawals.
  - Withdrawals are tax-free if used for qualified education expenses.

39

39

Parent Assets

- Section 529 prepaid tuition plans allow parents to purchase tuition credits at current college costs.
  - Rate of return is tied to tuition inflation rates.
    - Guarantees that investment will keep up with tuition inflation for a state school.
  - Most attractive to conservative investors since the plan guarantees to pay for tuition.

40

40

Parent Assets

- Section 529 savings plans are investment accounts.
  - Contributions allowed regardless of income.
  - Contribution limits are high.
  - Contributions not deductible for federal income tax purposes.
  - Rate of return is based upon the investments selected by the account owner.
  - Investment options are somewhat limited, and can only be changed once annually.

41

41

Parent Assets

- U.S. savings bonds include Series EE and I.
  - Considered free from default risk.
  - Backed by government and guarantee the principal will double in 20 years.
  - Series EE bonds have fixed rate, making them poor hedge against inflation.
  - Maximum purchase is $10,000 per year.
- U.S. savings bond purchased and held by parent is considered asset of the parent.

42

42

Parent Assets

- U.S. Savings bonds are tax-deferred until redemption.
  - Tax-free at redemption if used for education and income below threshold.
  - Free from most state and local taxation.
- Both series can be purchased electronically from the U.S. Treasury's website directly without administrative fees.

43

43

Parent Assets

- Parents can save for their children's education by contributing to standard savings accounts.
  - Considered parental asset for the purpose of calculating EFC.
  - Interest and capital gains are counted as parental income in the financial aid formula.

44

44

Practice

- Which one of the following statements is correct regarding Section 529 plans?
  - A. Every state sponsors and operates at least one 529 savings account or prepaid tuition plan.
  - B. High income taxpayers cannot contribute to these plans due to AGI phase-outs.
  - C. Account investment options are virtually unlimited and can be changed at any time.
  - D. Contributions are deductible for federal income tax purposes.

45

45

Practice

- Which of the following education savings vehicles would permit the highest contribution by a donor in a single year?
  - A. Coverdell Education Savings Account.
  - B. Series EE savings bonds.
  - C. Series I savings bonds.
  - D. Section 529 plan.

46

46

Practice

- Which of the following statements is correct regarding a Coverdell Education Savings Account?
  - A. The account is considered an asset of the student in the Expected Family Contribution formula.
  - B. The maximum annual contribution is $2,000 per student.
  - C. Once initially selected, the beneficiary cannot be changed without incurring taxes and a penalty.
  - D. Contributions to the account are deductible for federal income tax purposes.

47

47

Module 6

Retirement Planning

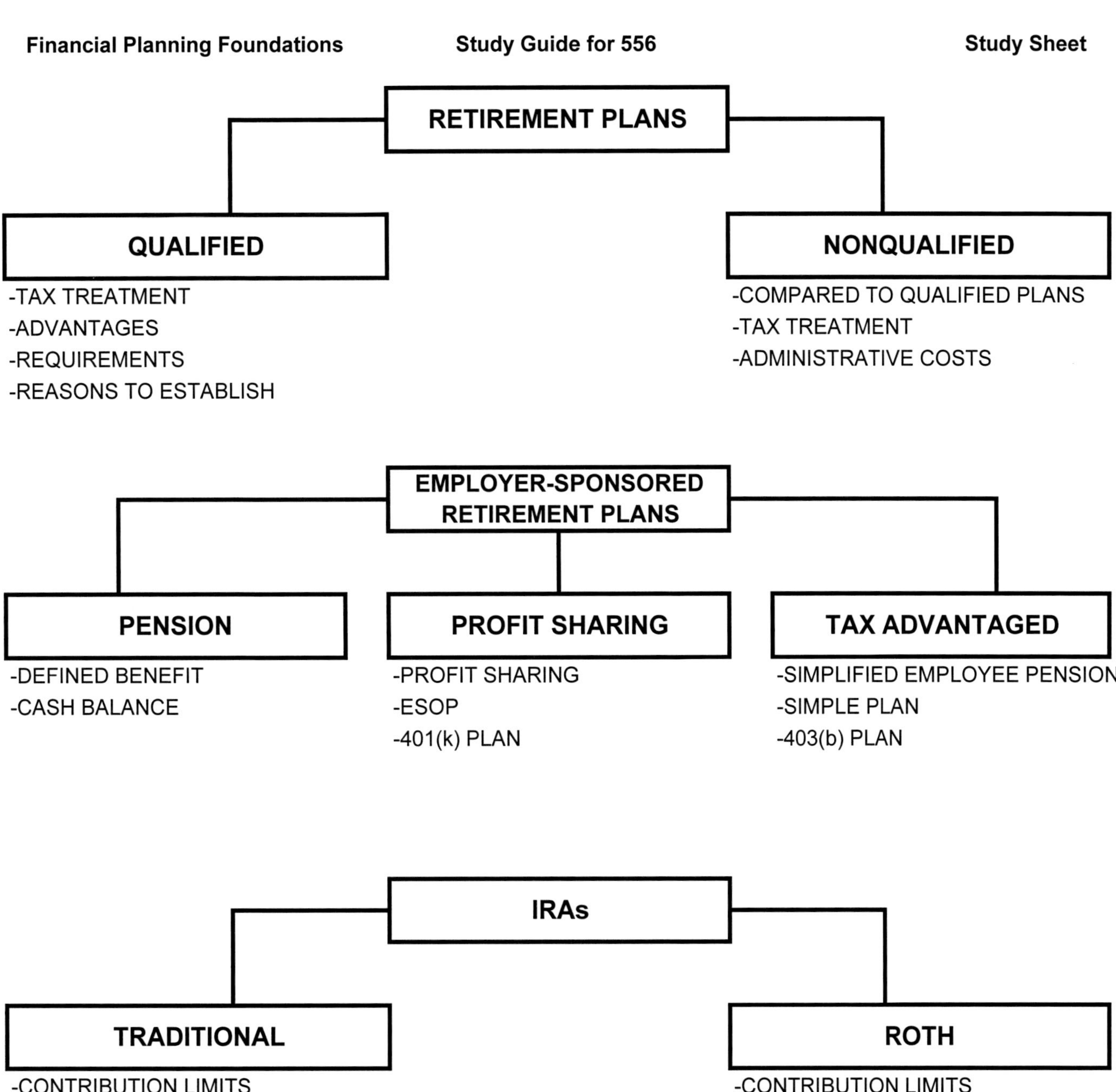
RETIREMENT PLANS
QUALIFIED
-TAX TREATMENT
-ADVANTAGES
-REQUIREMENTS
-REASONS TO ESTABLISH
NONQUALIFIED
-COMPARED TO QUALIFIED PLANS
-TAX TREATMENT
-ADMINISTRATIVE COSTS
EMPLOYER-SPONSORED RETIREMENT PLANS
PENSION
-DEFINED BENEFIT
-CASH BALANCE
PROFIT SHARING
-PROFIT SHARING
-ESOP
-401(k) PLAN
TAX ADVANTAGED
-SIMPLIFIED EMPLOYEE PENSION
-SIMPLE PLAN
-403(b) PLAN
IRAs
TRADITIONAL
-CONTRIBUTION LIMITS
-DEDUCTIBLE CONTRIBUTIONS
-AGI PHASE OUTS
-TAXATION OF DISTRIBUTIONS
ROTH
-CONTRIBUTION LIMITS
-NONDEDUCTIBLE CONTRIBUTIONS
-AGI PHASE OUTS
-TAXATION OF DISTRIBUTIONS

Retirement Planning

Module 6
Chapter 6

1

1

Objectives

- Obj I: Retirement Planning Process
- Obj II: Calculating Annual Savings Needs
- Obj III: Comparing Employer-Sponsored Plans
- Obj IV: Comparing IRAs
- Obj V: Retirement Income Choices

2

2

Retirement Planning Process

Objective I

3

3

Retirement Loss Exposure

- Individuals face the loss exposure of outliving their financial resources.
  - Retirement loss exposure.
- Retirement funding losses are influenced by:
  - Planning effectively.
  - Sufficient accumulation of retirement funds.
  - Aging population.
  - Inflation.

4

4

Planning Effectively

- Effective planning involves estimating:
  - Living expenses arising after employment income stops.
  - Length of retirement.
- Failure to accurately plan for retirement needs can result in a lower standard of living or the need to continue to work.

5

5

Planning Effectively

- Some individuals erroneously assume that expenses will decrease in retirement.
  - Healthcare costs typically increase.
- Planning should consider the potential costs of:
  - Long-term care.
  - Expenses related to hobbies, recreational activities, and travel.

6

6

Retirement Planning Process

- Steps in the retirement planning process:
  - Determining retirement goals.
  - Analyzing financial needs.
  - Arranging techniques.
  - Monitoring and revising the plan.

7

7

Determining Retirement Goals

- Meeting an individual's retirement goals is the ultimate objective of the planning process.
  - Goals should be stated clearly and objectively in writing as the planning process continues.
- The plan must examine the individual's expected standard of living during retirement.
  - Standard of living can include a desired lifestyle, ongoing support requirements, or payment in full of outstanding debts.

8

8

Analyzing Financial Needs

- Analysis of financial needs translates the retirement goals into an accumulation goal.
- Factors used to determine savings needed:
  - Amount of income needed at retirement.
  - Estimated retirement period.
  - Pension and Social Security estimates.
  - Estimated future value of existing resources.
  - Lump-sum necessary to fund any shortfall.
  - Additional amount that must be saved annually.

9

9

Analyzing Financial Needs

- Some individuals attempt to save amounts needed to meet their goals.
  - Many others decide to change their retirement goals and reduce the required funding.
  - A minority of individuals modify their inflation or return assumptions and increase their risk.

10

10

Arranging Techniques

- The third step in the process is to arrange risk financing and control techniques.
  - The financial professional and the individual determine the financial products needed.
- Categories of funding vehicles:
  - Tax-deductible and tax-deferred.
  - Tax-free.
  - Tax-deferred.
  - Taxable currently.

11

11

Arranging Techniques

- Tax-deductible, tax-deferred funding vehicles:
  - Most tax-efficient method of retirement saving.
  - Contribution needed to accumulate a sum at retirement is less than after-tax funds.
- These limitations apply:
  - Maximum contribution limits.
  - Early withdrawal penalty.
  - Minimum required distributions.
  - Access to funds may be limited.

12

12

Arranging Techniques

- Tax-deductible, tax-deferred funding vehicles:
  - Traditional IRAs.
  - Section 401(k) plans (other than Roth).
  - Section 403(b) plans (other than Roth).
  - Section 457 deferred compensation plans.
- These plans generally allow individuals to invest pre-tax funds and provide tax-deferred earnings.

13

13

Arranging Techniques

- Tax-free funding vehicles:
  - Offer investors nontaxable earnings.
  - Contributions are made with after-tax funds.
  - No penalty on withdrawal of contributions.
  - No required minimum distribution (RMD) rules apply.
- Examples:
  - Municipal bonds.
  - Roth IRAs.

14

14

Arranging Techniques

- Tax-deferred funding vehicles:
  - Taxation of earnings is deferred until earnings are distributed.
  - Contributions are made with after-tax funds.
- A nonqualified annuity is an example of a tax-deferred funding vehicle.
  - No contribution limitations or lifetime RMD.
  - Withdrawals may be subject to surrender charges and unfavorable LIFO tax treatment.

15

15

Arranging Techniques

- Currently taxable funding vehicles:
  - Contributions made with after-tax dollars.
  - Earnings are taxable in the year credited.
  - Primary benefit is the ease with which the individual can access the funds.
- Examples:
  - Certificates of deposit.
  - Savings accounts.
  - Money market accounts.

16

16

Monitoring and Revising the Plan

- A retirement plan should generally be monitored every year.
  - A significant event should cause the plan to be revised sooner.
- Factors to consider:
  - Individual's current financial situation.
  - Tax law changes.
  - Investment performance of retirement assets.
  - New investments.

17

17

Practice

- Which one of the following retirement funding vehicles is categorized as both tax-deferred and tax-deductible?
  - A. Nonqualified annuity.
  - B. Municipal bond.
  - C. Section 401(k) plan.
  - D. Money market mutual fund.

18

18

Practice

- Which one of the following retirement vehicles is subject to both contribution limits and required minimum distributions?
  - A. Municipal bond.
  - B. Traditional IRA.
  - C. Nonqualified annuity.
  - D. Roth IRA.

19

19

Calculating Annual Savings Needs

Objective II

20

20

Retirement Income Needs

- The main retirement goal for most individuals is to maintain their current lifestyle.
  - Determining retirement income needs is based on various assumptions.
- Methods used to estimate retirement income needs:
  - Income replacement ratio method.
  - Expense method.

21

21

Income Replacement Ratio Method

- The income replacement ratio method applies a percentage to average income to approximate the income required in the first retirement year.
  - Average income is usually the average of estimated earned income in the final three years of employment.
  - Specified percentage is typically 60%-80%.

22

22

Income Replacement Ratio Method

- Expenses decrease during retirement because:
  - Retirement contributions generally end.
  - Work-related expenses may end.
  - Home ownership expenses may decline/end.
  - Support for dependents may end.
  - Senior discounts may be available.
  - General expenses may decline as individual becomes less active.
  - Taxes typically decline.

23

23

Income Replacement Ratio Method

- Reasons taxes may decline during retirement:
  - Federal, state, and local governments often assess reduced taxes for retired individuals.
  - Social Security taxes usually end.
  - Standard deduction is increased for taxpayers age 65 and older.
  - Social Security benefits may be tax-free.
  - Some states don't tax pensions.
  - Local property taxes may be reduced.

24

24

Expense Method

- The expense method estimates an individual's retirement income needs.
  - Based on total estimated expenses in the first year of retirement.
  - A retiree's expense estimate is particularly speculative for younger individuals.

25

25

Accumulating Savings

- Once income needs have been determined, the funding vehicles must be chosen.
  - Vehicles used to accumulate cash.
  - Accumulation period is the period of time in which funds are saved for retirement.

26

26

Distributing Income

- In the distribution period, an individual can receive cash through:
  - Annual withdrawal plan – individual withdraws first-year retirement income shortfall from a fund.
    - Future withdrawals adjusted for inflation.
  - Annuity payments – based on the individual's life expectancy.
- An annuity guarantees payments throughout the individual's remaining lifetime.

27

27

Determining Annual Savings Need

- Calculating the annual savings needed requires assumptions related to these factors:
  - Annual income needed during retirement.
  - Length of time income will be provided.
  - Income provided by Social Security and defined benefit pension plans.
  - Projected value of existing retirement assets at retirement.
  - Inflation and investment return rates.

28

28

Determining Annual Savings Need

- Assumes 20 years until retirement; 25 years in retirement; 5% inflation rate.

Current Earned Income	$100,000
Replacement Percentage	80%
Income Target	80,000
Less: Pension and Social Security Income	(45,000)
Retirement Income Shortfall (Today's Dollars)	35,000
Multiply by: Future Value Factor (20 Years, 5%)	2.6533
Retirement Income Shortfall on Retirement Date	**92,866**

29

29

Determining Annual Savings Need

Retirement Income Shortfall on Retirement Date	92,866
Multiply by: Present Value of Annuity Due	14.7986
Fund Needed to Replace Shortfall	**1,374,279**

- The future value of the <u>existing</u> retirement assets is then determined using a Future Value Factor and subtracted from the fund needed to replace the shortfall.

30

30

Practice

- Fred plans to retire in 15 years. Based on a retirement sufficiency analysis, he has estimated that he will need a lump-sum amount saved of $2,000,000 on the day he retires. He currently has an account balance of $970,000.
- The following factors are taken from the "Future Value Factors for a $1 Single Sum" table, for a 15-year period:
  - 4% - 1.8009
  - 5% - 2.0789
  - 6% - 2.3966
  - 7% - 2.7590
- Assuming he does not set aside any additional funds for his retirement, what is the minimum interest rate he must earn on his current savings balance to realize his retirement planning goal?
  - A. 4%.
  - B. 5%.
  - C. 6%.
  - D. 7%.

31

31

Comparing Employer-Sponsored Plans

Objective III

32

32

Qualified Plans

- A qualified plan must:
  - Be established to benefit employees.
  - Prohibit the use of plan assets for purposes other than benefitting employees.
  - Satisfy age and service requirements.
  - Not discriminate with contributions/benefits.
  - Satisfy minimum vesting standards.
  - Meet benefit commencement requirements.
  - Offer survivor benefits as appropriate.

33

33

Defined Benefit Plans

- A defined benefit plan is a qualified plan with a guaranteed retirement benefit.
  - Must pay the promised benefit at retirement, regardless of the investment performance.
  - Future benefits can be accurately estimated.
  - Funded through employer contributions.
  - Annual contributions determined actuarially.
  - Annual contributions may vary substantially.
  - Funds guaranteed by PBGC.

34

34

Defined Contribution Plans

- A defined contribution plan is a type of qualified plan with these characteristics:
  - Individual account for each participant.
  - Contributions that are generally determined by formula (i.e. 3% of compensation).
  - Earnings allocated to participant's account.
- Defined contribution plans include money purchase plans, profit sharing plans, and 401(k) plans.

35

35

Pension Plans

- A pension plan is a type of qualified plan with these characteristics:
  - Requires annual employer contributions.
  - Benefits may be guaranteed by PBGC.
  - Provides a retirement benefit.
  - Distributions generally cannot begin until participant has terminated employment.
  - Limited to investing not more than 10% in the sponsoring company's stock.

36

36

Profit Sharing Plans

- A profit sharing plan is a type of qualified plan with these characteristics:
  - Does not require annual contributions.
    - Contributions should be recurring.
  - Benefits not guaranteed.
  - Does not necessarily provide retirement benefit.
  - May provide for in-service distributions.
  - No limit on investment in sponsoring company's stock.

37

37

Defined Benefit Plans

- Benefits promised under a defined benefit plan are stated in terms of a life income payable beginning at normal retirement age.
  - Flat benefit formula – benefit based solely on salary.
  - Unit benefit formula – benefit based on salary and service.

38

38

Cash Balance Plans

- A cash balance plan is a defined benefit plan whose benefit is defined more like that of a defined contribution plan.
  - Defines benefit in terms of a specified account balance.
  - Every plan participant has a hypothetical account that receives contributions and earnings.

39

39

Profit Sharing Plans

- A profit sharing plan is a type of qualified defined contribution plan.
  - Provides a way for employers to share tax-deferred profits with employees.
  - Must specify a formula for allocating contributions and earnings to each account:
    - Level contribution percentage.
    - Age-weighted contribution.
    - New comparability contribution.

40

40

401(k) Plans

- A Section 401(k) plan is a type of qualified defined contribution plan.
  - Participants may make elective deferral contributions to the plan with pre-tax dollars.
  - Employers may make matching contributions.
  - Some plans permit elective deferrals to a designated Roth 401(k) account.

41

41

403(b) Plans

- A Section 403(b) plan is not a qualified plan but is similar in structure to a 401(k) plan.
  - May only be established by tax-exempt organizations.
  - Participant may defer compensation pre-tax under an elective deferral arrangement.
  - Popular with schools.

42

42

ESOPs

- An ESOP is a defined contribution plan whose funds must be invested primarily in employer securities.
  - Employer contributions to an ESOP are flexible and discretionary.
  - ESOPs must permit distributions to be made in employer stock.
  - Creates a market for company stock and a method for financing company growth.

43

43

Simplified Employee Pension Plans

- Simplified employee pension plans permit employers to make discretionary contributions.
  - Employer funded type of IRA.
  - Employers can contribute lesser of:
    - 25% of compensation.
    - Defined contribution limit.
  - Generally less costly than a qualified plan.
  - Easy to install and administer.

44

44

SIMPLE Plans

- A SIMPLE plan allows both employee pre-tax and employer contributions.
  - Generally less costly than qualified plans.
  - Easy to install and administer.
  - Business must have 100 or fewer employees.
  - Employer must make either:
    - Matching contributions.
    - Nonelective contribution.

45

45

Nonqualified Plans

- Nonqualified plans are unfunded plans.
  - Salary reduction plan – plan participants defer compensation.
    - Can defer until retirement or a future event.
  - Supplemental executive retirement plan (SERP) – employer promises to pay a specified dollar amount beginning at the earlier of the participant's death or retirement.
    - Often act as "golden handcuffs."

46

46

Practice

- Which one of the following retirement plans is insured by the Pension Benefit Guarantee Corporation (PBGC)?
  - A. Profit sharing plan.
  - B. Defined benefit plan.
  - C. 401(k) plan.
  - D. 403(b) plan.

47

47

Practice

- Which one of the following represents a type of nonqualified plan?
  - A. Supplemental executive retirement plan.
  - B. Simplified employee pension plan.
  - C. Employee stock ownership plan.
  - D. Profit sharing plan.

48

48

Practice

- An advantage of a defined benefit plan is that:
  - A. Contributions are flexible for the employer.
  - B. In-service withdrawals are available once the employee attains age 50.
  - C. Future benefits can be accurately estimated.
  - D. Administrative costs are generally lower than other types of qualified plans.

49

49

Practice

- ABC Corporation wants to establish a retirement plan that closely resembles an IRA. The company would like to make all the contributions to the plan and would like to make higher annual contributions each year than those permitted under a traditional IRA or Roth IRA. Which one of the following would be the most appropriate plan for ABC Corporation?
  - A. 401(k) plan.
  - B. Simplified employee pension plan.
  - C. 403(b) plan.
  - D. Employee stock ownership plan.

50

50

Comparing IRAs

Objective IV

51

51

IRAs

- Two main types of IRAs are available – traditional IRA and Roth IRA.
  - Main difference is the tax treatment of contributions and distributions.
- Both IRAs have the following in common:
  - Contribution limits.
  - Permitted investments.
  - Loans are prohibited.
  - Immediate vesting of contributions.

52

52

Traditional IRAs

- Traditional individual retirement accounts (IRAs) may be funded in addition to an employer-sponsored retirement plan.
  - Must have earned income to contribute.
    - Includes salary, fees, tips, bonuses, commissions, and alimony.
    - Spousal IRA does not require the owner to have any earned income.

53

53

Traditional IRAs

- A traditional IRA contribution may be deductible for federal tax purposes.
  - Deduction is phased-out for active participants in other retirement plans.
  - Phase-out based on participant's AGI.
- Distributions from traditional IRAs of earnings and deductible contributions are taxable.
  - Nondeductible contributions are not taxed when distributed.

54

54

Roth IRAs

- Roth IRAs also permit owners to make annual contributions to fund their retirement income.
  - Contributions are never tax deductible.
  - Must have earned income to contribute.
    - Spousal IRA does not require the owner to have any earned income.
  - Ability to contribute is phased-out based on adjusted gross income.
  - Qualified plan or traditional IRA can be converted to Roth IRA.

55

55

Roth IRAs

- Minimum distribution rules do not apply while Roth IRA owner is alive.
- Distributions are taxed assuming FIFO basis.
  - Basis is distributed first and earnings are distributed last.
- Distributions of earnings can be tax-free.
  - Distribution must meet requirements of a qualifying distribution.

56

56

Distributions

- Qualifying distributions must meet two tests:
  - Made after five-year period beginning with first tax year of contribution -AND-
  - Meets ONE of the following conditions:
    - Participant is age 59½ or older.
    - Participant is deceased.
    - Participant is disabled.
    - Distribution made to pay first–time homebuyer expenses (lifetime limit of $10,000).

57

57

Stretch IRAs

- Stretch IRAs are designed to maximize the tax deferral of IRA assets.
  - Extends the minimum distributions for 10 years beyond the death of the IRA owner.
- Surviving spouse can treat decedent's IRA as his/her own.

58

58

Rollovers

- Funds may be transferred to and from IRAs without losing their tax-advantaged status.
- Rollover may be direct or indirect.
  - Direct rollover – funds sent directly from one plan to the IRA.
  - Indirect rollover – funds are sent from a tax-advantaged plan to a plan participant, who has 60 days to roll funds to IRA.
    - 20% withholding applies to indirect rollovers from qualified plans.

59

59

Practice

- Which one of the following is the main difference between a traditional IRA and a Roth IRA?
  - A. Eligible investment options.
  - B. Dollar amount of allowed contributions.
  - C. Accumulation of investment income.
  - D. Tax treatment of contributions and distributions.

60

60

Practice

- Which one of the following represents an advantage of a Roth IRA?
  - A. An individual can contribute to a Roth IRA regardless of their adjusted gross income.
  - B. No minimum distributions are required to be taken during the account owner's lifetime.
  - C. Amounts can be converted from a traditional IRA to a Roth IRA tax-free.
  - D. Contributions to the account are deductible for federal income tax purposes.

61

61

Retirement Income Choices

Objective V

62

62

Retirement Income Choices

- For most individuals, the largest percentage of retirement income is derived from Social Security benefits.
- Decisions that must be made when retiring:
  - Whether to purchase an annuity.
  - How and when to spend down savings.
  - When to begin pension benefits.
  - When to begin Social Security benefits.

63

63

Purchasing an Annuity

- The method of determining an appropriate retirement income for a client should be based on actual expenses.
  - Clients should identify what their essential living expenses will be in retirement.
- Expenses should be matched with income sources that are guaranteed.
  - If expenses exceed guaranteed income, client should consider purchasing a life annuity.

64

64

Purchasing an Annuity

- Steps an individual should take until they have an annuity that is able to cover any remaining essential living expenses:
  - Annuitize any deferred annuity cash value under a life income settlement option.
  - Roll over existing IRA, 401(k), or 403(b) balances to an immediate life annuity.
  - Consider using taxable assets to fund an immediate life annuity.

65

65

Spending Down Savings

- An alternative to purchasing an annuity is to spend down existing savings.
- One strategy involves liquidating 4% of assets in the first year.
  - Each year, the amount liquidated in the previous year would increase by inflation.
  - Unlikely that funds will be exhausted during lifetime.

66

66

Spending Down Savings

- Assets should be liquidated in this order:
  - Investments that have been losing money.
  - Available cash.
  - Investments that will produce long-term capital gains.
  - Investments that will produce short-term capital gains.
  - Tax-deferred assets such as 401(k) plans.

67

67

Beginning Pension Benefits

- An individual whose retirement income is insufficient may postpone his or her planned retirement date.
  - May increase pension benefit.
  - Provides additional period of asset accumulation.
  - Shortens period during which additional retirement income must be provided.

68

68

Beginning Social Security Benefits

- Social Security retirement benefits may begin as early as age 62 or as late as age 70.
- If individual has full retirement age of 66:
  - Begins at 62 – 25% reduction.
  - Begins at 63 – 20% reduction.
  - Begins at 64 – 13.3% reduction.
- If the individual elects to defer benefits beyond full retirement age, benefits increase by 8% for each year they are deferred.

69

69

Practice

- To maximize tax benefits, assets should be liquidated in which order?
  - A. Tax-deferred assets, long-term capital gain assets, short-term capital gain assets, cash, and loss investments.
  - B. Cash, long-term capital gain assets, short-term capital gain assets, tax-deferred assets, and loss investments.
  - C. Long-term capital gain assets, tax-deferred assets, cash, loss investments, and short-term capital gain assets.
  - D. Loss investments, cash, long-term capital gain assets, short-term capital gain assets, and tax-deferred assets.

70

70

Module 7

Estate Planning

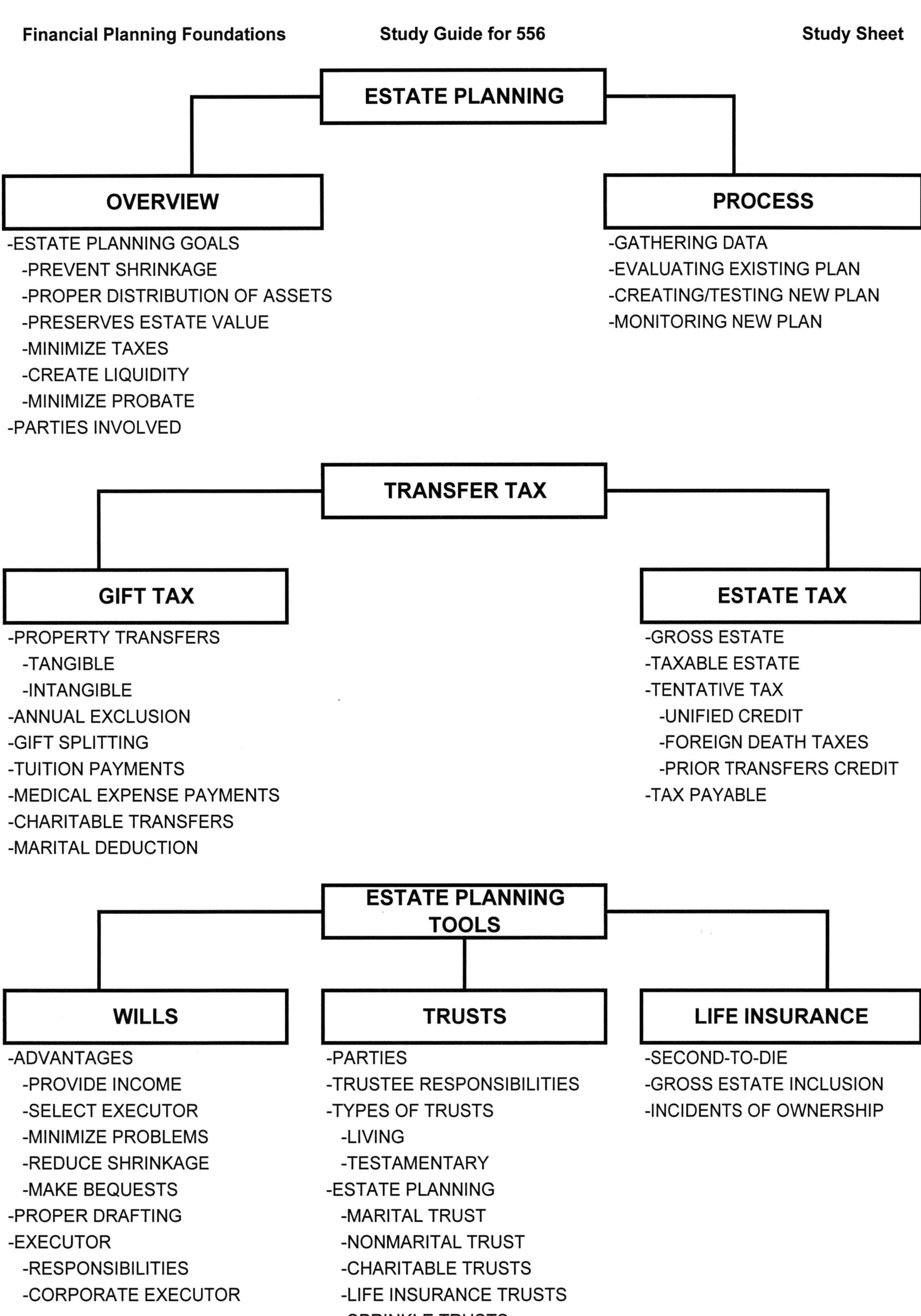
ESTATE PLANNING
OVERVIEW
-ESTATE PLANNING GOALS
-PREVENT SHRINKAGE
-PROPER DISTRIBUTION OF ASSETS
-PRESERVES ESTATE VALUE
-MINIMIZE TAXES
-CREATE LIQUIDITY
-MINIMIZE PROBATE
-PARTIES INVOLVED
PROCESS
-GATHERING DATA
-EVALUATING EXISTING PLAN
-CREATING/TESTING NEW PLAN
-MONITORING NEW PLAN
TRANSFER TAX
GIFT TAX
-PROPERTY TRANSFERS
-TANGIBLE
-INTANGIBLE
-ANNUAL EXCLUSION
-GIFT SPLITTING
-TUITION PAYMENTS
-MEDICAL EXPENSE PAYMENTS
-CHARITABLE TRANSFERS
-MARITAL DEDUCTION
ESTATE TAX
-GROSS ESTATE
-TAXABLE ESTATE
-TENTATIVE TAX
-UNIFIED CREDIT
-FOREIGN DEATH TAXES
-PRIOR TRANSFERS CREDIT
-TAX PAYABLE
ESTATE PLANNING TOOLS
WILLS
-ADVANTAGES
-PROVIDE INCOME
-SELECT EXECUTOR
-MINIMIZE PROBLEMS
-REDUCE SHRINKAGE
-MAKE BEQUESTS
-PROPER DRAFTING
-EXECUTOR
-RESPONSIBILITIES
-CORPORATE EXECUTOR
TRUSTS
-PARTIES
-TRUSTEE RESPONSIBILITIES
-TYPES OF TRUSTS
-LIVING
-TESTAMENTARY
-ESTATE PLANNING
-MARITAL TRUST
-NONMARITAL TRUST
-CHARITABLE TRUSTS
-LIFE INSURANCE TRUSTS
-SPRINKLE TRUSTS
LIFE INSURANCE
-SECOND-TO-DIE
-GROSS ESTATE INCLUSION
-INCIDENTS OF OWNERSHIP

Estate Planning

Module 7
Chapter 7

1

1

Objectives

- Obj I: Estate Planning Overview
- Obj II: Estate Planning Process
- Obj III: Gift and Estate Tax
- Obj IV: Estate Planning Tools

2

2

Estate Planning Overview

Objective I

3

3

Estate Planning Need

- Proper estate planning:
  - Prevents estate shrinkage – decrease in estate due to estate taxes, debts, and admin costs.
  - Allows individuals to have their estate distributed according to their wishes.
  - Preserves the value of an estate and passes the preserved value on to heirs.
- For those who do not have an estate plan, assets will be distributed based on intestacy laws.

4

4

Estate Planning Goals

- All individuals who own property or have accumulated even a small amount of wealth should establish an estate plan.
  - Few financial advisors have appropriate expertise to generate a complex estate plan for a client.

5

5

Estate Planning Goals

- Goals of estate planning:
  - Distributing assets according to wishes.
  - Minimizing estate and inheritance taxes.
  - Minimizing income taxes.
  - Creating needed liquidity.
  - Minimizing probate costs – include costs to distribute the estate and costs to defend against challenges to a Will.

6

6

Parties Involved

- Professionals potentially included in an estate planning team:
  - Attorney – provides overall legal advice.
    - Drafts Wills and other legal documents.
  - Accountant – provides technical advice on taxes and financial statements.
  - Trust officer – administers trust if trust is used to implement an estate plan.

7

7

Parties Involved

- Professionals potentially included in an estate planning team:
  - Investment counselor – provides advice about maintaining and increasing estate's value.
  - Life insurance specialist – serves two roles:
    - Initiates or reviews estate plan.
    - Recommends appropriate insurance products for estate plan.

8

8

Practice

- Probate costs must be considered when formulating an estate plan for an individual. Probate costs include:
  - A. Costs to distribute the estate.
  - B. Inheritance taxes.
  - C. Estate taxes.
  - D. Expenses associated with drafting a valid Will.

9

9

Practice

- Which one of the following statements is correct regarding estate planning?
  - A. Only individuals with estates exceeding $5,000,000 have a need for estate planning.
  - B. Most financial advisors have appropriate training to generate a complex estate plan for a client.
  - C. An estate planning team may include an investment advisor to advise ways to maintain or increase the estate's value.
  - D. A major goal of estate planning is to eliminate a client's liquid assets, which typically offer a very low rate of return.

10

10

Estate Planning Process

Objective II

11

11

Estate Planning Process

- The estate planning process provides a framework for effective estate planning.
  - Gathering data.
  - Evaluating existing plan.
  - Creating and testing a new plan.
  - Implementing and monitoring the new plan.

12

12

Gathering Data

- The first step in the estate planning process is to gather facts about the estate.
  - Questionnaires are often used to gather information about estate owner and family.
  - Complete description of assets and liabilities should be provided.
  - Estate owner's intentions for transferring property at death should be stated.
  - Executor should be identified – responsible for overseeing the settlement of estate.

13

13

Evaluating Existing Plan

- Existing plan can be tested by determining how property would be distributed if estate owner died immediately.
  - Property must be evaluated to determine if it will be included in the gross estate and/or the probate estate.
  - Attorney typically classifies property.

14

14

Evaluating Existing Plan

- Techniques to avoid probate:
  - Naming beneficiary.
  - Titling property as JTWROS or tenancy by the entirety.
  - Pay on Death arrangement.

15

15

Evaluating Existing Plan

- Analyzing existing plan helps determine need for cash at the estate owner's death.
  - Estate shrinkage at death must be estimated.
- Several alternative assumptions should be run:
  - Estate owner dies first.
  - Owner's spouse dies first.
  - Both spouses die simultaneously.
  - One spouse dies shortly after the other.

16

16

Creating New Plan

- The third step in the estate planning process is to formulate and test a new estate plan that:
  - Eliminates the existing plan's weaknesses.
  - Meets the estate owner's needs.
  - Avoids involuntary liquidation of estate assets.
- New plan should be tested with the same assumptions used in the existing plan.

17

17

Implementing New Plan

- The final step in the process is to execute the new estate plan, which may require:
  - Purchasing additional life insurance.
  - Drawing up new legal documents.
  - Revising existing legal documents.
  - Making gifts.
- Estate planning is an ongoing process.
  - It may be appropriate to review the estate plan annually.

18

18

Practice

- The purchase of additional life insurance will often take place during which step of the estate planning process?
  - A. Formulate and test a new estate plan.
  - B. Gather facts.
  - C. Execute and monitor the new estate plan.
  - D. Evaluate the existing estate plan.

19

19

Practice

- Mark owned the following assets at his death. Which one of the following assets will be included in Mark's probate estate?
  - A. Raw land owned as joint tenants with rights of survivorship with his brother.
  - B. Life insurance death benefits received by Mark's son as the named beneficiary.
  - C. A revocable trust that names Mark's cousin as the beneficiary of trust assets.
  - D. A small business transferred to Mark's wife through his Will.

20

20

Gift and Estate Tax

Objective III

21

21

Gift and Estate Tax

- Effective estate planning can maximize the amount of an estate's value that escapes taxation.
  - The effect of federal gift and estate taxes on the value of an estate must be considered in the estate planning process.
  - Laws regarding these taxes are subject to change.

22

22

Federal Gift Tax

- The federal gift tax applies to all transfers of property, whether tangible or intangible.
  - Tangible – real estate, equipment.
  - Intangible – stocks, patents.
- The law contains an annual gift tax exclusion for gifts of a present interest.
  - This exclusion is allowed for each donee and is available each year.
  - The federal gift tax is not designed to tax ordinary gifts, such as birthday presents.

23

23

Federal Gift Tax

- Other gift tax exclusions:
  - Gift splitting – spouses who give gifts jointly are deemed to each have given 50% of gift.
  - Gifts used to pay tuition (not room and board, or books).
  - Gifts used to pay medical expenses.
  - Gifts to charities.
- Individuals can combine up to five years of annual exclusions for 529 plan contributions.

24

24

Federal Gift Tax

- An unlimited marital deduction is available for gifts to spouses.
  - Facilitates making gifts between living spouses for estate planning purposes.
  - The value of property given to a spouse within the restrictions of the marital deduction escapes federal estate taxation.
- An appropriate gifting strategy is to gift property that is likely to appreciate.
  - Can also reduce federal estate taxes.

25

25

Federal Estate Tax

- The federal estate tax is imposed on property transferred at death.
- Steps in calculating estate tax:
  - Determine gross estate.
  - Determine taxable estate.
  - Determine tentative tax before credits.
  - Determine tax payable.

26

26

Gross Estate

- Gross estate includes assets owned at death.
  - Valued on date of death or alternate valuation date six months later.
- Gross estate value of jointly owned property:
  - Fractional interest rule – half of the value of property owned with a spouse is included in the gross estate of the first spouse to die.
  - Consideration furnished rule – property jointly owned by non-spouses is included in estate based on consideration furnished.

27

27

Taxable Estate

- The taxable estate is calculated by subtracting allowable deductions from the gross estate.
  - Administrative expenses.
  - Burial (funeral) expenses.
  - Casualty losses.
  - Debts.
  - Marital deduction.
  - Charitable deduction.

28

28

Tentative Tax and Tax Payable

- The tentative tax is determined based on the taxable estate.
  - Estate tax rates are graduated rates and are designed to tax large estates.
- The tentative tax is reduced by any applicable credits to determine the tax payable.
  - Unified credit.
  - Foreign death taxes.
  - Credit for taxes paid on prior transfers.

29

29

State Death Taxes

- Some states also impose a death tax.
  - State estate tax – patterned after federal estate tax and paid by the estate.
  - State inheritance tax – imposed on beneficiary's share of property received.

30

30

Practice

- The federal gift tax applies to:
  - A. All transfers of property, whether tangible or intangible.
  - B. Transfers of financial assets only.
  - C. All direct transfers of property but not indirect transfers.
  - D. Transfers of all real property but not transfers of personal property.

31

31

Practice

- Which one of the following represents a deduction from the gross estate in arriving at the taxable estate?
  - A. Prior gift tax paid.
  - B. Annual exclusion.
  - C. Executor's fees.
  - D. Unified credit.

32

32

Practice

- Jennifer and her brother, Harris, purchased real estate together for $300,000. Jennifer paid $200,000 for the property, and Harris paid $100,000, and each can prove their contribution. Jennifer died when the property was worth $900,000. What is the value of the real estate that will be included in Jennifer's gross estate for estate tax purposes?
  - A. $200,000.
  - B. $300,000.
  - C. $600,000.
  - D. $900,000.

33

33

Estate Planning Tools

Objective IV

34

34

Estate Planning Goals

- The goals of estate planning include:
  - Minimizing federal and state taxes paid.
  - Distributing estate property according to the estate owner's wishes.
- Tools that can help achieve these goals:
  - Wills.
  - Trusts.
  - Life Insurance.

35

35

Wills

- A Will is a legal expression of wishes about the disposition of property at death.
  - A Will is important for both small and large estate owners.
- Advantages of a Will:
  - Can provide income to surviving family members during probate process.
  - Allows decedent to select the estate executor.
  - Can minimize problems arising from distributions to minor children.

36

36

Wills

- Advantages of a Will:
  - Can include information about specific property and advice for its management.
  - Helps minimize estate shrinkage.
    - Can minimize estate taxes if drawn properly.
  - Can be used to make bequests and establish trusts.

37

37

Wills

- A properly-drafted Will should:
  - Be in writing and signed by the creator and at least two witnesses.
  - Identify heirs and property to be received.
  - Name the estate's executor.
  - Be reviewed and updated periodically with an attorney's help.

38

38

Wills

- The executor oversees the distribution of the estate and is responsible for:
  - Collecting the deceased's assets.
  - Determining and paying legal claims against the estate.
  - Distributing remaining assets to the proper individuals.

39

39

Wills

- Estate owners might choose individuals as executors because they are family members.
  - Individual executors are generally less expensive than corporate executors.
- Advantages of corporate executors:
  - Usually have more experience settling estates.
  - Cannot be disabled or die before or during the settlement process.
  - Lack emotional biases that some individual executors might have.

40

40

Trusts

- A trust is an arrangement by which one party holds title to property for the benefit of another.
- Parties to a trust:
  - Grantor – establishes the trust.
    - Also called settlor.
  - Trustee – administers the trust.
  - Property – corpus or res.
  - Beneficiary – person or organization.
  - Terms – based on trust document.

41

41

Trusts

- Responsibilities of a trustee include:
  - Administer trust solely for beneficiaries.
  - Retain (not delegate) trust administration.
  - Keep and provide accurate records.
  - Furnish information to beneficiaries.
  - Exercise reasonable care and skill.
  - Keep control of and preserve trust property.
  - Keep trust property separate from other property.

42

42

Trusts

- Responsibilities of a trustee include:
  - Make trust property productive.
  - Deal impartially with beneficiaries.
  - Cooperate with co-trustees.
  - Submit to the control of others who have legal authority to direct the trustee.

43

43

Trusts

- Two basic types of trusts:
  - Living (inter vivos) trusts – created during the grantor's life.
    - Revocable – becomes irrevocable at death.
      - Avoids probate.
    - Irrevocable – reduces estate taxes.
      - Avoids probate.
  - Testamentary trusts – created at death.

44

44

Trusts

- Trusts used in estate planning include:
  - Charitable remainder trusts.
  - Life insurance trusts.
  - Sprinkle trusts – trustee has discretion to distribute income to beneficiaries.

45

45

Life Insurance

- Life insurance payable to the estate is often an important source of liquidity.
- For married couples, second-to-die or survivorship life insurance is popular.
  - Pays the death benefit after the last surviving spouse dies.
  - Marital deduction can be used at the first spouse's death to minimize or eliminate estate taxes.

46

46

* State death taxes paid by a decedent's estate are allowed as a dedn against the federal estate tax due

Life Insurance

- Life insurance in which the insured has incidents of ownership is included in the gross estate.
  - Policy death benefit included in gross estate.
- Incidents of ownership include the power to:
  - Designate or change the policy's beneficiary.
  - Surrender the policy.
  - Assign or borrow the policy's cash value.
- Paying premiums is not considered an incident of ownership.

47

47

* portability feature of estate tax allows any unused portion of exemption to pass to a surviving spouse at the time of first spouse's death.

Practice

- Estate owners may choose either an individual or a corporation to be the executor of their estate. Which one of the following is a reason a corporate executor may be more appropriate than an individual executor?
  - A. A corporate executor usually employs a member of the family.
  - B. A corporate executor is generally less expensive than an individual executor.
  - C. A corporate executor is typically closer to the family than an individual executor.
  - ✓ D. A corporate executor may act more objectively than an individual executor.

48

48

* Mr X contributed the entire purchase price, entire value of the land will be included in X's gross estate because of consideration furnished rule.

Practice

- Which one of the following represents a statutory responsibility of a trustee?
  - A. Delegate the administration of the trust.
  - B. Make the trust property productive. ✓
  - C. Provide information to the grantor.
  - D. Act in the best interest of the settlor.

49

49

* Assets passed to heirs through the use of a will are included in probate estate.

* Property owned as JTWROS avoids probate because it ~~pas~~ automatically passes to the surviving tenants

* Life Ins death benefits will pass by contract to the named beneficiary upon insured's death thus avoiding probate.

* A revocable trust has a named beneficiary. The assets in the trust will pass by contract upon the grantor's death, thus avoiding probate.

* under fractional interest rule 50% of the death value of the property will be included in gross estate of the first spouse to die, irrespective of which spouse paid for the property

Module 8

Income Tax

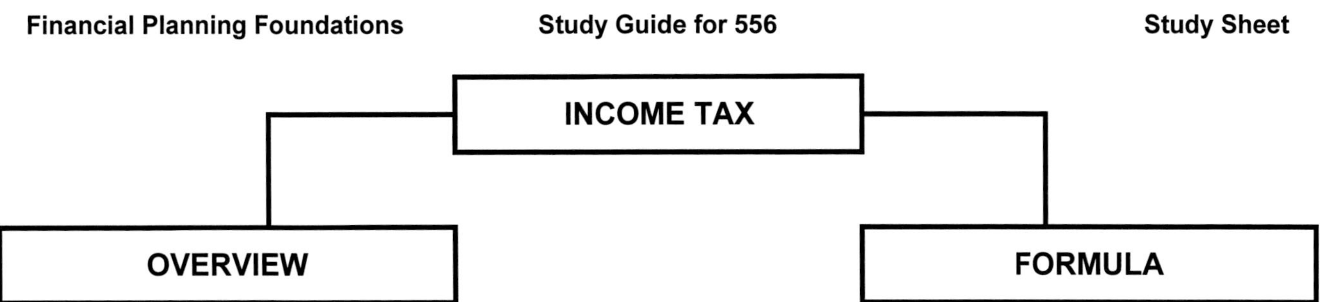

OVERVIEW

- OBJECTIVES OF TAX PLANNING
  - MINIMIZING TAX LIABILITY
  - SATISFYING GOALS AND OBJECTIVES
- TAX DEFERRAL
  - RETIREMENT PLANS
- TAX AVOIDANCE
  - INCOME SHIFTING
  - CHARITABLE CONTRIBUTIONS
  - TAX-FREE INCOME

FORMULA

- GROSS INCOME
- DEDUCTIONS FOR AGI
- ADJUSTED GROSS INCOME
- STANDARD OR ITEMIZED DEDUCTION
- TAXABLE INCOME

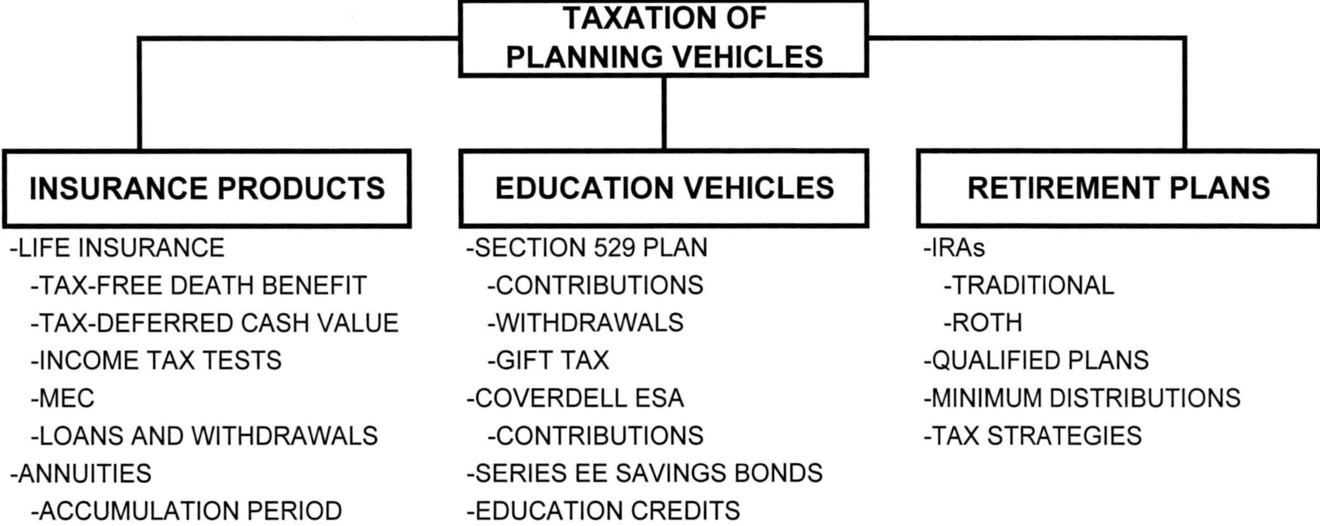

INSURANCE PRODUCTS

- LIFE INSURANCE
  - TAX-FREE DEATH BENEFIT
  - TAX-DEFERRED CASH VALUE
  - INCOME TAX TESTS
  - MEC
  - LOANS AND WITHDRAWALS
- ANNUITIES
  - ACCUMULATION PERIOD
  - ANNUITIZATION PERIOD
  - DEATH BENEFITS

EDUCATION VEHICLES

- SECTION 529 PLAN
  - CONTRIBUTIONS
  - WITHDRAWALS
  - GIFT TAX
- COVERDELL ESA
  - CONTRIBUTIONS
- SERIES EE SAVINGS BONDS
- EDUCATION CREDITS
- SCHOLARSHIPS

RETIREMENT PLANS

- IRAs
  - TRADITIONAL
  - ROTH
- QUALIFIED PLANS
- MINIMUM DISTRIBUTIONS
- TAX STRATEGIES

Income Tax

Module 8
Chapter 8

1

1

Objectives

- Obj I: Basic Tax Concepts
- Obj II: Taxation of Life Insurance and Annuities
- Obj III: Taxation of Education Funding Vehicles
- Obj IV: Taxation of Retirement Plans
- Obj V: Taxation of Transferred Property

2

2

Basic Tax Concepts

Objective I

3

3

Income Tax Planning

- The two primary objectives of income tax planning are:
  - Minimizing an individual's overall income tax liability.
  - Satisfying the individual's goals and objectives with minimal income tax consequences.

4

4

Gross Income

- Gross income includes all income from whatever source derived.
  - Includes earned income and investment income, as well as gain from sale of property.
- Capital gain can be long-term or short-term.
  - Long-term gains are taxed at favorable rates.
    - Qualified dividends also taxed at favorable rates.
  - Long-term if asset held > 12 months.

5

5

Adjusted Gross Income

- Adjusted gross income represents gross income, less certain deductions.
  - Deductions for AGI are referred to as "above-the-line" deductions.
  - Most "above-the-line" deductions are business related deductions.
- AGI is an important amount because it is used to determine many other phase-outs.
  - AGI is used for charitable contribution limitations.

6

6

Taxable Income

- Taxable income represents AGI less the greater of:
  - Standard deduction.
  - Itemized deductions.
    - Medical expenses.
    - Interest expense.
    - Charitable contributions.

7

7

Tax Due

- Income tax due is determined by applying the tax rate schedule to taxable income.
  - Based on filing status.
- Credits are then applied.
  - Retirement savings contribution credit, foreign tax credit, and child and dependent care credit.
- Other taxes may apply, such as self-employment tax.

8

8

Tax Deferral and Avoidance

- Tax deferral represents the delay of income taxation until a later date.
  - Contributing to a 401(k) plan, IRA, or annuity.
  - May be taxed at lower rate in future.
- Tax avoidance is the legal strategy of reducing or eliminating income taxation.
  - Shifting assets to children.
  - Charitable contributions.
  - Investing in tax-free bonds.

9

9

Practice

- Tom contributed the maximum allowable pre-tax amount to his 401(k) plan in the current year to lower his current tax liability. Tom has implemented the tax planning strategy of:
  - A. Tax deferral.
  - B. Tax avoidance.
  - C. Tax evasion.
  - D. Tax development.

10

10

Taxation of Life Insurance and Annuities

Objective II

11

11

Taxation of Life Insurance

- Life insurance has several tax advantages.
  - Death benefit is generally tax-free.
  - Cash value generally grows tax-deferred.
- If policy is sold or surrendered, a taxable gain may result.
  - Gain is based on excess of cash value of policy over the cost basis.
  - The cost basis of the policy is based on the premiums paid.

12

12

Modified Endowment Contract

- A MEC is a policy that meets the definition of life insurance but fails the seven-pay test.
  - Aggregate premiums paid in first 7 years must not exceed sum of net level premiums that would have been paid under a policy that would be paid up after 7 years.
- If the policy is a MEC, withdrawals and loans are subject to unfavorable tax treatment.

13

13

Withdrawals from Life Insurance

- Cash value withdrawals are subject to FIFO basis recovery.
  - MEC – cash value withdrawals subject to LIFO basis recovery.
- Loans are generally 100% tax-free.
  - MEC – loans subject to LIFO basis recovery.
- Example – Rick has a policy with a basis of $50,000 and a cash value of $60,000. He borrowed $15,000 from the policy.

14

14

Annuities

- During the accumulation period, interest credited to an annuity is tax-deferred.
  - Cash value withdrawals and loans are considered distributions and are taxed under LIFO basis recovery.
    - 10% penalty may also apply.
  - If a deferred annuity is surrendered, excess of cash value over cost basis is ordinary income.

15

15

Annuities

- Payments received during the annuitization period are partially taxable.
  - Exclusion ratio must be determined.
  - Tax-free portion = Basis / Number of Payments
- Death benefits are paid if the contract owner dies during the accumulation period.
  - Annuities do not receive a step-up in basis.
  - Beneficiary will pay tax on gain associated with the contract.

16

16

Practice

- Which one of the following statements is correct regarding the income tax consequences of life insurance?
  - A. The cost basis of a life insurance policy is equal to the policy's net cash value.
  - B. The death benefit received from a life insurance policy is generally taxable to the recipient.
  - C. If the policy is classified as a modified endowment contract, loans and withdrawals will generally be income tax-free.
  - D. Withdrawals from a life insurance policy are usually taxed FIFO basis recovery (basis first).

17

17

Practice

- Terri, age 60, purchased a nonqualified flexible premium deferred annuity several years ago. She has paid premiums totaling $20,000 over the years. The annuity was worth $25,000 yesterday. Today, Terri took a $3,000 loan from the annuity to purchase a car. How much of the loan will be subject to federal income taxation?
  - A. $0.
  - B. $600.
  - C. $2,400.
  - D. $3,000.

18

18

Taxation of Education Funding Vehicles

Objective III

19

19

Section 529 Plans

- Contributions are allowed regardless of the amount of the contributor's income.
  - Not deductible for income tax purposes.
- Withdrawals are tax-free if used for qualified higher education expenses.
  - Tuition, books, fees, supplies, room and board.
  - Nonqualified distributions are taxed and may be subject to a 10% penalty.

20

20

Coverdell Education Savings Acct.

- A Coverdell Education Savings Account is an education savings funding vehicle.
  - Contribution is limited to $2,000 per year.
    - No restrictions as to whom can contribute.
    - Not deductible for federal tax purposes.
  - Ability to make contributions phased-out.
  - Distributions to pay qualified education expenses are tax-free.

21

21

Series EE Savings Bonds

- Series EE bonds are U.S. Savings bonds.
  - Have fixed rate, making them poor hedge against inflation.
- Tax-free at redemption if used for education and income below threshold.
  - Bond holder must have been at least age 24 when the bond was purchased.
  - Room and board expenses are not eligible for purposes of the interest exclusion.

22

22

American Opportunity Tax Credit

- The American Opportunity Tax Credit is allowed for expenses incurred for the first four years of post-secondary education.
  - Applies on a per-student basis.
  - Phased-out for taxpayers whose MAGI exceeds a prescribed level.
  - Only available to a student enrolled at least half-time for at least one academic period.
  - Maximum credit of $2,500 per student.

23

23

Lifetime Learning Credit

- The Lifetime Learning Credit is allowed for expenses incurred for education.
  - Available for unlimited number of years.
  - Applies on a per-taxpayer basis.
  - Available even if not half-time student.
  - Phased-out based on AGI.
  - Maximum credit is $2,000.

24

24

Scholarships

- For purposes of tax-free scholarships, qualified education expenses include:
  - Tuition, books, fees.
  - Equipment and supplies.
- A scholarship is only tax-free if the student is a candidate for a degree.

25

25

Practice

- Which one of the following statements is correct regarding education funding vehicles?
  - A. Contributions to a Section 529 plan are deductible for federal income tax purposes.
  - B. Room and board expenses are not eligible expenses for purposes of the Series EE bond interest exclusion.
  - C. Amounts received for a scholarship are tax-free, even if used to pay for room and board.
  - D. The maximum permitted contribution to a Coverdell Education Savings Account is $5,000 per year.

26

26

Taxation of Retirement Plans

Objective IV

27

27

IRAs

- Contributions to either a Traditional or Roth IRA cannot exceed an individual's earned income.
- Includes:
  - Salary, bonuses, and professional fees.
  - Alimony payments received.
- Excludes:
  - Interest, dividends.
  - Rental income.
  - Annuities.

28

28

Traditional IRA

- Contributions to a traditional IRA cannot be made after participant attains age 70½.
- Contributions may be deductible for federal income tax purposes.
  - If participant is not an active participant in another plan, the contribution is deductible.
  - If participant is an active participant, deduction may be phased-out based on AGI.

29

29

Traditional IRA

- Distributions are taxed pro-rata basis.
  - Basis and earnings are pro-rated, so each distribution represents a portion in earnings.
  - Minimum distribution rules apply when participant attains age 70½.
  - Early withdrawal penalty (10%) may apply.

30

30

Roth IRA

- Roth IRA contributions are never deductible.
  - Minimum distribution rules do not apply while Roth IRA owner is alive.
- Distributions are taxed assuming FIFO basis.
  - Basis is considered distributed first, and earnings last.
  - Basis is tax-free, regardless of what distribution is used for.

31

31

Roth IRA

- Distributions of earnings can be tax-free.
  - Distribution must meet requirements of a qualifying distribution.
- Qualifying distributions must meet two tests:
  - Made after five-year period beginning with first tax year of contribution -AND-
  - Meets ONE of the following conditions:
    - Participant age 59½ or older, deceased, disabled, or buying a home.

32

32

Roth IRA

- Qualified plans and traditional IRAs may be converted to a Roth IRA.
  - Conversion subject to ordinary income tax in the year of the conversion.
  - Basis in traditional IRA is not taxed.
  - Conversion not subject to 10% penalty.

33

33

Qualified Plan

- Employer contributions to a qualified plan are deductible by the employer.
  - Employee contributions may be made on a pre-tax basis.
  - Roth contributions are after-tax.
- Plan earnings are tax-deferred until distributed.
- Distributions from the plan are generally taxable to the employee.

34

34

Qualified Plan

- Some qualified plans offer loan provisions.
  - Loans are not taxable.
- General requirements of plan loans:
  - Must typically be repaid within five years.
  - Repayment terms must call for payments involving principal and interest.
  - Maximum loan is $50,000.

35

35

Required Minimum Distributions

- Qualified plans and traditional IRAs generally require distributions to begin by April 1 after the year the participant attains age 72.
  - Roth IRAs do not require minimum distributions while account owner is alive.
- Failure to take required minimum distribution will result in a 50% penalty.

36

36

Tax Strategies

- Withdrawals from various accounts should be coordinated with the retiree's income tax liability:
  - If lower taxes are expected due to medical expenses or business losses, tax-deferred funds should be accessed.
  - If higher taxes are expected, currently taxable accounts or Roth IRAs should be accessed.
    - Currently taxable accounts may result in lower capital gains rates.

37

37

Practice

- Janet converted her traditional IRA to a Roth IRA. Which of the following statements is correct regarding the income tax treatment of this conversion?
  - A. The conversion will be tax-free and penalty-free.
  - B. The conversion will be subject to income tax but will be penalty-free.
  - C. The conversion will be tax-free but will be subject to a penalty.
  - D. The conversion will be subject to income tax and a penalty.

38

38

Taxation of Transferred Property

Objective V

39

39

Income in Respect of a Decedent

- IRD is income earned but not received at the time of death.
  - Included in decedent's gross estate.
  - Subject to income tax to recipient.
- IRD examples:
  - Salary.
  - Death benefit from qualified plan.
  - Traditional IRA.
  - Annuity.

40

40

Income in Respect of a Decedent

- Qualified plan death benefits are a significant source of IRD.
  - Tax treatment depends on when death occurs.
- If death occurs before retirement, death benefit paid in a lump-sum is taxed as follows:
  - Paid from life insurance – cash value less decedent's cost basis is taxable.
  - Not paid from life insurance – death benefit less cost basis is taxable.

41

41

Basis of Inherited Property

- Basis of inherited property is generally the value of the property on the date of death.
  - Step-up in basis.
  - All inherited property is long-term.
- Example – Janet purchased stock for $10,000 six months ago. Today, Janet died when the stock was worth $12,000. She left the stock to her son Rob.
  - Rob's basis in the stock is $12,000.

42

42

Basis of Gift Property

- The basis of property received as a gift is generally the donor's basis in the property.
  - Appreciated property – basis is equal to donor's basis
    - Plus allocable portion of any gift tax paid.
  - Loss property – basis is determined when property subsequently sold.
    - Sold at gain – use donor's basis.
    - Sold at loss – use fair market value at time of gift.

43

43

Trust Taxation

- If a trust is irrevocable, the income retained by the trust is generally taxed to the trust.
  - Income paid to the beneficiary is generally taxed to the beneficiary.
  - Income retains its character when passed to the beneficiary.

44

44

Trust Taxation

- If a trust is classified as a grantor trust, the grantor pays all tax on trust income.
  - Whether the income is retained or distributed is irrelevant.
- A trust will be considered a grantor trust if the trust is revocable, or the grantor can change the beneficiaries.

45

45

Practice

- When a donor gives a gift of appreciated property, the recipient's basis in the property is the:
  - A. Fair market value of the property reduced by any gift tax paid.
  - B. Donor's basis in the property plus a portion of any gift tax paid.
  - C. Fair market value of the property if subsequently sold at a gain, or the donor's basis if subsequently sold for a loss.
  - D. Average of the donor's cost basis and the fair market value on the date of the gift.

46

46

Practice

- If an irrevocable trust pays income to the trust beneficiary, the income is typically taxed to the:
  - A. Beneficiary.
  - B. Grantor.
  - C. Trustee.
  - D. Trust.

47

47

Module 9

Test Bank

MODULE 1

1. Which of the following best describes financial planning?
   A. It is a process used to select an investment advisor to make recommendations regarding investment products.
   B. It is the process by which individuals implement a comprehensive financial plan to help achieve their financial goals.
   C. It is a strategy used to eliminate loss exposures for individuals and families.
   D. It represents the techniques that are used to pass assets to future generations.

2. Which one of the following statements is correct regarding financial planning goals?
   A. Financial goals are similar among different individuals and remain fairly constant over time.
   B. Financial goals often create conflict because individuals have limited resources to satisfy their goals.
   C. Building wealth is the most basic financial goal for most individuals.
   D. Comprehensive financial plans are designed for ad hoc achievement of goals.

3. Which one of the following is considered a basic financial goal that is generally satisfied by individuals before focusing on other financial goals?
   A. Emergency fund establishment.
   B. Creating an estate plan.
   C. Saving for retirement.
   D. Protecting against loss of income.

4. Which one of the following represents characteristics of an empty nester?
   A. Peak earnings, focus on retirement planning and estate planning.
   B. Wealth declines, focus on long-term care insurance and wealth preservation.
   C. Peak earnings, focus on college funding.
   D. Income increases, focus on auto and health insurance.

5. Which one of the following statements is correct regarding the personal financial planning lifecycle?
   A. Married or single individuals with children in college typically focus on major purchases and college funding.
   B. Individuals in their early 20s are most likely to make a maximum effort to divert income toward retirement.
   C. During the retirement years, risk management typically focuses on health and long-term care costs.
   D. Tax planning is most likely to be simplistic and uncomplicated for empty nesters.

6. In which of the following phases of the personal financial planning life cycle would income increase, and the risk management focus would be on life insurance, building an emergency fund, and college funding?
   A. Early 20s.
   B. Single/married with children.
   C. Empty nester.
   D. Retired.

7. Which one of the following statements is correct regarding the personal financial planning life cycle?
   A. A primary focus for empty nesters should be on estate planning.
   B. Income typically reaches its peak for an individual during retirement.
   C. During the retirement years, planning typically refocuses on health costs.
   D. Wealth distribution is a major priority for a married individual with no children.

8. Which one of the following statements is correct regarding tax planning?
   A. Tax planning focuses on the efficient transfer of an individual's assets to family members and charity.
   B. Tax planning seldom requires a partnership with a professional tax planner.
   C. Efficient tax planning can reduce the after-tax cost of health insurance.
   D. Tax planning does not have any influence on an individual's investment decisions.

9. In comprehensive financial planning, which one of the following loss exposures is typically handled without the use of insurance?
   A. Health loss exposures.
   B. Property loss exposures.
   C. Premature death loss exposures.
   D. Unemployment loss exposures.

10. The primary method of risk management planning for individuals is:
   A. Risk avoidance.
   B. Separation.
   C. Insurance.
   D. Retention.

11. A strategy of investing the same amount of money in an investment every period, regardless of the movement of the stock market, is referred to as:
   A. Dollar-cost averaging.
   B. Dividend reinvestment.
   C. Market timing.
   D. Risk control.

12. Which one of the following statements is correct regarding personal financial planning techniques?
   A. Tax planning focuses exclusively on minimizing federal taxes.
   B. A special needs trust allows an individual to receive benefits from an inheritance without losing government assistance.
   C. A deductible in a health insurance plan is an example of the risk management technique of risk avoidance.
   D. Most financial planners suggest individuals accumulate assets sufficient to replace 40-50% of preretirement income each year.

13. Which one of the following statements is correct regarding personal financial planning techniques?
   A. Social Security benefits were originally designed to be the sole source of income for retirees.
   B. A formal Will eliminates the need for comprehensive estate planning.
   C. For individuals, the number of investment strategies tends to be somewhat limited.
   D. Short-term investment horizons typically call for little or no risk of principal loss.

14. Tom's 12-year-old granddaughter was permanently disabled in an automobile accident. She is currently receiving government benefits. Tom would like to provide her with financial support, but he is concerned that a direct gift will cause her to lose her government benefits. What would be the best strategy for Tom?
    - A. Will.
    - B. Life insurance.
    - C. Special needs trust.
    - D. Market timing.

15. Bob and Clarissa, both age 28, are married. They have no children. Bob earns $3,000 per month after taxes, and Clarissa earns $4,000 per month after taxes. Their monthly rent expense is $1,000, insurance is $400, and their monthly credit card bill is $800. Clarissa may lose her job due to downsizing at her employer's company. Which one of the following statements best describes their current financial situation with respect to the job loss risk exposure?
    - A. Based on their current cash flow, it is highly likely they will have to declare bankruptcy if Clarissa loses her job.
    - B. If Clarissa lost her job, they would actually be in a better financial position because she would receive tax-free unemployment benefits that would fully replace her income.
    - C. Although they would experience some impact long-term if Clarissa lost her job, Bob's income is sufficient to satisfy their current cash flow needs.
    - D. The job loss risk exposure is actually higher with respect to Bob losing his job than it is with respect to Clarissa losing her job.

16. Which one of the following represents a social insurance program that must be incorporated into a risk management plan?
    - A. Life insurance.
    - B. Annuity.
    - C. Disability insurance.
    - D. Unemployment insurance.

17. Which one of the following statements is correct regarding the role of property and liability insurance in personal financial planning?
    - A. Homeowners insurance policies include liability exposure coverage as part of the package.
    - B. An individual's automobile is typically the largest asset and therefore the largest property expense.
    - C. Flood exposures are covered in the typical homeowners insurance policy.
    - D. Most families are able to adequately cover their auto liability exposures by purchasing the state limits of auto liability insurance.

18. Which one of the following statements is correct regarding life insurance and annuity products?
    - A. One of the most effective ways a family can manage the premature death loss exposure is to purchase an annuity.
    - B. Term insurance provides a greater death benefit per dollar of premium than a cash value life insurance policy.
    - C. The human life value approach attempts to estimate a family's financial needs to determine the appropriate amount of life insurance.
    - D. Annuities are primarily designed to provide income in the case of a disability.

19. Which one of the following methods of determining life insurance needs uses the estimated present value of the insured's financial contribution to the family to determine the income the family could lose in the event of the insured's death?
    A. Income replacement ratio approach.
    B. Annuity approach.
    C. Human life value approach.
    D. Needs-based approach.

20. Which one of the following statements is correct regarding health and disability insurance?
    A. Most disability policies cover custodial care for older individuals.
    B. Medicare is the major source of health insurance in the United States.
    C. Disability insurance may be more important to a family than life insurance.
    D. Employer-sponsored health plans usually waive any deductibles and coinsurance provisions.

21. Which one of the following statements is correct regarding Social Security?
    A. Medicaid provides health insurance benefits for those who opt out of employer-sponsored retiree health insurance plans.
    B. Retirement benefits are based on a worker's lifetime earnings.
    C. By the year 2027, the full retirement age will be age 65.
    D. A retiree can begin collecting benefits as early as age 60.

22. Which one of the following statements is correct regarding unemployment insurance?
    A. Benefits are typically provided for up to five years.
    B. All state governments sponsor unemployment compensation programs.
    C. These programs are funded exclusively by employer-paid premiums.
    D. Benefits are uniform from state-to-state.

23. The first step of the financial planning process is:
    A. Implementing the plan.
    B. Gathering data.
    C. Identifying and evaluating alternatives.
    D. Establishing financial goals.

24. Creation of a balance sheet and cash flow statement occurs during which phase of the financial planning process?
    A. Gathering information.
    B. Implementing the plan.
    C. Analyzing the current situation.
    D. Establishing and prioritizing goals.

25. Which one of the following occurs during the "Identify and Evaluate Alternatives" step of the financial planning process?
    A. Create a balance sheet and cash flow statement.
    B. Drafting Wills and incapacity documents.
    C. Revising the financial plan.
    D. Determine appropriate insurance policies.

26. Tom and Laura, a married couple, have a 2-year-old daughter. They would like to begin saving for their daughter's education, so they had a financial plan created by a local personal financial planner. The plan indicated that they need to save $10,000 per year to fund the education. Tom opened a Section 529 plan and deposited $10,000 yesterday. This is an example of which step of the financial planning process?
    A. Establishing financial goals.
    B. Monitoring the plan.
    C. Analyzing the current situation.
    D. Implementing the plan.

MODULE 2

27. Which one of the following statements is correct regarding yearly renewable term insurance?
    - A. It represents a pure protection policy with no cash value.
    - B. It requires the policyowner to provide evidence of insurability before renewing.
    - C. It is the most comprehensive form of insurance offered by life insurance companies.
    - D. The premium is determined by the death rate at the insured's original age when the policy was first issued.

28. Which one of the following is the best description of a decreasing term life insurance policy during the policy period?
    - A. Increasing premium, level face amount.
    - B. Decreasing premium, level face amount.
    - C. Level premium, decreasing face amount.
    - D. Decreasing premium, decreasing face amount.

29. Which one of the following would be the best application of a decreasing term policy?
    - A. Funding of a buy-sell agreement.
    - B. To provide a higher face amount over time to an insured who cannot currently afford the premiums.
    - C. To cover the outstanding balance on a mortgage.
    - D. Insured needs a policy with lower premiums in the early years.

30. Which one of the following statements is correct regarding term insurance?
    - A. Most level term insurance policies contain a conversion provision allowing the policy to be converted into a decreasing term life insurance policy.
    - B. These policies contain a cash value that increases based on a guaranteed interest rate.
    - C. Absent any secondary guarantees, term life insurance coverage terminates without value at the end of the specified period of coverage.
    - D. The death benefit under straight line decreasing term insurance is meant to coincide with the decreasing principal balance as a mortgage is paid down over time.

31. Which one of the following statements is correct regarding the renewability feature of a term life insurance policy?
    - A. This feature allows the insured to renew the policy for a period of time without providing evidence of insurability.
    - B. Renewable term insurance is satisfactory for an individual and the insurance company when coverage extends into higher ages.
    - C. The premiums will not increase if this feature is used to renew the policy.
    - D. The chief function of this feature is to protect the insurance company from adverse selection.

32. Which one of the following statements is correct regarding the convertibility provision contained in some term life insurance policies?
    A. The provision permits the policy owner to exchange the term contract for a permanent contract if the owner can provide evidence of insurability.
    B. The provision serves those who want permanent insurance but are temporarily unable to afford higher premiums.
    C. The provision allows an insured to purchase temporary insurance and permanent insurance in the same policy.
    D. The convertibility provision is similar to a renewability provision in that both provisions guarantee access to permanent insurance in the future.

33. Which one of the following represents a characteristic of a universal life insurance policy?
    A. Shifting of mortality and expense risk to the insurance company.
    B. The insurer is prohibited from imposing a surrender charge.
    C. Policyowners are prohibited from withdrawing against the cash value.
    D. The premium charges are separated into three traditional elements.

34. The net amount at risk remains constant in a universal life insurance policy under which death benefit option?
    A. Option A.
    B. Option B.
    C. Option C.
    D. Option D.

35. Which one of the following statements is correct regarding universal life insurance?
    A. The Option B death benefit features a generally increasing death benefit equal to the specified amount plus premiums paid.
    B. The cash value of the policy is increased by a fixed rate each year, as specified in the policy illustration.
    C. The amount at risk in the policy has no effect on the tax treatment of the cash value.
    D. Withdrawals from the policy are considered partial surrenders and may be subject to surrender charges.

36. Gene applied for a universal life insurance policy and specified a death benefit equal to $200,000 plus the total premiums paid. Gene elected a death benefit option referred to as:
    A. Option A.
    B. Option B.
    C. Option C.
    D. Option D.

37. Jimmy is age 25, married, and has a 2-year-old son. He just started a new job and would like to purchase a home in the next 3 years. His employer offers him term insurance equal to 2 times his salary, at no cost to Jimmy. Jimmy expects his life insurance need to increase over the next few years and would like to purchase a permanent policy. Jimmy would like premium flexibility, as he may experience uncertain cash flow in the future and would like a death benefit that can be adjusted to satisfy his increasing insurance needs. He does not want to absorb the risk of investment losses with respect to the policy and has no desire to manage policy investments. The most appropriate type of policy for Jimmy to purchase is a:
   A. Variable universal policy.
   B. Universal policy.
   C. Whole life policy.
   D. Term policy.

38. Brittney is age 38, and a single mother with two teenage children. She is in good health and is concerned that there will be insufficient funds to pay for their college education if she should die prematurely. Assuming she is insurable, she should purchase a(n):
   A. Annual renewable term insurance policy.
   B. 10-year term insurance policy.
   C. Universal life insurance policy.
   D. Variable life insurance policy.

39. Scott and Stacy would like to purchase a permanent insurance policy on Scott's life. They would like premium flexibility, and the ability to borrow against the cash value. In addition, they are risk tolerant and would like to be able to invest the cash value in equity-type investments. Which of the following types of insurance policies would be most appropriate?
   A. Whole life policy.
   B. Variable universal policy.
   C. Universal policy.
   D. Limited pay whole life policy.

40. Which one of the following statements is correct regarding types of annuities?
   A. Indexed annuities are the most regulated of the three types of deferred annuities.
   B. A variable annuity allows the annuity purchaser to participate in the investment of the annuity funds.
   C. Immediate annuities typically accept additional premiums after the first premium has been paid.
   D. A deferred annuity is an annuity that accepts pre-tax dollars from an employer-sponsored retirement program or IRA.

41. Which one of the following statements is correct regarding the characteristics of annuities?
   A. Immediate annuities have an accumulation period.
   B. Distributions from a qualified annuity may be subject to a 20% penalty if made before age 55.
   C. A fixed annuity's value fluctuates with that of an underlying securities portfolio.
   D. With a nonqualified annuity, the investment in the contract is not taxed when distributed.

42. Which one of the following types of annuities will provide a monthly benefit for the longer of the participant's life or some specified period of time?
   A. Life annuity with period certain guarantee.
   B. Joint and survivor annuity.
   C. Annuity certain.
   D. Installment payments.

43. Which one of the following represents a refund annuity?
   A. Periodic payments continuing for the annuitant's life and ceasing at the time of the annuitant's death.
   B. Periodic payments continuing for an individual's life, with payments to continue for a certain period of time if the individual dies before that period has elapsed.
   C. Periodic payments continuing for an individual's life, with a balance to be paid at the time of the annuitant's death if the annuitant's basis has not been fully recovered.
   D. Periodic payments continuing for an individual's life, with decreasing periodic payments continuing to the individual's spouse at the time of the individual's death.

44. Which one of the following statements is correct regarding an indexed annuity?
   A. Similar to a variable annuity, an indexed annuity can only be sold by a registered representative.
   B. Some indexed annuities are tied to a stock index, and some are tied to a bond index.
   C. The account value will experience a loss if market conditions deteriorate.
   D. Indexed annuities are immediate annuities.

45. In the case of a variable annuity, the insurer is subject to the risk that the annuitant will outlive their table life expectancy. To compensate for this risk, the insurer includes which one of the following in the premium?
   A. Surrender charge.
   B. 12b-1 fee.
   C. Mortality and expense charge.
   D. Front-end sales load.

46. Jennifer would like to accumulate money for her planned retirement in 15 years. To satisfy her retirement goal, Jennifer should purchase:
   A. An immediate annuity with a single premium.
   B. A deferred annuity with periodic premiums.
   C. A deferred annuity with a single premium.
   D. An immediate annuity with periodic premiums.

47. Donna purchased a flexible premium deferred annuity 15 years ago. To date, she has paid $275,000 in total premiums, and the annuity is now worth $325,000. She begins taking monthly payments from the annuity in the amount of $2,000. Assuming Donna has a remaining life expectancy of 18 years, the taxable portion of each monthly payment is:
   A. $0.
   B. $472.
   C. $536.
   D. $727.

48. Karl, age 62, deposited $10,000 into a nonqualified flexible premium deferred annuity. Today, the annuity is worth $11,000, and Karl borrows $1,500 from the account to fund a vacation. What are the tax consequences of this loan?
    A. The entire amount of the loan is tax-free and penalty-free.
    B. $1,000 of the loan is taxable to Karl but will not be subject to a penalty.
    C. $1,500 will be taxable to Karl, and $1,000 will be subject to a penalty.
    D. $1,000 will be taxable to Karl, and $1,500 will be subject to a penalty.

49. John is age 65 and retiring. His wife is age 70 and has been retired for several years. Both are in excellent health. Which of the following will provide the couple with the largest monthly payment over a short-term time horizon?
    A. Single life annuity.
    B. Single life annuity with five-year sum certain.
    C. Joint and 50% survivor annuity.
    D. Joint and 100% survivor annuity.

50. Dodie recently received a $300,000 inheritance, and she has decided to use the money to purchase an annuity. She does not want her account value to decline if investment markets decline, and she would like to ensure that if she dies before recovering the $300,000, any shortfall will be paid to her surviving children. What would be the best type of annuity for Dodie to purchase?
    A. Variable annuity.
    B. Flexible premium annuity.
    C. Refund annuity.
    D. Straight life annuity.

51. Byron wants to purchase an annuity. He receives a bonus from his employer every year, but the amount fluctuates, so he wants an annuity that permits varying premiums from year-to-year. He also wants his annuity to benefit from gains in the stock market, even if it means his account value will drop when market conditions deteriorate. He expects to start receiving annuity payments in approximately 15 years when he retires. Which of the following represents the best option for Byron?
    A. Single premium fixed immediate annuity.
    B. Flexible premium fixed deferred annuity.
    C. Single premium variable immediate annuity.
    D. Flexible premium variable deferred annuity.

52. Stan's wife recently died, leaving Stan with a $500,000 life insurance benefit. Stan is retired, and currently receives income from Social Security and some of his personal investments. He wants to supplement his retirement income by purchasing an annuity. All of Stan's children are adults and are self-sufficient. He is not concerned with leaving them an inheritance when he dies. Assuming Stan wants guaranteed monthly income for the remainder of his life, the best annuity for him to purchase is a:
    A. Joint and survivor fixed annuity.
    B. Straight life immediate fixed annuity.
    C. Deferred refund annuity.
    D. Flexible premium variable deferred annuity.

53. Which one of the following statements is correct regarding structured settlements?
    A. Interest income received by the claimant is taxed in the year received.
    B. They represent a high risk to the claimant due to the potential insolvency of the payer.
    C. Attorneys failing to recommend a structured settlement run the risk of being sued if a client wastes a lump sum payment.
    D. The claimant typically receives a stream of periodic payments from a fund administered by the Social Security Administration.

54. Which one of the following statements is correct regarding structured settlements?
    A. Because of a structured settlement, an injured party is more likely to become a ward of the state.
    B. Courts cannot influence the method by which the structured settlement payment will be made.
    C. The settlement places the claimant at risk because the payments are typically discontinued after 10-15 years have elapsed.
    D. The settlement may need to be approved by the Centers for Medicare and Medicaid Services.

55. Which one of the following statements is correct regarding a substandard annuity?
    A. It is written by insurers that have financial ratings that are lower than the national averages.
    B. Premiums are determined in a similar fashion to substandard life insurance.
    C. Premiums are typically lower than for a standard annuity.
    D. It is a type of deferred annuity.

56. Tiffany was driving her car on the highway when she was struck by a drunk driver. Tiffany escaped injury, but her 10-year-old daughter Stephanie suffered a broken neck, which left her a quadriplegic. A lawsuit was filed against the drunk driver, and the claim was resolved via a structured settlement, funded with a qualifying annuity. The terms of the settlement provide for a monthly payment to Stephanie to help pay her medical expenses and meet her basic living needs. A correct statement about this structured settlement is:
    A. None of the settlement will be taxed.
    B. Settlement proceeds are subject to claims of victim's creditors.
    C. The settlement must remain a fixed amount once payments have started.
    D. Settlement proceeds will not be counted as income for purposes of receiving Medicaid benefits.

MODULE 3

57. Which one of the following statements is correct regarding Social Security disability benefits?
    A. Benefits may be reduced by workers compensation benefits or federal disability benefits received by the individual.
    B. As long as an individual has been employed for three consecutive years, they will be eligible for benefits after satisfying the definition of disability.
    C. The definition of disability is similar to the "own occupation" definition of disability found in many private disability income insurance policies.
    D. Payment of benefits begins 30 days after an individual has satisfied the disability requirements.

58. Which one of the following statements is correct regarding provisions found in a disability income policy?
    A. The definition of disability under the policy may be based on an inability to perform duties, or on the amount of earned income lost.
    B. Individuals often choose the shortest waiting period because it lowers the overall premiums on the policy.
    C. Group disability insurance is usually cheaper than individual disability insurance because of government restrictions on pricing related to group insurance.
    D. Although a disability policy will pay a benefit due to loss of income resulting from an accident or illness, it will not pay a benefit for a loss of a limb or blindness.

59. Which one of the following definitions of disability used in a group disability income plan is the most liberal for the insured employee?
    A. The inability of the employee to engage in any occupation for compensation.
    B. The inability of the employee to engage in any occupation for which he or she is qualified by experience, education, or training.
    C. The inability of the employee to engage in his or her own occupation for 36 months and any occupation for which he or she is qualified thereafter.
    D. The inability of the employee to perform each and every duty of his or her own occupation.

60. Which one of the following types of disability insurance policies cannot be cancelled by the insurance company but can include a premium increase by the insurance company at the time of renewal?
    A. Conditionally renewable.
    B. Guaranteed renewable.
    C. Cancelable.
    D. Noncancelable.

61. Which one of the following statements is correct regarding individual disability insurance policies?
    A. Membership in a group is required to purchase coverage.
    B. Disability benefits received by the insured are tax-free.
    C. Benefits are typically inferior to those offered in group policies.
    D. These policies typically replace 30-40% of an insured's income.

62. Which one of the following statements is correct regarding group disability income plans?
    A. Most long-term disability plans have shorter probationary periods than short-term disability plans.
    B. Group disability programs cannot require an individual to provide evidence of insurability in order to receive coverage.
    C. Most long-term disability plans have provisions enabling an insured to convert the plan to an individual disability income policy.
    D. Most group policies have a coordination-of-benefits provision defining how other benefits affect benefits from the disability policy.

63. Which one of the following statements is correct regarding Social Security disability benefits?
    A. The period of disability is counted in determining an individual's insured status for Social Security.
    B. In order to qualify as disabled, an individual must have an impairment that prevents them from performing any substantial gainful activity for the remainder of their life.
    C. The waiting period for benefits is generally nine months for a worker who becomes disabled for the first time.
    D. Benefits may be paid to the disabled worker, and auxiliary benefits may also be paid to eligible dependents of the disabled worker.

64. David works for a package delivery company delivering packages within two zip codes. He injured his leg, preventing him from performing his regular job duties. However, he can perform alternate duties for the company, such as entering delivery requests into the company's computer system. Under his disability insurance plan, David is eligible to receive full benefits for the first 9 months that he is performing the alternate duties. After the 9-month period, if David is not able to resume his regular job of delivering packages, the disability benefits cease. This policy uses which definition of disability?
    A. Own occupation.
    B. Any occupation.
    C. Split definition.
    D. Modified own occupation.

65. Byron purchased a disability insurance policy that cannot be cancelled by the insurance company. In addition, the insurance company cannot increase premiums and cannot change the policy benefits. What type of policy did Byron purchase?
    A. Conditionally renewable.
    B. Guaranteed renewable.
    C. Cancelable.
    D. Noncancelable.

66. Danny wants to purchase a disability policy that will pay him a benefit if his salary decreases by 20% or more due to an accident or sickness. What type of coverage would be best suited for Danny?
    A. Partial disability coverage.
    B. Guaranteed renewal coverage.
    C. Residual disability coverage.
    D. Salary continuation coverage.

67. Tara purchased an individual disability policy from a national insurance company. The policy guarantees insurability and allows Tara to increase the monthly benefit as her income increases, provided she can provide documented evidence of her increases in income. What type of rider did Tara purchase for her policy?
    A. Cost of living adjustment.
    B. Future increase option.
    C. Waiver of premium.
    D. Automatic increase rider.

68. Which one of the following represents a type of managed care health organization that provides the most flexible access to non-network physicians?
    A. Health Maintenance Organization (HMO).
    B. Medicare Part A.
    C. Flexible Spending Organization.
    D. Preferred Provider Organization.

69. Which one of the following statements is correct regarding health insurance plans?
    A. Managed-care plans differ from traditional health insurance plans by offering more types of services and broader coverage.
    B. The majority of individuals in the U.S. obtain their medical expense insurance through individual medical expense coverage.
    C. Basic medical insurance coverage usually provides coverage for prescription drugs and home healthcare services.
    D. Major medical insurance typically has a deductible, which gives the insured a financial incentive to obtain less costly services.

70. Which one of the following statements is correct regarding preferred-provider organizations (PPOs)?
    A. PPOs are one of the most cost-effective forms of managed-care plans.
    B. The majority of PPOs provide benefits for a wider selection of medical procedures if non-network providers are used.
    C. Employees insured by a PPO may see a specialist without a referral by a gatekeeper physician.
    D. Members can choose any physician, but network physicians are more expensive and have higher deductibles.

71. Which one of the following managed-care plans charges insurers an access fee for use of the network, negotiates with healthcare providers to set fee schedules for guaranteed service levels, and helps resolve issues between insurers and healthcare providers?
    A. Health maintenance organization.
    B. Point-of-service plan.
    C. Exclusive provider organization.
    D. Preferred provider organization.

72. Which one of the following managed-care plans typically features a gatekeeper physician and provides all the care needed by its members in exchange for a fixed fee?
    A. Health maintenance organization.
    B. Point-of-service plan.
    C. Exclusive provider organization.
    D. Preferred provider organization.

73. Which one of the following statements is correct regarding a consumer-directed health plan?
    A. Individuals that are covered pay lower premiums because the insureds act as a large group that can result in economies of scale.
    B. These arrangements often incorporate a network of health care professionals.
    C. It is a type of managed-care plan that combines a health maintenance organization (HMO) and a preferred provider organization (PPO).
    D. Employees generally do not like these plans because employer contributions to a savings account will be taxed to the employee.

74. Scott's employer recently implemented a high-deductible health insurance plan. The plan features extremely low premiums and permits Scott to contribute to a health savings account on a pre-tax basis. What type of health insurance plan was implemented by Scott's employer?
    A. Health maintenance organization.
    B. Preferred provider organization.
    C. Point-of-service plan.
    D. Consumer-directed health plan.

75. Which one of the following is a requirement of Medicare for an unmarried individual?
    A. The individual must be retired.
    B. The individual must be a U.S. citizen.
    C. The individual must generally be age 65 or older.
    D. The individual must be collecting Social Security benefits.

76. Which one of the following statements is correct regarding the Medicare system?
    A. Individuals are generally eligible for Medicare coverage upon attaining age 62.
    B. State assistance is available to pay for Medicare Part B if the individual has limited income or resources.
    C. An individual who is deferring Social Security benefits cannot begin Medicare until the Social Security benefits have begun.
    D. Medicare Part A is largely funded through a monthly premium paid by beneficiaries and the federal government's general revenues.

77. Which one of the following expenses is covered by Medicare Part A?
    A. Inpatient hospital care.
    B. Elective cosmetic surgery.
    C. Custodial care.
    D. Physicians' services.

78. Which one of the following expenses is covered by Medicare Part B?
    A. Prescription drugs.
    B. Skilled-nursing facility benefits.
    C. Doctors' services.
    D. Orthopedic shoes.

79. Which one of the following statements is correct regarding Medicare Advantage (Part C) plans?
    A. Under the program, beneficiaries can choose to be covered under a guaranteed insurability plan.
    B. They can exclude certain benefits that otherwise would have been provided under Medicare Part A or Part B.
    C. They are means-tested federal-state welfare programs that cover medical expenses for low-income individuals.
    D. Some plans limit members' annual out-of-pocket spending to protect against catastrophic medical costs.

80. Which one of the following statements is correct regarding Medicare Part D (prescription drug) coverage?
    A. It is available to all Medicare beneficiaries entitled to Medicare Part A.
    B. It is designed to fill the gaps in coverage associated by Medicare Part A and Part B.
    C. It is financed by payroll taxes and self-employment taxes.
    D. It features an annual deductible and coinsurance.

81. Which one of the following statements is correct regarding Medicaid?
    A. The largest group of Medicaid recipients is persons with disabilities.
    B. Disabled children may be eligible, even if their parents are not.
    C. The program is funded exclusively by the various states.
    D. Individuals with 10 years of work experience are automatically eligible upon attaining age 65.

82. Which one of the following statements is correct regarding long-term care insurance policies?
    A. Most policies pay for care the insured receives from a family member.
    B. A physician certification provision is used to determine the criteria for approved nursing care facilities.
    C. Most policies are issued on a noncancelable basis.
    D. A qualified policy features tax-deductible premiums and tax-free benefits.

83. The primary factor in determining the cost of a long-term care policy is:
    A. Geographic region.
    B. Marital status.
    C. Age.
    D. Health.

84. Long-term care insurance typically excludes coverage for:
    A. Services related to drug addiction.
    B. Respite care.
    C. Adult day healthcare centers.
    D. Skilled nursing care services.

85. Sam purchased a long-term care policy 15 years ago with a $150 daily benefit. He chose to stop his premium payments. The policy is currently paid up for a reduced benefit of $110 per day. The reason for this is because the policy contained:
    A. A waiver of premium.
    B. A nonforfeiture option.
    C. A guaranteed renewability provision.
    D. Inflation protection.

MODULE 4

86. Which one of the following statements is correct regarding investment return?
    A. Investors wanting capital appreciation should invest the majority of their portfolio in fixed income securities.
    B. Total return on an investment is the sum of the capital appreciation and the investment income.
    C. The tax rate applied to interest income is often lower than the rate applied to capital appreciation.
    D. Investment income is the amount by which an asset's selling price exceeds the asset's purchase price.

87. Which one of the following statements is correct regarding investment income?
    A. Bonds typically focus on capital appreciation.
    B. The primary type of investment return on an apartment building is capital appreciation.
    C. Growth stocks tend to pay high dividends as compared to value stocks.
    D. The return for a certificate of deposit is comprised completely of investment income.

88. The compound annual rate of return is a better measure of total return than the rate of return, because the compound annual rate of return:
    A. Relies on the holding period of the investment.
    B. Adjusts the overall return for inflation.
    C. Includes an increase in return based on the risk assumed.
    D. Considers the return on invested income.

89. Five years ago, Sara purchased stock in a publicly traded company for $50,000. Today, the stock is worth $70,000. Sara plans on holding on to the stock until she retires in 10 years. The stock has experienced a $20,000:
    A. Realized capital gain.
    B. Realized capital loss.
    C. Unrealized capital gain.
    D. Unrealized capital loss.

90. Martha is looking to purchase an investment product that derives its entire return from investment income. What would be the best investment for Martha to purchase to satisfy her investment objective?
    A. Value stock.
    B. Certificate of deposit.
    C. Municipal bond.
    D. Apartment building.

91. Mildred purchased common stock for $1,000. She received the following dividends:
Year 1 - $50
Year 2 - $55
Year 3 - $60
At the end of Year 3, she sold the stock for $1,100. What is her average annual rate of return on the stock?
A. 5.51%
B. 7.42%
C. 8.83%
D. 9.11%

92. Stan invested $1,000 in common stock. One year later, the value of the stock was $980, and he had received a $30 dividend. Which one of the following statements is correct regarding Stan's rate of return?
A. Stan had an unrealized capital gain.
B. Stan suffered an income loss from the stock.
C. Stan had a total rate of return that was negative.
D. Stan had an unrealized loss that was more than offset with investment income.

93. Which one of the following statements is correct regarding risk?
A. Market risk is the risk that a security cannot be sold quickly at the current market value.
B. Business risk is the risk from events that affect a particular company.
C. Inflation risk is the risk that the general level of prices will grow at a slower rate.
D. Investment risk is the risk an investment's return will be absorbed by taxes.

94. Which one of the following statements is correct regarding risk?
A. Financial risk is the risk of the loss of purchasing power.
B. Interest rate risk is the risk that the interest rate on a margin loan will exceed the rate of return on the investment.
C. Liquidity risk is the risk that a security cannot be sold quickly at the current market value.
D. Systematic risk is risk that can be reduced through diversification.

95. Which one of the following statements is correct regarding inflation risk?
A. Inflation risk represents uncertainty about an investment's performance due to changes in the market for that investment.
B. Assets that emphasize capital appreciation are immune to inflation risk.
C. Inflation risk is reduced as long as the value of the investment moves in the opposite direction as inflation.
D. What matters most to investors is the level of inflation over the life of their investment.

96. Which one of the following statements is correct regarding interest rate risk?
A. If interest rates rise, the market price of older bonds will rise relative to the price of newer bonds.
B. Assets that emphasize capital appreciation are less susceptible to inflation risk than fixed-income securities.
C. An important source of interest rate risk is the change in demand for the company's products or services.
D. Interest rate risk is the uncertainty about an investment's future value due to changes in general rates of inflation.

97. Which one of the following statements is correct regarding various categories of investment risk?
   A. Exchange rate risk applies to any investment that is based on a currency other than the investor's home country.
   B. Market risk only applies to investments in stocks and bonds.
   C. As a general rule, investments that have more liquidity risk have a higher market price than they otherwise would.
   D. A company's financial risk generally does not affect the value of the company's common stock.

98. Which one of the following represents an example of systematic risk?
   A. Taking on an excessive amount of debt.
   B. Announcement of lower-than-expected earnings.
   C. Downturn in the economy.
   D. Increase in overhead costs.

99. Which one of the following statements is correct regarding elements of investment risk?
   A. Interest rate risk is the uncertainty about future performance due to the amount of debt assumed.
   B. As the amount of investment risk increases, the average investor will usually want a lower rate of return.
   C. The goal of diversification is to achieve maximum return without regard to investment risk.
   D. Unsystematic risk, or specific risk, is diversifiable risk that is specific to a particular investment.

100. Which one of the following statements is correct regarding the use of leverage in investing?
   A. Financial leverage magnifies any losses incurred.
   B. Leverage reduces the amount of investment risk.
   C. Leverage represents the systematic investing of the same amount of money periodically.
   D. Leverage can be used to eliminate systematic risk.

101. Which one of the following is an appropriate investment for an emergency fund?
   A. Precious metals.
   B. Real estate.
   C. S&P 500 index mutual fund.
   D. Savings account.

102. Five years ago, Johnny purchased several 30-year, AAA-rated corporate bonds, each having a coupon rate of 5%. Market interest rates recently increased by 1%. Johnny can expect the value of his bond portfolio to:
   A. Increase by 1%.
   B. Decrease because there is an inverse relationship between market interest rates and bond prices.
   C. Increase by slightly less than 1%.
   D. Remain unchanged because only newly issued bonds are affected by changes in market interest rates.

103. ABC Company took on excessive amounts of debt. As a result, its interest expense increased tremendously, causing ABC Company to experience a decrease in earnings and a stock market price decline. The risk most likely to have caused this stock price decline is:
   A. Business risk.
   B. Financial risk.
   C. Market risk.
   D. Liquidity risk.

104. A manufacturing company announced that it was laying off 5,000 workers because of a fire that occurred in its main production facility. The company's common stock price immediately declined by 10% per share. The decline in share price is an example of:
   A. Purchasing power risk.
   B. Business risk.
   C. Credit risk.
   D. Reinvestment rate risk.

105. Which one of the following statements is correct regarding the strategy of dollar cost averaging?
   A. Laddering is a dollar cost averaging strategy that is appropriate for common stock.
   B. Dollar cost averaging can reduce the risk of purchasing investments when prices are high.
   C. Dollar cost averaging involves the purchase of fewer shares when market prices drop.
   D. Laddering helps an investor reduce interest rate risk in a portfolio.

106. All of the following statements are correct regarding dividend reinvestment plans, EXCEPT:
   A. Participants reinvesting dividends will still be required to pay federal income tax on the total amount of dividends reinvested.
   B. Plans involving new share purchases reduce the issuing company's debt-to-equity ratio.
   C. They reduce an investor's ability to increase portfolio diversification because dividends are not available to purchase stock of different companies.
   D. They paid higher dividends on the shares than the dividend paid on shares owned outside the plan.

107. Which one of the following statements is correct regarding reinvestment?
   A. Reinvestment of dividends is only available for mutual funds.
   B. Shares purchased in a dividend reinvestment plan are often provided without assessing any fees or commissions.
   C. If dividends are reinvested into more shares, the dividends are not taxed until those shares are subsequently sold.
   D. Reinvestment refers to the systematic contribution of cash towards an investment every month.

108. Which one of the following statements is correct regarding asset allocation?
   A. The primary purpose of asset allocation as an investment strategy is to maximize an investor's rate of return.
   B. Asset allocators generally attempt to outperform the market by selecting underpriced securities.
   C. Asset allocation is independent of an investor's age.
   D. Asset allocation allows an investor to tailor a portfolio to his or her own risk tolerance.

109. Which one of the following statements is correct regarding dividend reinvestment plans (DRIPs)?
   A. DRIPs generally are available only for shares of preferred stock of private companies.
   B. Dividends are used to purchase convertible bonds of the underlying company.
   C. Shares are often purchased without having to pay fees.
   D. Dividends that are reinvested under the plan are not subject to income taxes.

110. Which one of the following represents a savings and investment planning technique?
   A. Purchase of term insurance.
   B. Creating a Will.
   C. Charitable giving.
   D. Dollar cost averaging.

111. Doris, age 45, just received an inheritance of $200,000 from her late Aunt. She would like to invest the proceeds in both equities and fixed income currently, with a gradual shift from equities to fixed income over the next 20 years. Which one of the following types of mutual funds would be most suitable to satisfy her asset allocation goal over the next 20 years?
   A. Growth fund.
   B. Specialty fund.
   C. Life-cycle fund.
   D. Sector fund.

112. Warren has decided that he would like to begin a monthly dollar cost averaging program. He purchased 10 shares of ABC Mutual Fund at a cost of $50 per share. What should Warren do in the second month, assuming the price of the mutual fund has increased to $100 per share?
   A. Purchase 10 shares of ABC Mutual Fund.
   B. Sell 5 shares of ABC Mutual Fund.
   C. Purchase 10 shares of XYZ Mutual fund.
   D. Purchase 5 shares of ABC Mutual Fund.

113. Valerie has $10,000 to invest. She wants to implement a laddering strategy. Which one of the following would satisfy her investment objective?
   A. Investing a portion of the portfolio in stocks, bonds, and precious metals.
   B. Investing the $10,000 in 5 bonds with maturities of 1, 2, 3, 4, and 5 years respectively.
   C. Investing the $10,000 in 2 certificates of deposit, one short-term and one long-term.
   D. Investing in $500 of common stock per month until the $10,000 is exhausted.

114. Peggy is interested in investing in a mutual fund that is required to maintain an asset allocation consisting of stocks, bonds, and money market instruments. She would like the fund to automatically reduce the portfolio risk as she gets older. The best type of mutual fund for Peggy to purchase is a:
   A. Balanced mutual fund.
   B. Fixed income mutual fund.
   C. Life-cycle mutual fund.
   D. International mutual fund.

115. Which one of the following statements is correct regarding savings accounts?
    A. The main advantage of savings accounts is their high rate of return.
    B. Money market mutual funds are insured, up to certain limits, by the Federal Deposit Insurance Corporation.
    C. Substantial interest penalties may apply if a certificate of deposit is redeemed before maturity.
    D. Savings accounts offer an investor both capital appreciation and investment income.

116. Which one of the following statements is correct regarding Treasury securities?
    A. Because of their short time horizon, Treasury bills do not have a secondary market.
    B. Treasury notes are not subject to state and local income taxation.
    C. Treasury bonds have maturities ranging from 2-5 years.
    D. Treasury bills are always issued at a premium over their face value.

117. Which one of the following statements is correct regarding corporate bonds?
    A. Debentures are corporate bonds that are backed by specific collateral.
    B. Income bonds provide the lowest priority on payment of all corporate bonds.
    C. Most bonds only pay interest at the time of maturity.
    D. The capital appreciation on the bond is tax-free if held to maturity.

118. Bonds are typically the least susceptible to which of the following risks?
    A. Interest rate risk.
    B. Default risk.
    C. Inflation risk.
    D. Exchange rate risk.

119. Which one of the following statements is correct regarding stocks?
    A. Value stocks are issued by companies with earnings that are growing at a faster rate than the general economy.
    B. Cyclical stocks are issued by companies whose earnings are correlated with economic expansions and recessions.
    C. Penny stocks are issued by companies with an established record of dividend payments.
    D. Defensive stocks trade for less than $1.

120. Which one of the following statements is correct regarding the investment in stocks?
    A. The beta of a stock measures the stock's unsystematic risk.
    B. A company's stock price represents the discounted value of future earnings.
    C. Non-dividend paying stocks are subject to inflation risk.
    D. Common stocks trading on organized exchanges are illiquid.

121. An investor looking for a mutual fund that offers a diversified portfolio that emphasizes safety and performance should purchase a(n):
    A. Stock mutual fund.
    B. Precious metals mutual fund.
    C. International mutual fund.
    D. Blended mutual fund.

122. Which one of the following statements is correct regarding types of mutual funds?
   A. International funds invest both in the United States and in foreign markets.
   B. Asset allocation funds are designed for individuals in certain phases of the life cycle.
   C. Sector funds are not well diversified and should represent a small portion of the portfolio.
   D. Index funds typically have higher costs because they are actively managed by the investment company.

123. Christy wants to purchase a municipal bond that is backed by revenues generated from the projects financed by the bond. Christy should purchase a:
   A. General obligation bond.
   B. Revenue bond.
   C. Assessment bond.
   D. Treasury bond.

124. Ted and Alice, a married couple, consider themselves aggressive investors. They would like to purchase an investment that will have a high potential for price appreciation. They would like a return that exceeds the general return of the market and are not interested in current dividends. Which one of the following would be the best investment selection for Ted and Alice?
   A. Treasury bonds.
   B. Defensive stocks.
   C. Value stocks.
   D. Money market mutual funds.

MODULE 5

125. Which one of the following statements is correct regarding the costs and benefits of postsecondary education?
    - A. There is no correlation between salary and the level of postsecondary education attained.
    - B. There is a higher unemployment rate among the more highly education.
    - C. Government funding for universities and colleges has been decreasing.
    - D. The number of Americans pursuing postsecondary education has declined in recent years.

126. Which one of the following represents the largest single cost category when planning for postsecondary education?
    - A. Supplies and books.
    - B. Entertainment, clothing, and personal expenses.
    - C. Housing expenses.
    - D. Tuition and fees.

127. Which one of the following statements is correct regarding costs associated with funding a postsecondary education?
    - A. Expenses associated with funding the education generally rise at a pace that is slightly lower than the Consumer Price Index (CPI).
    - B. A four-year bachelor's degree is more costly than a vocational certificate obtained from a trade school.
    - C. Online degrees from two-year and four-year academic institutions provide a significant tuition savings compared to brick-and-mortar institutions.
    - D. Saving for a postsecondary education complements other investment goals.

128. Which one of the following statements is correct regarding investing for postsecondary education goals?
    - A. The closer the saver is to the college funding need, the more aggressive the portfolio allocations should be.
    - B. The accepted rule for determining an education investment portfolio is to assume costs will remain constant over the planning horizon.
    - C. When calculating the annual savings needed to fund the education, the investment rate of return is offset by the education inflation rate.
    - D. Once the investment strategy has been determined, it is critical that the investments selected remain constant.

129. Kim has two children, ages 4 and 15. She is unmarried and has sought the advice of a financial planning professional to help her determine the amount she must save to fund her children's education. She plans on sending each child to an in-state university for a five-year education and will be saving for their education completely on her own. Which of the following represents the most important data the professional should gather to help project the future cost of the education?
    - A. Kim's expected return on her investment portfolio.
    - B. Historical inflation rate applicable to education costs.
    - C. Annual earned and unearned income received by Kim.
    - D. Kim's acceptable risk tolerance.

130. Which of the following formulas would be used to determine the future value of a principal sum?
   A. $P * (1 + i)^n$
   B. $i * (1 – P)^n$
   C. $n/P * (1 + i)$
   D. $P / (1 + i)^n$

131. The parents of a five-year-old girl are determining the amount that needs to be saved for a college education. One year of tuition costs $20,000 in today's dollars, and the girl will begin college in 13 years. Assuming an education inflation rate of 5%, what will be the future value cost of her freshman year in college?
   A. $25,525.
   B. $28,421.
   C. $37,713.
   D. $48,132.

132. The Amits are calculating the amount needed to be saved for their son's education. He will begin his freshman year in 8 years, and the tuition inflation rate is 6%. Assuming tuition costs $15,000 per year in today's dollars, what is the future value of the son's tuition for his freshman year?
   A. $19,420.
   B. $22,162.
   C. $23,908.
   D. $26,863.

133. Which one of the following statements is correct regarding the Free Application for Federal Student Aid (FAFSA)?
   A. It requires both the student and parents to report current assets.
   B. It is used solely to obtain financial aid from the federal government for education.
   C. It does not require parents to report tax-exempt interest income received during the year as a resource.
   D. It must be filed only once within three months of any financial assistance is received.

134. Which one of the following statements is correct regarding the Free Application for Federal Student Aid (FAFSA)?
   A. It includes only the parents' income.
   B. It weighs the parents' assets more heavily than the student's assets.
   C. It represents the final step in the process of obtaining financial aid.
   D. It is affected by the size of the family.

135. Which one of the following statements is correct regarding the Expected Family Contribution (EFC) formula used to measure financial strength?
   A. The EFC formula weighs the parents' assets up to three times more heavily than the student's assets.
   B. The institutional EFC formula determines a student's eligibility for government-backed grants and loans.
   C. The EFC formula considers cash value life insurance policies owned by the parents.
   D. The EFC formula reduces the income component by a credit for single parent households.

136. Which one of the following items is not considered under the Expected Family Contribution (EFC) formula?
   A. Investments in mutual funds.
   B. Assets of noncustodial parents.
   C. Money market securities.
   D. Savings account balances.

137. Which one of the following items is not considered under the Expected Family Contribution (EFC) formula?
   A. Municipal bond investments.
   B. Checking account balances.
   C. Equity in a principal residence.
   D. Business interests.

138. Which one of the following strategies would most likely reduce the Expected Family Contribution?
   A. Take a withdrawal from a 401(k) plan to pay for college costs.
   B. Use excess cash to pay off credit card debt.
   C. Maximize savings levels.
   D. Pay for college costs with the parents' assets first.

139. Which one of the following statements is correct regarding Pell grants?
   A. They can be used to pay for online vocational programs.
   B. They are available to graduate students who have already earned a bachelor's degree.
   C. They are typically given only to individuals with a high school GPA above a threshold level.
   D. They will begin accruing interest if not repaid within 10 years after graduation.

140. Which one of the following statements is correct regarding student aid programs?
   A. Pell grants are only available to full-time students.
   B. Stafford loans must be repaid within five years after receipt.
   C. Federal Perkins loans are the major source of education borrowing from the federal government.
   D. Interest is charged on a Parent Loans for Undergraduate Students beginning on the date the loan proceeds are received.

141. Which one of the following federal student aid programs is available regardless of financial need?
   A. Unsubsidized Stafford Loans.
   B. Federal Pell Grants.
   C. Supplemental Education Opportunity Grant.
   D. Perkins loans.

142. Which one of the following statements is correct regarding education loans?
   A. Perkins loans are serviced by and repaid to the federal government.
   B. PLUS loans can be obtained by the parent to pay education costs of a dependent.
   C. Subsidized Stafford loans typically have a higher interest rate than unsubsidized loans.
   D. Loans offered under the Federal Direct Loan Program are variable-rate loans.

143. Which one of the following parental assets is included in the computation of the Expected Family Contribution formula in determining eligibility for federal student financial aid?
   A. Income of a noncustodial parent.
   B. Brokerage account.
   C. Primary residence.
   D. Section 401(k) plan balance.

144. The Lemoines decided not to save for their daughter's postsecondary education because they are not sure she will continue beyond high school. If she does attend college, they are willing to provide help financially. They expect their daughter to pay a significant portion of any college costs she incurs and would like her to be in a position to obtain the maximum financial aid available. Which of the following actions would minimize the Expected Family Contribution?
   A. Decrease their includable assets by purchasing municipal bonds.
   B. Start an annual gift-giving program of cash to their daughter for her to invest.
   C. Place excess savings in a brokerage account for the purchase of equity securities.
   D. Transfer some of their checking account balance to a deferred annuity.

145. The two types of Section 529 plans are:
   A. Prepaid tuition plans and savings plans.
   B. Lending plans and investment plans.
   C. Tuition credit plans and student plans.
   D. Tuition plans and equipment plans.

146. Which one of the following statements is correct regarding Uniform Transfer to Minors Act (UTMA) and Uniform Gift to Minors Act (UGMA) accounts?
   A. The maximum annual contribution to the account is $15,000.
   B. Under the EFC formula, all account income is considered income of the student.
   C. These accounts are more expensive than most trusts.
   D. Funds may be used by the custodian for the minor's basic needs.

147. Which one of the following statements is correct regarding Uniform Transfer to Minors Act (UTMA) accounts?
   A. The account beneficiary can be changed until the minor attains the age of majority.
   B. They do not permit the accounts assets to be invested in real estate.
   C. Income earned by account assets may be taxed at the parents' tax rate.
   D. They are considered assets of the parents in the EFC formula.

148. Which one of the following statements is correct regarding a Coverdell Education Savings Account?
   A. The account beneficiary can be changed by the custodian at any time.
   B. A parent can contribute to the account regardless of their income level.
   C. The maximum contribution to the account is $5,000 per year.
   D. The account is considered an asset of the student for purposes of the EFC formula.

149. Which one of the following statements is correct regarding a Coverdell Education Savings Account?
    - A. The account can only be established by the student's parents.
    - B. Contributions to the account are deductible for federal income tax purposes.
    - C. Funds can be withdrawn tax-free to pay for elementary school expenses.
    - D. The account must be distributed within 30 days of the student's attainment of age 21.

150. Which one of the following statements is correct regarding a Section 529 savings plan?
    - A. Contributions to the plan are deductible for federal income tax purposes.
    - B. Contributions are allowed regardless of the amount of the contributor's income.
    - C. Plan participation is usually limited to residents of the sponsoring state.
    - D. The rate of return on investments inside the plan is tied to the tuition inflation rate at a particular college.

151. Which one of the following statements is correct regarding state-run Section 529 prepaid college tuition plans?
    - A. They are most attractive to aggressive investors since their return typically exceeds that of equity securities.
    - B. They can be used for private schools, as well as out-of-state schools.
    - C. They guarantee admission to a state college.
    - D. The plan balance will be forfeited if the student chooses not to go to college.

152. An advantage of a Section 529 plan is that:
    - A. The account owner can withdraw amounts penalty-free for any reason upon attaining age 59½.
    - B. The beneficiary can be changed to the account owner's spouse, brother, or sister, without resulting in a gift.
    - C. Individual stocks, bonds, and mutual funds are permitted investments in most accounts.
    - D. Contributions made to the plan are deductible in arriving at the donor's federal taxable income.

153. Which one of the following statements is correct regarding Series EE bonds?
    - A. They are considered the student's asset even if purchased and held by the parents.
    - B. They pay a relatively high rate of return.
    - C. The maximum allowable purchase for an individual is $25,000 per calendar year.
    - D. They are not subject to state income taxes.

154. Darryl is a single father with a 4-year-old daughter. He wants to begin saving for his daughter's college education. Which one of the following would be the best strategy if Darryl's primary objective is to guarantee the cost of future tuition?
    - A. Coverdell Education Savings Account.
    - B. Section 529 plan.
    - C. Uniform Transfer to Minors Act (UTMA) account.
    - D. Series EE savings bonds.

155. John and Sue Garcia, a married couple, would like to save for their son's education but have limited resources. They would like to begin a funding strategy that will enable their son to qualify for the maximum amount of financial aid. Which of the following would be considered the least appropriate strategy to achieve their goal?

A. Establish a Coverdell Education Savings Account and make maximum annual contributions.
B. Open up a brokerage account titled JTWROS between John and Sue.
C. Purchase U.S. Series EE bonds and hold them in Sue's name.
D. Contribute to a Uniform Transfer to Minors Act account on behalf of their son.

156. Agnes is a widow with five grandchildren. She has a net worth in excess of $4,000,000 and would like to establish a savings plan to help her grandchildren pay for their college educations. She plans on contributing at least $5,000 per year to the education fund of each of her grandchildren. Agnes wants to be sure the funds will be used for education purposes and would like to reclaim the funds if they will not be used for this purpose. Which of the following represents the best funding vehicle to satisfy Agnes' objectives?

A. Coverdell Education Savings Account.
B. Section 529 plan.
C. Annual gifting program to the grandchildren.
D. Uniform Transfer to Minors Act (UTMA) account.

157. Angie, age 71, is a widow with three grandchildren ranging in age from 10-12. She has a net worth in excess of $4,000,000, and she is in excellent health. Angie would like to pay for each of the grandchildren's college tuitions, regardless of what school they attend. Angie has eliminated from consideration a Section 529 plan, due to limited investment options and high management fees. She doesn't want to give the grandchildren control over the assets when they attain age 18, which is the age of majority. Which of the following strategies would be most appropriate for Angie, assuming taxes are not a major concern for her?

A. Establish a brokerage account, invest the proceeds, and give the grandchildren gifts each year they are in college.
B. Create and fund a Uniform Transfer to Minors Act (UTMA) account for each grandchild.
C. Invest her own funds in a brokerage account, then pay the college tuition directly to the college when due.
D. Purchase U.S. Series EE savings bonds for each grandchild.

MODULE 6

158. Which one of the following represents the first step of the retirement planning process?
    A. Monitoring and revising the plan.
    B. Determining retirement goals.
    C. Analyzing financial needs.
    D. Arranging appropriate techniques.

159. Which one of the following statements is correct regarding the retirement planning process?
    A. The principal benefit of accumulating funds in a currently taxable funding vehicle is the ease with which the individual can access the funds.
    B. A retirement plan should be monitored every five years at a minimum.
    C. Financial needs analysis translates an individual's retirement goals into a method for distributing retirement assets.
    D. Most individuals modify their inflation or return assumptions and increase their risk in order to reduce the annual funding required for retirement.

160. Which one of the following retirement funding vehicles is categorized as both tax-deferred and tax-deductible?
    A. Nonqualified annuity.
    B. Municipal bond.
    C. Section 401(k) plan.
    D. Money market mutual fund.

161. Which one of the following retirement funding vehicles is categorized as both tax-deferred and tax-deductible?
    A. Nonqualified annuity.
    B. Roth IRA.
    C. Traditional IRA.
    D. Certificate of deposit.

162. Which one of the following retirement vehicles is subject to both contribution limits and required minimum distributions?
    A. Municipal bond.
    B. Traditional IRA.
    C. Nonqualified annuity.
    D. Roth IRA.

163. Which one of the following retirement vehicles is generally subject to a 10% penalty if withdrawals are made prior to age 59½?
    A. Municipal bond.
    B. Roth IRA.
    C. Money market account.
    D. Section 401(k) plan.

164. A disadvantage of investing in tax-free funding vehicles for retirement is that:
    A. Contributions to these vehicles are not deductible for tax purposes.
    B. Access to funds may be prohibited before retirement.
    C. Specific required minimum distributions dates must be satisfied.
    D. Withdrawals prior to age 59½ are subject to a 10% penalty.

165. Timmy and Jack are twin brothers. Beginning at the age of 25, they each contributed annually to a retirement funding vehicle. Timmy and Jack contributed the exact same amount each year to the respective vehicles, and neither of them made any withdrawals. They are now both 50 years old, and Timmy's vehicle has left him with more current spendable money than Jack's vehicle. The likely reason for this is because Timmy's vehicle:
    A. Was the only one that was tax-deferred.
    B. Was the only one that featured tax-deductible contributions.
    C. Was the only one that imposed an early withdrawal penalty.
    D. Was invested more aggressively.

166. Rob wants to save for his retirement by contributing a small amount into a retirement vehicle each month. He has the following objectives:
    - Contribute $800 per month.
    - Tax-deductible contributions.
    - Tax-deferred earnings.

    Assuming Rob is not concerned about paying taxes on his eventual distributions, what would be the best vehicle to satisfy his objectives?
    A. Nonqualified annuity.
    B. Roth IRA.
    C. Section 401(k) plan.
    D. Savings account.

167. Stan wants to save for his retirement by contributing a small amount into a retirement vehicle each month. He has the following objectives:
    - Contribute $400 per month.
    - Tax-free distributions.
    - No minimum distribution requirements.

    What would be the best vehicle to satisfy his objectives?
    A. Nonqualified annuity.
    B. Roth IRA.
    C. Section 401(k) plan.
    D. Traditional IRA.

168. Which one of the following represents an expense that usually decreases with retirement?
    A. Medical expenses.
    B. Home ownership expenses.
    C. Travel expenses.
    D. Hobby expenses.

169. Which one of the following statements is correct regarding the determination of retirement savings needs?
   A. The income replacement ratio method usually uses an income replacement ratio of 45%-55%.
   B. The expense method for estimating retirement income needs is especially appropriate for younger clients.
   C. Taxes typically increase during retirement due to the receipt of taxable retirement plan distributions.
   D. The income replacement ratio method usually begins by estimating income during the final three years of employment.

170. Which one of the following types of expenses is most likely to increase during retirement?
   A. Taxes.
   B. Vacation expenses.
   C. Retirement contributions.
   D. Home-ownership expenses.

171. Which one of the following types of expenses is most likely to increase during retirement?
   A. Work-related expenses.
   B. Support for dependent children.
   C. Medical expenses.
   D. General expenses.

172. The most significant difference between systematic withdrawals from a fund vs. systematic withdrawals from an annuity is that systematic withdrawals from a fund:
   A. Are completely taxable to the recipient, while an annuity offers tax-free distributions.
   B. Are tax-free to the recipient, while an annuity has completely taxable distributions.
   C. Guarantees payments for life, which an annuity provides income only as long as assets remain.
   D. Provides income only as long as assets remain, while an annuity guarantees payments for life.

173. Which one of the following statements is correct regarding the determination of retirement savings needs?
   A. The retirement payout from a defined contribution plan is affected by an individual's Social Security benefit.
   B. Retirement income needs are usually determined using either the income replacement ratio method or the expense method.
   C. If the determination of annual savings needs for retirement is done properly, little review of the amount determined is necessary.
   D. The annual savings requirement must be determined before pension and Social Security benefits are subtracted from income needs.

174. Johnny has a retirement fund that is earning a rate of return of 6%. He wants to take withdrawals from the fund that keeps pace with inflation, which is currently 2%. Assuming a first-year withdrawal amount of $20,000, what should Johnny withdraw in the second year?
   A. $20,400.
   B. $20,800.
   C. $21,200.
   D. $21,600.

175. Which one of the following represents an advantage of a defined benefit plan?
   A. Contributions are flexible.
   B. Funds are guaranteed by the Pension Benefit Guarantee Corporation.
   C. In-service withdrawals are permitted by employees.
   D. Communication of benefits to employees is generally straight-forward.

176. Which one of the following statements is correct regarding benefit formulas in a defined benefit plan?
   A. If an employer desires long-service employees, the plan's benefit formula should contain a years-of-service cap.
   B. The flat-percentage-of-earnings formula is the most frequently used benefit formula in a defined benefit plan.
   C. Employers typically provide an income-replacement ratio of approximately 80% of an employee's career average salary.
   D. The unit-benefit formula considers both the participant's service and salary in the calculation of the pension benefit.

177. Which one of the following represents a type of defined benefit plan with a benefit that is defined more like a defined contribution plan?
   A. Simplified employee pension.
   B. Profit sharing plan.
   C. 401(k) plan.
   D. Cash balance plan.

178. Which one of the following statements is correct regarding a profit sharing plan?
   A. The employer must specify a formula for allocating contributions.
   B. In-service withdrawals by employees are prohibited.
   C. The plan can invest up to 10% in employer stock.
   D. The plan can provide for past service.

179. Which one of the following statements is correct regarding Section 401(k) plans?
   A. They can include employee after-tax contributions and employer matching contributions.
   B. Internal Revenue Service contribution limits do not apply.
   C. They can only be established by tax-exempt organizations.
   D. Future benefits of these plans can be accurately estimated.

180. Which one of the following is a correct statement regarding a simplified employee pension (SEP)?
   A. The maximum contribution is $5,000 for an employee under age 50.
   B. It is a plan that closely resembles an individual retirement account (IRA).
   C. It is a type of defined benefit plan.
   D. Employee pre-tax elective deferrals can be offered in the plan.

181. Which one of the following statements is correct regarding a SIMPLE IRA?
    A. Employees can make elective deferral contributions equal in amount to those allowed in a 401(k) plan.
    B. Mandatory employer contributions may be matching contributions or nonelective contributions.
    C. The plan can offer loans to participants provided that the loan bears a reasonable rate of interest and is repaid within five years.
    D. To sponsor a SIMPLE, an employer has to have 75 or fewer employees.

182. Which one of the following statements is correct regarding nonqualified deferred-compensation plans?
    A. They must be funded to satisfy requirements of the Internal Revenue Code.
    B. They can be rolled over into other tax-advantaged plans.
    C. They can give an employer an immediate income tax deduction.
    D. They can provide for deferral of taxation until the benefit is received.

183. Which one of the following statements is correct regarding nonqualified supplemental executive retirement plans (SERPs)?
    A. They are typically set up as profit sharing plans.
    B. Forfeiture provisions are common.
    C. They must provide benefits to rank-and-file employees.
    D. They are funded by employee contributions.

184. A salary reduction nonqualified plan is:
    A. A plan that allows executives to voluntarily elect to defer their compensation until retirement or another stated event.
    B. A supplemental executive retirement plan in which the executive receives greater benefits both below and above the limits applicable to a qualified plan.
    C. A type of defined contribution plan.
    D. A plan designed to provide a survivor benefit at the participant's death.

185. Which one of the following statements is correct regarding a Roth IRA?
    A. A Roth IRA contribution can be made regardless of a taxpayer's AGI.
    B. An individual under age 50 can contribute the maximum to a Traditional IRA and a Roth IRA in the same year.
    C. A taxpayer with only investment income can contribute to a Roth IRA.
    D. Contributions to a Roth IRA are nondeductible.

186. Which one of the following statements is correct regarding the tax treatment of contributions to a traditional IRA and a Roth IRA?
    A. Contributions to both a traditional IRA and a Roth IRA are always deductible.
    B. Contributions to both a traditional IRA and a Roth IRA are always nondeductible.
    C. Contributions to a traditional IRA may be deductible, but contributions to a Roth IRA are never deductible.
    D. Contributions to a Roth IRA may be deductible, but contributions to a traditional IRA are never deductible.

187. Anna, age 35, made $50,000 of pre-tax contributions to a traditional IRA over a ten-year period. The account is now worth $70,000, and she has decided to convert the traditional IRA to a Roth IRA. If she completes the conversion, what will be the income tax consequences?
   A. $20,000 will be subject to income tax and a 10% penalty.
   B. $50,000 will be subject to income tax and a 20% penalty.
   C. $70,000 will be subject to income tax but no penalty.
   D. $70,000 will be subject to income tax and a 10% penalty.

188. Which one of the following individuals would be eligible to make the maximum allowable contribution to a traditional IRA?
   A. John, an unmarried 40-year-old individual, whose only income is $60,000 of dividends.
   B. Kristen, a college student who earns $3,500 from a part-time job.
   C. Sandra, an unemployed homemaker, whose husband earns a $100,000 salary.
   D. Bob, an unmarried 55-year-old individual, who only income is $100,000 of rental income.

189. Which one of the following statements is correct regarding retirement income choices?
   A. The largest percentage of retirement income is derived from Social Security benefits.
   B. Both the maximum Social Security benefit and the age at which a retiree can receive full Social Security benefits are decreasing.
   C. The principal employer-sponsored plans in which employees are investing are simplified employee pensions.
   D. Recent reports indicate that savings in 401(k) plans contain an adequate amount of assets needed to maintain retirees' standard of living.

190. To maximize tax benefits, assets should be liquidated in which order?
   A. Tax-deferred assets, long-term capital gain assets, short-term capital gain assets, cash, and loss investments.
   B. Cash, long-term capital gain assets, short-term capital gain assets, tax-deferred assets, and loss investments.
   C. Long-term capital gain assets, tax-deferred assets, cash, loss investments, and short-term capital gain assets.
   D. Loss investments, cash, long-term capital gain assets, short-term capital gain assets, and tax-deferred assets.

191. If an individual has a Social Security full retirement age of 66, and he begins taking benefits at age 62, the reduction in benefits received will be:
   A. 20%.
   B. 25%.
   C. 30%.
   D. 35%.

192. Jamie, age 25, is interested in saving for her retirement. She currently earns a salary of $50,000 and is willing to set aside $5,000 per year to fund her retirement. Her employer offers a Section 401(k) plan, with a dollar-for-dollar match up to 5% of compensation. Which of the following retirement savings vehicles should Jamie first consider when saving for her retirement?
   A. Traditional IRA.
   B. Nonqualified deferred annuity.
   C. Roth IRA.
   D. 401(k) plan.

193. Stan and Cindi, a married couple, retired several years ago. They fund their annual expenses with a combination of Social Security benefits, employer-sponsored retirement plan benefits, and an annuity. They want to take an expensive vacation and are wondering which account to withdraw the money. Their goal is to minimize the income taxes associated with the withdrawal, since they are currently in a high income tax bracket. From which of the following accounts should they take the needed funds?
   A. Currently taxable account.
   B. Roth IRA.
   C. Annuity.
   D. 401(k) plan.

MODULE 7

194. Which one of the following is an example of a probate cost?
    A. Legal costs to defend against challenges to a Will.
    B. Burial expenses.
    C. Mortgage liability on the decedent's home.
    D. Legal fees to draft a Will.

195. The sum of property owned by a person at the time of death is referred to as:
    A. Net worth.
    B. An estate.
    C. Liquid assets.
    D. Tax base.

196. A decrease in the size of an estate due to the payment of probate costs, estate taxes, and claims of creditors is referred to as:
    A. Estate shrinkage.
    B. Estate liability.
    C. Estate liquidation.
    D. Estate minimization.

197. Which one of the following statements is correct regarding estate planning?
    A. Only individuals with estates exceeding $5,000,000 have a need for estate planning.
    B. Most financial advisors have appropriate training to generate a complex estate plan for a client.
    C. An estate planning team may include an investment advisor to advise ways to maintain or increase the estate's value.
    D. A major goal of estate planning is to eliminate a client's liquid assets, which typically offer a very low rate of return.

198. Which one of the following represents a goal of estate planning?
    A. Eliminate the need for a Will.
    B. Minimize income taxes.
    C. Decrease estate liquidity.
    D. Maximize the amount of assets included in the probate estate.

199. Which one of the following represents a tax imposed on property received by heirs and beneficiaries?
    A. Estate tax.
    B. Income tax.
    C. Generation-skipping transfer tax.
    D. Inheritance tax.

200. A party named in a decedent's Will to administer the estate is referred to as a(n):
    A. Probate supervisor.
    B. Executor.
    C. Administrator.
    D. Trustee.

201. The purchase of additional life insurance will often take place during which step of the estate planning process?
   A. Formulate and test a new estate plan.
   B. Gather facts.
   C. Execute and monitor the new estate plan.
   D. Evaluate the existing estate plan.

202. Which one of the following represents the first step in the estate planning process?
   A. Formulate and test a new estate plan.
   B. Gather facts.
   C. Execute and monitor the new estate plan.
   D. Evaluate the existing estate plan.

203. Which one of the following represents an action that would take place during step 1 (Gather Facts) of the estate planning process?
   A. Determine the estate owner's intentions for transferring property at death.
   B. Classify the estate property to determine if it will be included in the probate estate.
   C. Estimate and minimize estate shrinkage.
   D. Create and revise legal documents.

204. Which one of the following represents an action that would take place during step 2 (Evaluate the existing estate plan) of the estate planning process?
   A. Determine the estate owner's intentions for transferring property at death.
   B. Classify the estate property to determine if it will be included in the probate estate.
   C. Estimate and minimize estate shrinkage.
   D. Create and revise legal documents.

205. Which one of the following statements is correct regarding the estate plan?
   A. Once the estate plan has been implemented, it should be reviewed every 10 years.
   B. A new estate plan should be tested using the same assumptions used in analyzing the existing estate plan.
   C. Estate shrinkage should be estimated solely under the assumption that the older spouse dies first.
   D. The estate plan should be designed to automatically liquidate illiquid assets at the estate owner's death.

206. If the insured has incidents of ownership over a life insurance policy, the policy proceeds will be included in the insured's gross estate. Incidents of ownership include all of the following EXCEPT:
   A. The right to change the policy's beneficiary.
   B. The ability to surrender the policy.
   C. The right to pay the policy premiums.
   D. The ability to take a loan against the policy.

207. Mark owned the following assets at his death. Which one of the following assets will be included in Mark's probate estate?
   A. Raw land owned as joint tenants with rights of survivorship with his brother.
   B. Life insurance death benefits received by Mark's son as the named beneficiary.
   C. A revocable trust that names Mark's cousin as the beneficiary of trust assets.
   D. A small business transferred to Mark's wife through his Will.

208. Which one of the following statements is correct regarding the federal gift tax?
   A. The recipient of the gift is responsible for any tax due.
   B. It applies to direct and indirect gifts of either tangible or intangible property.
   C. A flat 35% tax applies to all gifts given to children.
   D. It is imposed on the individual's last gift.

209. The alternate valuation date for estate tax purposes is:
   A. 1 month after death.
   B. 3 months after death.
   C. 6 months after death.
   D. 9 months after death.

210. Which one of the following represents a deduction from the gross estate in arriving at the taxable estate?
   A. Prior gift tax paid.
   B. Annual exclusion.
   C. Executor's fees.
   D. Unified credit.

211. Which one of the following represents a state death tax imposed on the right of a beneficiary to receive property from a decedent?
   A. Sponge tax.
   B. Inheritance tax.
   C. Pickup tax.
   D. Estate tax.

212. Which one of the following represents the nature of the portability feature associated with the estate tax applicable exclusion amount?
   A. It allows any unused portion of the exemption to pass to a surviving spouse at the time of the first spouse's death.
   B. It reduces a surviving spouse's gross estate by the amount of any property held jointly with the other spouse.
   C. It provides for a carryover basis in a decedent's assets to a surviving spouse.
   D. It effectively allows for gift-splitting between spouses at the time of the first spouse's death.

213. Which one of the following statements is correct regarding state death taxes?
   A. All states apply a standard 20% state death tax rate to a decedent's assets exceeding $2,000,000.
   B. State death taxes paid by a decedent's estate are allowed as a deduction against the federal estate tax due.
   C. Only transfers to a surviving spouse are subject to state death tax.
   D. There are two types of state death taxes – state transfer tax and state bequest tax.

214. Alexander, age 60, is unmarried. During the current year, he paid the following expenses for his adult son, Rex:

- Medical bills incurred due to an injury suffered by Rex - $25,000.
- Tuition payments for Rex - $20,000.
- Rex's apartment rent - $24,000.
- New car for Rex - $40,000.

Assuming an annual exclusion of $15,000, what is the amount of the taxable gift?
   A. $49,000.
   B. $69,000.
   C. $74,000.
   D. $94,000.

215. Pete gave a $200,000 cash gift to his son, John, so John can build a new home. Which of the following statements is correct regarding the gift?
   A. The entire amount will be considered a taxable gift.
   B. John will be required to include the gift in his income for income tax purposes.
   C. Pete will be entitled to an income tax deduction for the gift given.
   D. Pete is responsible for any gift tax due relating to the gift.

216. John made several gifts during the year. Which one of the following gifts, made by John, will constitute a taxable gift for gift tax purposes?
   A. Donation of $150,000 to the United Way.
   B. Gift of a $15,000 diamond ring to his wife, Joann.
   C. Gift of $40,000 of stock to his cousin, Lisa.
   D. Gift of a $10,000 boat to his son, Ron.

217. Stephen purchases a tract of land for $50,000. Two years after the purchase, when the land was valued at $80,000, Stephen added his daughter's name to the title as a joint tenant with rights of survivorship. Stephen died when the land was worth $100,000. How much is included in Stephen's gross estate?
   A. $40,000.
   B. $50,000.
   C. $80,000.
   D. $100,000.

218. Scott and Natalie, a married couple, own a tract of land titled as joint tenants with rights of survivorship. The entire purchase price of $500,000 was paid by Natalie. Natalie predeceased Scott. At the time of her death, the land was valued at $2,000,000. What is the amount that will be included in Natalie's gross estate relating to the land?

A. $250,000.
B. $500,000.
C. $1,000,000.
D. $2,000,000.

219. Which one of the following statements is correct regarding a Will?

A. It is only necessary for an estate that will be subject to estate or inheritance tax.
B. It can provide income to family members during estate settlement.
C. It can replace a comprehensive estate plan.
D. It represents the most common method to establish a revocable trust.

220. Which one of the following is a correct statement regarding a revocable trust?

A. It can be set up by the executor after the individual's death.
B. The trust assets will avoid inclusion in the grantor's gross estate for estate tax purposes.
C. The grantor reserves the right to reclaim the property at any time before death.
D. It can be established without a trustee.

221. Which one of the following represents a trust provision that can provide flexibility in a trust by permitting a trustee to distribute income to the beneficiaries as needed?

A. Spendthrift provision.
B. Terminable interest provision.
C. Sprinkle provision.
D. Survivorship provision.

222. Tito owned a life insurance policy on his own life, with his son, Jerome, named as the policy beneficiary. The policy had a death benefit of $300,000, and a cash value of $40,000. Tito paid premiums over the years totaling $35,000. Which one of the following statements is correct, assuming Tito died today?

A. The policy will be excluded from Tito's gross estate.
B. The policy will be excluded from Tito's probate estate.
C. Jerome must include $5,000 in his gross income for income tax purposes.
D. Jerome must include $260,000 in his gross income for income tax purposes.

MODULE 8

223. The two primary objectives of income tax planning are:
   A. Maximizing capital gains and reducing gross income subject to taxation.
   B. Minimizing alternative minimum tax liability and structuring an investment portfolio to achieve tax efficiency.
   C. Satisfying financial objectives and deferring the maximum amount of tax possible.
   D. Minimizing overall tax liability and satisfying financial goals with minimal tax consequences.

224. Which one of the following statements is correct regarding deductions allowable to a taxpayer?
   A. "Above-the-line" deductions are only available if a taxpayer itemizes his or her deductions.
   B. Most "above-the-line" deductions represent expenditures of a personal nature.
   C. Deductions in arriving at adjusted gross income are sometimes referred to as "below-the-line" deductions.
   D. The reduction of an individual's adjusted gross income may result in the increased availability of other tax benefits.

225. Which one of the following represents an itemized deduction (below-the-line deduction) for an individual taxpayer?
   A. Deductible contributions to a traditional IRA.
   B. Cash donations to a qualified charity.
   C. Business expenses incurred by the taxpayer.
   D. Alimony paid to a former spouse.

226. Which one of the following statements is correct regarding elements of personal income taxation?
   A. Charitable contribution limits are determined based on an individual's taxable income.
   B. The standard deduction amount for each filing status is indexed for inflation annually.
   C. Qualified dividends are taxed at a flat 10% rate.
   D. A "below-the-line" deduction is a deduction from total income to determine adjusted gross income.

227. Which one of the following statements is correct regarding the taxation of capital gains and losses?
   A. Capital assets held more than six months will be considered long-term.
   B. The determination of whether a capital gain is short-term or long-term is affected by the taxpayer's marital status.
   C. Individuals may deduct capital losses in full against capital gains.
   D. Short-term capital gains are subject to more favorable tax rates than long-term capital gains.

228. Which one of the following represents a credit available to individual taxpayers?
   A. Foreign tax credit.
   B. Unreimbursed medical expense credit.
   C. Self-employment tax credit.
   D. Casualty loss credit.

229. Which one of the following items is subtracted from the income tax due to arrive at the total tax owed by the taxpayer?
   A. Penalties.
   B. Credits.
   C. Deductions.
   D. Exclusions.

230. Scott purchased $10,000 worth of tax-free municipal bonds for his investment portfolio. Scott has implemented the tax planning strategy of:
   A. Tax deferral.
   B. Tax avoidance.
   C. Tax evasion.
   D. Tax development.

231. Which one of the following statements is correct regarding the income tax consequences of life insurance?
   A. The cost basis of a life insurance policy is equal to the policy's net cash value.
   B. The death benefit received from a life insurance policy is generally taxable to the recipient.
   C. If the policy is classified as a modified endowment contract, loans and withdrawals will generally be income tax-free.
   D. Withdrawals from a life insurance policy are usually taxed FIFO basis recovery (basis first).

232. A permanent insurance policy has a:
   - Death benefit - $200,000
   - Cash value - $80,000
   - Cost basis - $60,000

   If the policy meets the statutory definition of insurance, and the insured dies, how much of the policy death benefit will be taxable to the beneficiary?
   A. $0.
   B. $20,000.
   C. $140,000.
   D. $200,000.

233. Janice, age 61, decided to take a withdrawal from her deferred annuity before the annuity start date. Which of the following statements is correct regarding Janice's decision?
   A. Janice will be subject to a 10% early withdrawal penalty.
   B. If Janice completely surrenders her annuity, she can reduce the taxable amount by any surrender charges.
   C. Her withdrawal will be taxed at capital gains rates.
   D. If the contract was entered into in 1986, the FIFO basis recovery rule will apply.

234. Delores has been contributing to an annuity over the last 25 years and has made total after-tax contributions equaling $170,000. Based on her remaining life expectancy of 16 years, she can receive a monthly annuity payment of $1,400. The annuity has a current value of $215,000. Assuming Delores begins annuitizing her flexible premium deferred annuity on July 1 of the current year, what is the taxable portion of the monthly payment received?
   A. $515.
   B. $937.
   C. $1,400.
   D. $10,625.

235. Tommy is 60 years old and is the owner of a fixed annuity that he purchased several years ago for $200,000. Tommy decided to begin taking his annuity payments this year and will receive $20,000 annually from the contract for the remainder of his life. Which one of the following statements is correct, assuming Tommy has a remaining life expectancy of 25 years?
   A. The expected return under the contract is $200,000.
   B. The exclusion ratio for the contract is 60%.
   C. The tax-free portion of this year's annuity payment is $8,000.
   D. The taxable portion of this year's annuity payment is $18,000.

236. Stacy, age 45, purchased a single premium nonqualified annuity several years ago, paying a non-deductible premium of $50,000. The annuity currently has a cash value of $75,000. Assuming Stacy takes a $9,000 loan from the cash value today, how much would be included in her gross income for federal income tax purposes?
   A. $0.
   B. $3,000.
   C. $6,000.
   D. $9,000.

237. Which one of the following statements is correct regarding education funding vehicles?
   A. Contributions to a Section 529 plan are not subject to gift taxes.
   B. Room and board expenses are not eligible expenses for purposes of the Series EE bond interest exclusion.
   C. Distributions from a qualified tuition program that are used to pay for room and board are taxable.
   D. The maximum permitted contribution to a Coverdell Education Savings Account is $5,000 per year.

238. Which one of the following statements is correct regarding a Section 529 savings plan?
   A. Contributions to the plan are deductible for federal income tax purposes.
   B. Contributions are allowed regardless of the amount of the contributor's income.
   C. Plan participation is usually limited to residents of the sponsoring state.
   D. Plan contributions are limited to $20,000 per donor, per year.

239. All of the following are requirements that must be met to exclude interest income from a Series EE savings bond from a taxpayer's gross income, EXCEPT:
   A. The interest and principal must be used to pay for qualified educational expenses of the taxpayer, spouse, or dependents.
   B. The bond must have been issued to an individual at least 24 years old.
   C. At least 5% of the redeeming party's gross income must be in the form of interest, dividends, or capital gains.
   D. The redeeming party must be the original purchaser of the bond, or his or her spouse.

240. Which one of the following statements is correct regarding the Lifetime Learning credit?
   A. A credit of up to $5,000 per year may be claimed by the taxpayer.
   B. The credit is only allowed for expenses incurred for the first two years of the student's postsecondary education.
   C. Like the American Opportunity Tax Credit, the lifetime learning credit applies on a per-student basis.
   D. The credit is phased-out for taxpayers whose modified adjusted gross income exceeds a prescribed level.

241. Which one of the following statements is correct regarding the American Opportunity Tax Credit?
   A. An individual can claim both the American Opportunity Tax Credit and the Lifetime Learning Credit in the same year for the same student.
   B. The credit is available for all years of post-secondary education and for courses taken to improve job skills.
   C. The credit is phased-out for taxpayers whose modified adjusted gross income exceeds a prescribed level.
   D. Only 75% of the credit is available to taxpayers who do not have an income tax liability.

242. Which one of the following statements is correct regarding a Uniform Transfers to Minors Account (UTMA)?
   A. Income earned by investments inside the account may be taxed to the parent due to the kiddie tax rules.
   B. The corpus of the account is transferred to the beneficiary upon attainment of age 30.
   C. The account can contain only liquid investments, such as cash or money market securities.
   D. The amount transferred to the account is revocable and can be rescinded by the donor parent.

243. Phil received a merit scholarship from a local university. The scholarship was valued at $20,000, based on the following:
   - Tuition - $12,000
   - Room and board - $5,000
   - Books and fees - $2,000
   - Equipment - $1,000

   How much of the scholarship will Phil be required to include in his gross income for federal income tax purposes?
   A. $0.
   B. $5,000.
   C. $6,000.
   D. $8,000.

244. Which one of the following statements is correct regarding loans from qualified plans?
   A. Plan administrators can offer below market interest rates on loans to owner-employees.
   B. Loans must bear adequate security, such as the participant's accrued benefit.
   C. Loans must be repaid within three years unless the loan is used to acquire a principal residence.
   D. Loans will be taxable to the participant, unless the proceeds are used for certain hardships.

245. Which one of the following statements is correct regarding the income tax treatment of qualified retirement plans?
   A. If an employer contribution is made to the plan, the employee will be taxed on the contribution.
   B. Employer contributions made to the plan are nondeductible by the employer.
   C. Qualified plan earnings are tax-free at the time of distribution.
   D. A designated Roth account is permitted, allowing tax-free distributions at retirement.

246. Which one of the following statements is correct regarding the required minimum distribution rules applicable to retirement plans?
   A. The required beginning date for a retired participant is March 1 of the calendar year in which the participant attains age 70½.
   B. Under the rules, the entire account balance must be distributed before the owner attains age 85.
   C. There is a 50% penalty attributable to a required minimum distribution that should have been taken but was not.
   D. Roth IRAs are subject to the rules when the participant attains age 75.

247. If an individual earns $300,000 per year, contributions to which of the following retirement vehicles would create the largest reduction in current tax liability?
   A. 401(k) plan.
   B. Traditional IRA.
   C. Flexible premium deferred annuity.
   D. Roth IRA.

248. Which one of the following represents an advantage of having an irrevocable living trust?
   A. The trust is included in the grantor's gross estate for estate tax purposes.
   B. The grantor can retrieve the trust assets at any time prior to death.
   C. The assets held in the trust are never subject to federal income taxation.
   D. The trust avoids the expenses and delays associated with the probate process.

249. Andy wants to convert his traditional IRA to a Roth IRA. The balance in his traditional IRA is $110,000, and he has made after-tax contributions over the years of $15,000 to the traditional IRA. What is the federal tax ramification of this transaction?
   A. He will include $95,000 in his gross income and will be subject to a 10% penalty.
   B. He will include $95,000 in his gross income but will not be subject to a 10% penalty.
   C. He will include $110,000 in his gross income and will be subject to a 10% penalty.
   D. He will include $110,000 in his gross income but will not be subject to a 10% penalty.

250. Over the last 15 years, Brooke, age 42, contributed $18,000 pre-tax and $10,000 after-tax to a traditional IRA. The account is now worth $40,000. Brooke took a $20,000 distribution to purchase a new car. How much of the distribution will be subject to an early withdrawal penalty?
   A. $0.
   B. $5,000.
   C. $15,000.
   D. $20,000.

251. Marissa, age 56, just retired from her employer of 20 years. She has a 401(k) balance of $300,000, comprised of the following:
   - $120,000 of pre-tax elective deferral contributions made by Marissa.
   - $60,000 of matching contributions made by Marissa's employer.
   - $70,000 of additional non-elective contributions made by Marissa's employer.
   - $50,000 of plan earnings.

   Marissa converted the 401(k) plan to a Roth IRA. How much must Marissa include in her gross income for federal income tax purposes as a result of the conversion?
   A. $50,000.
   B. $110,000.
   C. $180,000.
   D. $300,000.

252. Jay, age 62, has a $40,000 balance in his traditional IRA. Over the years, he made tax-deductible contributions to the IRA in the amount of $24,000. He recently took a $10,000 distribution from the IRA to fund a vacation. What are the tax consequences of this distribution?
   A. The distribution will be completely tax-free.
   B. Only $4,000 of the distribution is subject to income tax but no penalty.
   C. The entire $10,000 distribution is subject to income tax as well as a 10% penalty.
   D. The entire $10,000 distribution is subject to income tax but no penalty.

253. Which one of the following statements is correct regarding income in respect of a decedent (IRD)?
   A. IRD is included in the gross estate of the decedent, and therefore it is not subject to income tax to the recipient.
   B. IRD includes investments in stock held by the decedent in a taxable brokerage account.
   C. The recipient of IRD may be eligible for an income tax deduction for the amount of federal estate taxes paid on the IRD item.
   D. IRD results in favorable tax consequences when the IRD owner dies.

254. Which one of the following would be considered income in respect of a decedent?
   A. Interest income earned by the executor on corporate bonds owned by the estate.
   B. Capital gain resulting from the executor's sale of estate common stock.
   C. Proceeds of a wrongful death suit brought by the decedent's executor against the drunk driver who caused the decedent's death.
   D. The decedent's final paycheck received by the estate two weeks after the decedent's death.

255. When a donor gives a gift of appreciated property, the recipient's basis in the property is the:
   A. Fair market value of the property reduced by any gift tax paid.
   B. Donor's basis in the property plus a portion of any gift tax paid.
   C. Fair market value of the property if subsequently sold at a gain, or the donor's basis if subsequently sold for a loss.
   D. Average of the donor's cost basis and the fair market value on the date of the gift.

256. Which one of the following statements is correct regarding the income taxation of trusts?
   A. Income from a grantor trust is taxed to the beneficiaries of the trust.
   B. Amounts distributed from a trust to beneficiaries are taxed as ordinary income.
   C. Similar to individuals, a trust is entitled to a personal exemption.
   D. Trust income retained by the trust is tax-free until distributed to the beneficiaries.

257. Trust income from an irrevocable trust that is accumulated in the trust is generally taxed to the:
   A. Donor.
   B. Grantor.
   C. Trust.
   D. Beneficiary.

258. Five years ago, Tara purchased publicly traded stock for $20,000. Two years ago, when the value of the stock was $30,000, Tara gifted the stock to her daughter, Jessica. Last month, Jessica sold the stock for $35,000. What was Jessica's basis in the stock at the time of the sale?
   A. $15,000.
   B. $20,000.
   C. $30,000.
   D. $35,000.

259. Maria died one year before her planned retirement date. She had a qualified profit sharing plan with a balance of $200,000. Her cost basis in the plan was $50,000. A lump sum death benefit of $200,000 was paid to her son, Stan. Assuming the death benefit was not payable from life insurance, what is the tax treatment of the death benefit to Stan?
   A. The entire death benefit will be received by Stan income tax-free.
   B. Stan will be taxed on $50,000.
   C. Stan will be taxed on $150,000.
   D. Stan will be taxed on the full $200,000 amount received.

260. A mother gifted property with a basis of $2,000,000 and a fair market value of $1,500,000 to her son. If the mother paid $20,000 of gift tax, and the son later sold the asset for $2,200,000, what would be the son's taxable gain?
   A. $0
   B. $200,000
   C. $500,000
   D. $700,000

261. Marion created and funded a trust last year. The trust document provides that Marion's mother will receive $2,000 of income from the trust each month. Marion retained the right to revoke the trust at any time. If the trust earns $30,000 of income this year, what will be the income tax ramifications?

A. $30,000 of income will be taxed to Marion.
B. $6,000 will be taxed to Marion, and $24,000 will be taxed to her mother.
C. $6,000 will be taxed to the trust, and $24,000 will be taxed to her mother.
D. $6,000 will be taxed to the mother, and $24,000 will be taxed to the trust.

MODULE 1

1. B is correct. (Obj 1 – Type A).

Financial planning is the process by which individuals and families develop and implement a comprehensive financial plan to help achieve their financial goals.

2. B is correct. (Obj 1 – Type A).

A is incorrect. Financial goals are different among individuals and families and change over time.
C is incorrect. Basic financial goals typically include providing for basic living expenses and protecting against loss of income or wealth. Building wealth is considered a secondary goal.
D is incorrect. Many individuals attempt to satisfy their goals on an ad hoc basis. Comprehensive financial plans attempt to avoid this problem.

3. D is correct. (Obj 1 – Type A).

The two basic financial planning goals that most people have throughout their life are:
-Providing basic living essentials (such as food and clothing).
-Protecting against loss of income or wealth.

4. A is correct. (Obj 1 – Type A).

An empty nester typically experiences peak earnings, as well as an ability to build wealth due to decreased expenses. In addition, there is a focus on retirement planning and funding, as well as estate planning and long-term care needs.

5. C is correct. (Obj 1 – Type A).

A is incorrect. Married or single individuals with children in college typically focus on retirement planning and funding.
B is incorrect. Empty nesters are most likely to make a maximum effort to divert income toward retirement.
D is incorrect. Tax planning is most likely to be simplistic and uncomplicated for individuals in their early 20s.

6. B is correct. (Obj 1 – Type A).

A is incorrect. An individual in their early 20s has relatively low income and low wealth.
C is incorrect. An empty nester focuses on retirement planning, long-term care insurance, and estate planning.
D is incorrect. A retired individual usually has decreased income and focuses on preserving wealth.

7. A is correct. (Obj 1 – Type A).

B is incorrect. Income usually peaks for an individual when their child/children are in college and continues to peak up until retirement.
C is incorrect. During the retirement years, planning often shifts to preserving wealth and estate planning.
D is incorrect. Wealth distribution is a major priority for a retired individual.

8. C is correct. (Obj 2 – Type A).

A is incorrect. Tax planning focuses on minimizing federal, state, and local taxes.
B is incorrect. Professional tax planners are necessary partners in planning, as tax laws have become complex.
D is incorrect. Investment decisions are often influenced by tax law.

9. D is correct. (Obj 2 – Type A).

Retirement loss exposures and unemployment loss exposures are typically not handled through the use of insurance.

10. C is correct. (Obj 2 – Type A).

Insurance is the primary method of risk management planning.

11. A is correct. (Obj 2 – Type A).

Dollar-cost averaging is a strategy of investing the same amount of money in an investment every period, regardless of the movement of the stock market. It tends to lead to an investor earning the long-term average return, regardless of short-term market fluctuations.

B is incorrect. Dividend reinvestment involves immediate reinvestment of a stock's dividend into more shares of that stock.
C is incorrect. Market timing attempts to purchase securities when the price is low and sell when the price is high.
D is incorrect. Risk control is a risk management technique, not an investment strategy.

12. B is correct. (Obj 2 – Type A).

A is incorrect. Tax planning focuses on minimizing federal, state, and local taxes. Efficient tax planning can ensure that more assets are available for retirement.
C is incorrect. A deductible in a health insurance plan is an example of the risk management technique of risk retention.
D is incorrect. Most financial planners suggest individuals accumulate assets sufficient to replace 70-100% of preretirement income each year.

13.D is correct. (Obj 2 – Type A).

A is incorrect. Social Security benefits were never designed to be the sole source of retirement income for retirees.
B is incorrect. Although it is important for all individuals to have a Will, the Will does not eliminate the need for formal estate planning. A Will specifies how property will be distributed at the time of death.
C is incorrect. For individuals, there are many financial instruments and investment strategies.

14.C is correct. (Obj 2 – Type B).

A special needs trust allows an individual to receive benefits from an inheritance without losing government assistance.

15.C is correct. (Obj 2 – Type B).

Bob's income is sufficient to satisfy their current cash flow needs.

16.D is correct. (Obj 3 – Type A).

The following types of social insurance programs must be incorporated into a risk management plan:
-Social Security.
-Medicare and Medicaid.
-Unemployment insurance.

A is incorrect. Life insurance is a type of private insurance product.
B is incorrect. Annuities are a type of private insurance product.
C is incorrect. Disability insurance is a type of private insurance product.

17.A is correct. (Obj 3 – Type A).

B is incorrect. An individual's home is typically the largest asset and therefore the largest property expense.
C is incorrect. Flood exposures are not covered in the typical homeowners insurance policy. Instead, the homeowner must purchase a separate flood insurance policy.
D is incorrect. The state minimum limits of automobile liability coverage are usually not adequate for a family. Most families purchase higher limits of liability.

18.B is correct. (Obj 3 – Type A).

A is incorrect. One of the most effective ways a family can manage the premature death loss exposure is to purchase life insurance.
C is incorrect. The needs-based approach attempts to estimate a family's financial needs to determine the appropriate amount of life insurance.
D is incorrect. Annuities are primarily designed to provide income that the annuitant cannot outlive.

19.C is correct. (Obj 3 – Type A).

The human life value approach uses the estimated present value of the insured's financial contribution to the family to determine the income the family could lose in the event of the insured's death.

20.C is correct. (Obj 3 – Type A).

A is incorrect. Disability policies don't cover most types of custodial care. Custodial care is typically only covered by a long-term care policy.
B is incorrect. Employer-sponsored health plans are the major source of health insurance in the United States.
D is incorrect. Employer-sponsored health plans have deductibles and co-insurance provisions.

21.B is correct. (Obj 3 – Type A).

A is incorrect. Medicaid provides health insurance benefits for low-income individuals.
C is incorrect. By the year 2027, the normal retirement age will be age 67.
D is incorrect. A retiree can begin collecting benefits as early as age 62.

22.B is correct. (Obj 3 – Type A).

A is incorrect. Benefits are usually not paid for more than one year unless poor economic conditions provide for additional benefits.
C is incorrect. Benefits are funded by a combination of employer-paid premiums, taxes, and government contributions.
D is incorrect. Unemployment benefits are limited and vary from state-to-state.

23.D is correct. (Obj 4 – Type A).

The steps of the financial planning process are:
1) Establishing and prioritizing goals.
2) Gathering information.
3) Analyzing the current situation.
4) Identifying and evaluating alternatives.
5) Developing a plan.
6) Implementing the plan.
7) Monitoring and revising the plan.

24.A is correct. (Obj 4 – Type A).

During phase 2 of the financial planning process (Gathering Information), financial statements are created.

25. D is correct. (Obj 4 – Type A).

A is incorrect. Creation of a balance sheet and cash flow statement occurs during the "Gathering Information" phase of the financial planning process.
B is incorrect. Drafting Wills and other documents would occur during the "Implementing a Plan" phase of the financial planning process.
C is incorrect. Revising the financial plan occurs during the "Monitoring the Plan" phase of the financial planning process.

26. D is correct. (Obj 4 – Type B).

Implementing the selected techniques, such as opening a Section 529 plan or purchasing insurance occurs during the "Implementing the plan" phase of the financial planning process.

MODULE 2

27.A is correct. (Obj 1 – Type A).

B is incorrect. Yearly renewable term insurance allows the policyowner to renew without providing evidence of insurability.
C is incorrect. Yearly renewable term insurance is the most basic form of insurance offered by life insurance companies.
D is incorrect. The premium is determined using the insured's attained age.

28.C is correct. (Obj 1 – Type A).

A decreasing term life insurance policy features level premiums with a death benefit that decreases over time.

29.C is correct. (Obj 1 – Type A).

The best application of a decreasing term policy would be to cover the outstanding balance on a mortgage. A decreasing term life insurance policy features a face amount that decreases over time. Therefore, as the mortgage is paid off over time, the face amount of the policy will more closely match the liability.

30.C is correct. (Obj 1 – Type A).

A is incorrect. Many term insurance policies have conversion provisions that allow for the conversion to a permanent policy.
B is incorrect. Term insurance does not have a cash value.
D is incorrect. The death benefit under mortgage protection decreasing term insurance is meant to coincide with the decreasing principal balance as a mortgage is paid down over time.

31.A is correct. (Obj 1 – Type A).

The main function of a renewability feature of a life contract is to ensure that the insured may renew without a medical exam or evidence of insurability as long as the renewal is within the periods outlined in the contract and there has been no lapse in payment of premiums.

B is incorrect. Insurance companies typically do not allow renewals beyond a certain age.
C is incorrect. If a term policy is renewed, the premiums will most likely increase upon renewal.
D is incorrect. The chief function of the renewability provision is to protect the insurability of the named insured.

32.B is correct. (Obj 1 – Type A).

A is incorrect. Term policies may contain a convertibility provision permitting the owner to exchange the contract for a permanent plan without evidence of insurability.
C is incorrect. Convertible term insurance provides temporary (term) insurance with an option to convert the same policy to permanent coverage.
D is incorrect. The renewability provision only guarantees availability to term insurance, not permanent insurance, coverage in the future.

33. D is correct. (Obj 2 – Type A).

A is incorrect. The mortality and expense risk is shifted to the policyowner.
B is incorrect. Universal life policies often contain a surrender charge.
C is incorrect. Unlike most whole life policies, universal life insurance policies permit the policyowners to take a permanent withdrawal of the cash value.

34. B is correct. (Obj 2 – Type A).

Option B offers an increasing death benefit, equal to the specified amount plus the cash value. This results in a constant net amount at risk.

35. D is correct. (Obj 2 – Type A).

A is incorrect. The Option B death benefit features a generally increasing death benefit equal to the specified amount plus the cash value.
B is incorrect. Each year, cost deductions and interest credits are reflected in the cash value. These expenses and credits are not based on a fixed rate.
C is incorrect. In order for the cash value to maintain the tax-advantage normally seen with other types of life insurance, the net amount at risk associated with a universal life insurance policy must satisfy certain tests.

36. C is correct. (Obj 2 – Type B).

Option C is an increasing death benefit equal to the specified amount plus total premiums paid.

A is incorrect. Option A is a level death benefit equal to the specified amount.
B is incorrect. Option B is an increasing death benefit equal to the specified amount, plus the policy's cash value.
D is incorrect. Option D is not a type of death benefit offered.

37. B is correct. (Obj 2 – Type B).

A universal policy offers flexibility with respect to the premium and death benefit and is a permanent policy.

A is incorrect. A variable universal policy may experience investment losses and often requires investment management by the policyowner.
C is incorrect. A whole life policy does not offer premium flexibility, nor does it offer death benefit flexibility.
D is incorrect. A term policy is a temporary (not permanent) insurance policy.

38. B is correct. (Obj 2 – Type B).

A 10-year term insurance policy would offer guaranteed low-cost level premiums for the next 10 years, which would provide funds to pay for college if Brittney dies. At the end of the 10-year term, the children would most likely be out of college, and the insurance would no longer be needed.

A is incorrect. Annual renewable term insurance would have increasing premiums each year and would most likely need to be renewed each year until the children are out of college.
C is incorrect. A permanent insurance policy is not needed at this point.
D is incorrect. A permanent insurance policy is not needed at this point.

39. B is correct. (Obj 2 – Type B).

Since Scott and Stacy are risk tolerant, a variable policy would be appropriate because it would allow them to invest the cash value. Since they want premium flexibility, a universal policy would be appropriate as well. Therefore, the best policy would be a variable universal policy.

40. B is correct. (Obj 4 – Type A).

A is incorrect. Variable annuities are the most regulated of the three types of deferred annuities.
C is incorrect. Immediate annuities, by their very nature, do not accept additional deposits. They are funded by a single premium.
D is incorrect. A qualified annuity is an annuity that accepts pretax dollars from an employer-sponsored retirement program or IRA.

41. D is correct. (Obj 4 – Type A).

A is incorrect. Immediate annuities do not have an accumulation period. Deferred annuities have an accumulation period, which is the distinguishing factor between immediate and deferred annuities.
B is incorrect. Distributions from a qualified annuity may be subject to a 10% penalty if made before age 59½.
C is incorrect. A variable annuity's value fluctuates with that of an underlying securities portfolio. A fixed annuity features guaranteed interest at a rate no less than that in the contract.

42. A is correct. (Obj 4 – Type A).

A life annuity with period certain guarantee will provide a monthly benefit for the longer of the participant's life or some specified period of time.

B is incorrect. A joint and survivor annuity will pay a benefit over the longer of two lives.
C is incorrect. An annuity certain ends at the end of the term, regardless of whether the annuitant is alive.
D is incorrect. Installment payments provide for a refund of the premiums.

43. C is correct. (Obj 4 – Type A).

A is incorrect. This is an example of a straight life annuity.
B is incorrect. This is an example of a life annuity with a period certain guarantee.
D is incorrect. This is an example of a joint and survivor annuity.

44.B is correct. (Obj 4 – Type A).

A is incorrect. Indexed annuities can be sold by a non-registered representative, unlike a variable annuity.
C is incorrect. Indexed annuities have limited participation in equity markets but also have the protection offered by a fixed annuity.
D is incorrect. Indexed annuities are typically deferred annuities.

45.C is correct. (Obj 4 – Type A).

An insurer includes a mortality and expense charge to compensate the insurer for the risk that 1) the death benefit will exceed the annuity's cash value on the date of death and 2) the annuitant will outlive their table life expectancy.

46.B is correct. (Obj 4 – Type B).

Immediate annuities do not provide for asset accumulation and must be purchased with a single premium. Therefore, she should purchase a deferred annuity. This annuity should be purchased with periodic premiums to satisfy her goal of accumulating money for retirement.

47.D is correct. (Obj 4 – Type B).

The amount of basis recovery per year is:
Basis Recovery = $275,000 / 18 years
Basis Recovery = $15,278

The amount of basis recovery per monthly payment is:
Basis Recovery Per Payment = $15,278 / 12 Months
Basis Recovery Per Payment = $1,273

Therefore, the taxable amount of each payment is: $727 ($2,000 - $1,273).

48.B is correct. (Obj 4 – Type B).

When a loan or distribution is taken from a nonqualified annuity, it is taxed using the Last-In, First-Out method for basis. In other words, the earnings are taxed first. Karl's account has $1,000 of earnings ($11,000 - $10,000). Therefore, $1,000 of the $1,500 loan is subject to income tax.
Since Karl is over age 59½, there is no penalty associated with the loan.

49.A is correct. (Obj 4 – Type B).

A single life annuity will provide the largest payment over the short term.

All other options will provide a lower initial monthly annuity payment. Annuity payments are based on the amount of risk the underlying insurance company must assume. The higher the risk, the lower the annuity payment received by the annuitant.

B is incorrect. The insurance must pay for a minimum of 5 years, thus increasing their risk.
C and D are incorrect. A joint life expectancy will always be longer than a single life expectancy, thereby increasing the insurance company's risk.

50.C is correct. (Obj 4 – Type B).

A refund annuity guarantees that the principal will be repaid, regardless of when the annuitant dies.

51.D is correct. (Obj 4 – Type B).

The flexible premiums would accommodate his fluctuating bonus. The variable annuity would allow him to invest in an underlying portfolio of securities. The deferred annuity would allow him to begin payments in the future.

52.B is correct. (Obj 4 – Type B).

Stan is not worried about leaving an inheritance, so a refund annuity or a period certain annuity is not necessary. A straight life annuity would provide him with the largest monthly payment, because there are no guarantees.

53.C is correct. (Obj 5 – Type A).

A is incorrect. Structured settlements are income tax-free.
B is incorrect. Structured settlements are typically funded using an immediate annuity. These annuities are issued by life insurance companies with solid ratings. Therefore, they represent a very low risk to the claimant.
D is incorrect. The claimant typically receives a stream of periodic payments from an immediate annuity.

54.D is correct. (Obj 5 – Type A).

A is incorrect. Because of a structured settlement, an injured party is less likely to become a ward of the state.
B is incorrect. In cases involving minors, courts can require a structured settlement to guarantee income, rather than a lump sum award.
C is incorrect. Structured settlements are often paid in the form of an immediate annuity that lasts for the claimant's lifetime.

55.C is correct. (Obj 5 – Type A).

A is incorrect. An annuity is considered substandard based on the health and life expectancy of the applicant, not on the financial strength of the insurance company.
B is incorrect. Premiums are higher for substandard life insurance than for regular life insurance. Premiums for substandard annuities are lower than for regular annuities.
D is incorrect. A substandard annuity is a type of immediate annuity.

56.A is correct. (Obj 5 – Type B).

The structured settlement is not taxed because the victim was paralyzed and the settlement was used for medical expenses.

B is incorrect. Structured settlements cannot be attached by creditors, nor can they be assigned or alienated by the victim.
C is incorrect. Structured settlements are very flexible and can often be modified once payments have begun. Some structured settlements permit the victim to receive additional funds above the normal payment in the case of medical need.
D is incorrect. Settlement proceeds are counted as income for purposes of receiving Medicaid benefits. There is no indication that a special needs trust was used. The special needs trust would have allowed Stephanie to receive her monthly distribution, without counting the income for purposes of Medicaid.

MODULE 3

57. A is correct. (Obj 1 – Type A).

B is incorrect. Eligibility for benefits varies based upon the individual's age.
C is incorrect. The definition of disability is similar to the "ANY occupation" definition of disability.
D is incorrect. Payment of benefits requires a five-month waiting period.

58. A is correct. (Obj 1 – Type A).

B is incorrect. The shorter the waiting period, the higher the premium. Individuals usually choose a waiting period based on the amount of premiums they can afford.
C is incorrect. Group disability insurance is usually cheaper than individual disability insurance because group insurance creates economies of scale through the purchase of many policies.
D is incorrect. Some disability policies pay a benefit for permanent injuries, including the loss of a limb.

59. D is correct. (Obj 1 – Type A).

A is incorrect. This is the most restrictive (harsh) definition of disability for the insured employee.
B is incorrect. This definition is not as liberal as "the inability of the employee to perform each and every duty of his or her own occupation" because the employee would not be eligible for benefits if he or she could perform one or more duties based upon qualifications.
C is incorrect. This definition is very liberal for 36 months but becomes less liberal thereafter.

60. B is correct. (Obj 1 – Type A).

A guaranteed renewable policy cannot be cancelled by the insurance company. However, the insurance company can raise premiums periodically.

61. B is correct. (Obj 1 – Type A).

A is incorrect. An advantage of individual disability insurance over group insurance is that no membership in a group is required to purchase coverage.
C is incorrect. Individual and group disability policies typically offer similar benefits.
D is incorrect. These policies typically replace 60-80% of an insured's income.

62. D is correct. (Obj 1 – Type A).

A is incorrect. The probationary period is usually longer for long-term disability plans than it is for short-term disability plans.
B is incorrect. Evidence of insurability is a common eligibility requirement in group disability products.
C is incorrect. Most long-term disability plans do not allow an insured to convert the plan to an individual disability income policy.

63. D is correct. (Obj 1 – Type A).

A is incorrect. The period of disability is not counted in determining an individual's insured status for Social Security.
B is incorrect. In order to qualify as disabled, an individual must have an impairment that prevents them from performing any substantial gainful activity. This impairment must last at least 12 months or result in death.
C is incorrect. The waiting period for benefits is generally five months for a worker who becomes disabled for the first time.

64. C is correct. (Obj 1 – Type B).

The policy provides an "own occupation" definition for the first 9 months, then switches to an "any occupation" definition for the remainder of the policy.

65. D is correct. (Obj 1 – Type B).

A noncancelable policy cannot be cancelled by the insurance company. In addition, the insurance company cannot change benefits or rates associated with the policy. A noncancelable policy is the most attractive policy to the insured.

66. C is correct. (Obj 1 – Type B).

Residual disability coverage is coverage that becomes effective if a person's salary drops below a certain level due to accident or sickness.

67. B is correct. (Obj 1 – Type B).

A is incorrect. A cost-of-living adjustment increases the benefit by a percentage or amount specified in the rider.
C is incorrect. A waiver of premium ceases the required premium payment during a period of disability.
D is incorrect. An automatic increase rider increases the benefit based on inflation, not on income increases.

68. D is correct. (Obj 2 – Type A).

A is incorrect. An HMO is a type of managed care organization. However, access to non-network physicians may be limited due to the requirement of a primary care physician that must approve various visits and services.
B is incorrect. Medicare Part A is not a type of managed care plan.
C is incorrect. A flexible spending organization is not a type of managed care organization.

69. D is correct. (Obj 2 – Type A).

A is incorrect. Managed-care plans differ from traditional health insurance plans by providing negotiated benefits and fees with a network of healthcare providers.
B is incorrect. The majority of individuals in the U.S. obtain their medical expense insurance through group health insurance plans.
C is incorrect. Basic medical insurance coverage does not provide coverage for prescription drugs and home healthcare services. These items are often covered under a major medical policy.

70. C is incorrect. (Obj 2 – Type A).

A is incorrect. PPOs are one of the most expensive forms of managed-care plans.
B is incorrect. PPOs generally provide coverage for the same medical procedures regardless of whether network or non-network providers are used. In some cases, some procedures are only covered if network providers are used.
D is incorrect. Members can choose any physician, but network physicians are less expensive and have lower deductibles.

71. C is correct. (Obj 2 – Type A).

An exclusive provider organization charges insurers an access fee for use of the network, negotiates with healthcare providers to set fee schedules for guaranteed service levels, and helps resolve issues between insurers and healthcare providers.

72. A is correct. (Obj 2 – Type A).

A health maintenance organization typically features a gatekeeper physician and provides all the care needed by its members in exchange for a fixed fee.

73.B is correct. (Obj 2 – Type A).

A is incorrect. Individuals covered under a consumer-directed health plan pay lower premiums because the deductibles and out-of-pocket fees are high.
C is incorrect. A point-of-service plan (POS) is a type of managed-care plan that combines a health maintenance organization (HMO) and a preferred provider organization (PPO).
D is incorrect. Contributions to a savings account by the employer will be tax-free to the employee.

74.D is correct. (Obj 2 – Type B).

A consumer-directed health plan is the only type of plan that permits the use of a health savings account.

75.C is correct. (Obj 3 – Type A).

A is incorrect. There is no requirement that an individual must be retired to receive Medicare benefits.
B is incorrect. A non-citizen is eligible for Medicare benefits if they are a permanent resident of the U.S.
D is incorrect. Even if an individual defers Social Security benefits, they are still eligible (if meeting the other requirements) to receive Medicare benefits.

76.B is correct. (Obj 3 – Type A).

A is incorrect. Individuals are generally eligible for Medicare coverage upon attaining age 65.
C is incorrect. Medicare benefits can begin at age 65, even if Social Security benefits are deferred to a later age.
D is incorrect. Medicare Part A is largely funded through payroll taxes.

77.A is correct. (Obj 3 – Type A).

Inpatient hospital care is covered under Medicare Part A.

B is incorrect. Elective cosmetic surgery is not covered under Medicare.
C is incorrect. Custodial care is not covered under Medicare.
D is incorrect. Physicians' services are covered under Medicare Part B.

78.C is correct. (Obj 3 – Type A).

A is incorrect. Prescription drugs are covered under Medicare Part D.
B is incorrect. Skilled-nursing-facility benefits are covered under Medicare Part A.
D is incorrect. Orthopedic shoes are not covered under Medicare Part B.

79.D is correct. (Obj 3 – Type A).

A is incorrect. Under the program, beneficiaries can choose to be covered under a managed care plan.
B is incorrect. Medicare Advantage plans must provide all benefits available under Parts A and B of Medicare.
C is incorrect. Medicaid is a means-tested federal-state welfare program that covers medical expenses for low-income individuals.

80. D is correct. (Obj 3 – Type A).

A is incorrect. Part D is available to individuals eligible for Part A and enrolled in Part B of Medicare.
B is incorrect. Medicare Supplemental Insurance is designed to fill the gaps in coverage associated by Medicare Part A and Part B.
C is incorrect. Part D is financed by a premium paid by participants and the federal government.

81. B is correct. (Obj 3 – Type A).

A is incorrect. The largest group of Medicaid recipients is children.
C is incorrect. The program is partially funded by the various states. However, the federal government pays almost 60% of all Medicaid expenses.
D is incorrect. Medicaid is a means-tested federal-state welfare program that covers medical expenses for low-income individuals.

82. D is correct. (Obj 4 – Type A).

A is incorrect. Most policies do not pay for care the insured receives from a family member.
B is incorrect. A physician certification provision is used to determine whether the insured is eligible for benefits under the policy.
C is incorrect. Most long-term care policies issued are issued on a guaranteed renewable basis.

83. C is correct. (Obj 4 – Type A).

Age is the primary factor in determining the cost of a long-term care policy.

84. A is correct. (Obj 4 – Type A).

Services or care for alcoholism or drug addiction are typically excluded from coverage under long-term care policies.

85. B is correct. (Obj 4 – Type B).

A nonforfeiture option allows for a reduced benefit, or a return of premiums, if the insured cancels the policy.

MODULE 4

86. B is correct. (Obj 1 – Type A).

A is incorrect. Investors wanting capital appreciation should invest some portion of their portfolio in stocks or other equity-based securities.
C is incorrect. The tax rate applied to capital appreciation is often lower than the rate applied to interest income.
D is incorrect. Capital appreciation is the amount by which an asset's selling price exceeds the asset's purchase price.

87. D is correct. (Obj 1 – Type A).

A is incorrect. Bonds focus on investment income.
B is incorrect. The primary type of investment return on an apartment building is rental income (investment income).
C is incorrect. Value stocks tend to pay high dividends as compared to growth stocks.

88. D is correct. (Obj 1 – Type A).

The compound annual rate of return, unlike the rate of return, takes into account the return on invested income.

89. C is correct. (Obj 1 – Type B).

The capital gain or loss is realized only when the owner of the investment sells the investment. Since Sara did not sell the investment, the $20,000 of appreciation represents an unrealized capital gain.

90. B is correct. (Obj 1 – Type B).

A is incorrect. A value stock does generate investment income (dividend income), but it also may have capital appreciation if the value of the stock increases due to market conditions.
C is incorrect. A bond does generate investment income (interest income), but it also may have capital appreciation if the value of the bond increases due to market conditions.
D is incorrect. An apartment building does generate investment income (rental income), but it also may have capital appreciation if the value of the building increases due to market conditions.

91. C is correct. (Obj 1 – Type B).

The total investment return for the stock was $265, which represents capital appreciation of $100 ($1,100 sales price less $1,000 purchase price) and investment income of $165 ($50 + $55 + $60).
Therefore, her total return was 26.5% ($265 / $1,000). Since she held the investment for three years, the average rate of return was 8.83% (26.5% / 3).

92. D is correct. (Obj 1 – Type B).

A is incorrect. Stan had an unrealized capital loss because the value of the stock declined.
B is incorrect. Stan received dividend income of $30.
C is incorrect. Although the stock suffered an unrealized capital loss, Stan had a total rate of return that was positive due to the dividend income.

93. B is correct. (Obj 2 – Type A).

A is incorrect. Liquidity risk is the risk that a security cannot be sold quickly at the current market value.
C is incorrect. Inflation risk is the risk of the loss of purchasing power, caused by changes in the overall price level of goods and services in the economy.
D is incorrect. Investment risk is the possible variation in total return on an investment.

94. C is correct. (Obj 2 – Type A).

A is incorrect. Financial risk is the risk that a company has taken on too much debt.
B is incorrect. Interest rate risk is the risk that a change in market interest rates will affect the value of an investment.
D is incorrect. Unsystematic risk is risk that can be reduced through diversification.

95. D is correct. (Obj 2 – Type A).

A is incorrect. Market risk represents uncertainty about an investment's future performance due to changes in the market for that investment.
B is incorrect. Assets that emphasize capital appreciation, such as stocks and real estate, are less susceptible to inflation risk, but still possess some inflation risk.
C is incorrect. Inflation risk is reduced as long as the value of the investment moves in the same general direction as overall inflation.

96. B is correct. (Obj 2 – Type A).

A is incorrect. If interest rates rise, the market price of older bonds will fall relative to the price of newer bonds.
C is incorrect. An important source of business risk is the change in demand for the company's products or services.
D is incorrect. Inflation risk is the uncertainty about an investment's future value due to changes in general rates of inflation.

97. A is correct. (Obj 2 – Type A).

B is incorrect. Market risk applies to investments other than stocks or bonds, including real estate and commodities.
C is incorrect. As a general rule, investments that have more liquidity risk have a lower market price than they otherwise would.
D is incorrect. A company's financial risk affects the value of both the company's stock and bonds.

98. C is correct. (Obj 2 – Type A).

Systematic risk is a risk common to all securities, such as a downturn in the economy. Systematic risk cannot be diversified.

99. D is correct. (Obj 2 – Type A).

A is incorrect. Financial risk is the uncertainty about future performance due to the amount of debt assumed.
B is incorrect. As the amount of investment risk increases, the average investor will usually want a higher rate of return.
C is incorrect. The goal of diversification is to achieve maximum investment return while minimizing investment risk.

100. A is correct. (Obj 2 – Type A).

B is incorrect. Leverage actually increases the amount of investment risk, because it increases the variation of the investment return.
C is incorrect. Leverage represents the use of debt to invest.
D is incorrect. Leverage does not reduce systematic risk.

101. D is correct. (Obj 2 – Type A).

An emergency fund should be comprised of investments that are both liquid and marketable. A savings account, money market mutual fund, checking account, and very short-term CD are examples of investments that are appropriate for an emergency fund.

102. B is correct. (Obj 2 – Type B).

There is an inverse relationship between market interest rates and bond prices. Therefore, when market interest rates increase, bond price will drop.

103. B is correct. (Obj 2 – Type B).

Financial risk is the uncertainty about future investment returns because of the amount of debt assumed by an organization on which the investment is based.

104. B is correct. (Obj 2 – Type B).

Business risk is the exposure a company has to factor(s) that will lower its profits or lead it to fail. Anything that threatens a company's ability to achieve its financial goals is considered a business risk. Business risk is a type of unsystematic risk.

105. B is correct. (Obj 3 – Type A).

A is incorrect. Laddering is an appropriate strategy for bonds.
C is incorrect. Dollar cost averaging involves the purchase of more shares as market prices decline.
D is incorrect. Since laddering involves the purchase of longer-term bonds, it actually increases the interest rate risk of a portfolio.

106. D is correct. (Obj 3 – Type A).

Regardless of whether shares are held inside a dividend reinvestment plan or outside a plan, all shares of common stock for a company will pay the same dividend.

107. B is correct. (Obj 3 – Type A).

A is incorrect. Many publicly traded stocks offer dividend reinvestment plans.
C is incorrect. The dividends are taxed immediately, regardless of whether the dividends are reinvested.
D is incorrect. Dollar cost averaging refers to the systematic contribution of cash towards an investment every month.

108. D is correct. (Obj 3 – Type A).

A is incorrect. The primary purpose of asset allocation as an investment strategy is to ensure the risk of the portfolio is appropriate for the investor.
B is incorrect. Asset allocators generally do not make an effort to identify underpriced securities.
C is incorrect. The asset allocation changes as an investor gets older. Typically, as an investor gets older, the allocation is changed to reduce the overall risk of the portfolio.

109. C is correct. (Obj 3 – Type A).

A is incorrect. DRIPs are usually offered by publicly traded companies.
B is incorrect. Dividends are reinvested under the plan and the reinvested dividends are used to purchase additional shares (either whole or fractional) of stock of the company.
D is incorrect. Dividends that are reinvested under dividend reinvestment plans are taxed as though the dividends were received in cash by the shareholders.

110. D is correct. (Obj 3 – Type A).

A is incorrect. Term insurance is a type of risk management planning technique.
B is incorrect. The creation of a Will is an estate planning technique.
C is incorrect. A charitable remainder annuity trust is an example of an income tax and estate planning technique.

111. C is correct. (Obj 3 – Type B).

Life-cycle funds are asset allocation funds in which the share of each asset class is automatically adjusted to lower risk as the desired retirement date approaches. A lifecycle fund's asset allocation reflects what its investment managers have determined is the optimal risk and return profile for a given time horizon ending with the fund's target year.

112. D is correct. (Obj 3 – Type B).

A dollar cost averaging plan represents the systematic investing of the same dollar amount each period. Warren purchased ABC Company Mutual Fund shares for $500 (10 shares x $50 per share) in the first month and should therefore purchase $500 worth of shares in the second (and subsequent) month.

113. B is correct. (Obj 3 – Type B).

A is incorrect. This is an example of asset allocation.
C is incorrect. This is an example of a dumbbell strategy.
D is incorrect. The purchase of equal dollar amounts of stock on a periodic basis represents dollar cost averaging, not laddering.

114. C is correct. (Obj 3 – Type B).

A life-cycle mutual fund, or asset allocation fund, maintains an asset allocation consisting of stocks, bonds, and money market instruments. The percentage in each asset class changes and becomes less risky with the passage of time.

115. C is correct. (Obj 4 – Type A).

A is incorrect. The main advantage of savings accounts is their liquidity and safety. Savings accounts offer a relatively low rate of return.
B is incorrect. Although market accounts are insured by the Federal Deposit Insurance Corporation, money market mutual funds are not.
D is incorrect. Savings accounts typically only offer an investor investment income.

116. B is correct. (Obj 4 – Type A).

A is incorrect. Treasury bills have an active secondary market.
C is incorrect. Treasury bonds have maturities ranging from 11-30 years.
D is incorrect. Treasury bills are always issued at a discount from their face value.

117. B is correct. (Obj 4 – Type A).

A is incorrect. Debentures are only backed by the issuer's full faith and credit. They are not secured bonds, which are backed by specific collateral.
C is incorrect. Most corporate bonds pay interest semi-annually.
D is incorrect. If held to maturity, the capital appreciation on a corporate bond is taxed as a capital gain.

118. D is correct. (Obj 4 – Type A).

Although certain bonds, such as Eurobonds, are subject to exchange rate risk, most bonds are not subject to this risk. Most bonds are subject to interest rate risk, default risk, and inflation risk.

119. B is correct. (Obj 4 – Type A).

A is incorrect. Growth stocks are issued by companies with earnings that are growing at a faster rate than the general economy. Value stocks are issued by companies that are considered undervalued.
C is incorrect. Income stocks are issued by companies with an established record of dividend payments.
D is incorrect. Penny stocks trade for less than $1. Defensive stocks are issued by companies that have earnings that are not affected by the economy, such as grocery stores.

120. B is correct. (Obj 4 – Type A).

A is incorrect. The beta of a stock measures the stock's systematic risk.
C is incorrect. Only income stocks are subject to inflation risk.
D is incorrect. Common stocks trading on organized exchanges very liquid.

121. D is correct. (Obj 4 – Type A).

A blended mutual fund invests in both bonds and stocks. It offers a diversified portfolio that emphasizes safety and performance.

122. C is correct. (Obj 4 – Type A).

A is incorrect. Global funds invest both in the United States and in foreign markets. International funds invest outside the United States.
B is incorrect. Life cycle funds are designed for individuals in certain phases of their life cycle. Many of these funds have a retirement date that is set, and as the date draws closer, the asset allocation becomes more conservative.
D is incorrect. Index funds are passively managed, resulting in lower fund costs.

123. B is correct. (Obj 4 – Type B).

A is incorrect. General obligation bonds are municipal bonds backed by the taxes collected by the government body.
C is incorrect. An assessment bond is backed by taxes and assessments.
D is incorrect. Treasury bonds are not municipal bonds.

124. C is correct. (Obj 4 – Type B).

Valued stocks have a higher potential for price appreciation because the stocks are generally considered undervalued.

MODULE 5

125. C is correct. (Obj 1 – Type A).

A is incorrect. Census data reflects that there is a positive correlation between salary and the level of postsecondary education attained.
B is incorrect. Census data indicates that there is a lower unemployment rate among the more highly educated.
D is incorrect. The number of Americans pursuing postsecondary education has increased substantially in recent years.

126. D is correct. (Obj 1 – Type A).

Tuition and fees represent the largest single cost category to consider when planning for postsecondary education.

127. B is correct. (Obj 1 – Type A).

A is incorrect. Expenses associated with funding a postsecondary education have risen at a pace that exceeds the Consumer Price Index (CPI).
C is incorrect. Online degrees from two-year and four-year academic institutions have similar tuition costs as brick-and-mortar institutions. However, housing and transportation costs are much lower for online institutions.
D is incorrect. Saving for a postsecondary education typically competes with other investment goals.

128. C is correct. (Obj 1 – Type A).

A is incorrect. The closer the saver is to the college funding need, the more conservative the portfolio allocations should be.
B is incorrect. The accepted rule for determining an education investment portfolio is to determine an appropriate asset allocation based on the student's age and number of years until the education is scheduled to begin.
D is incorrect. The investment strategy must be reevaluated and adjusted periodically as plans and costs change.

129. B is correct. (Obj 1 – Type B).

Although it is important for the professional to review Kim's investment portfolio, asset allocation, and income, these factors are only important in determining the amount Kim must save to fund the children's education. The question asks for the most important factor needed to determine the future cost of the education. The education inflation rate is the most important factor of those listed in projecting future education costs.

130. A is correct. (Obj 2 – Type A).

To determine the future value of a principal sum, the principal sum (P) must be multiplied by 1 plus the growth rate (1 + i) to the power of the number of years for which the future value is being calculated (n).

131. C is correct. (Obj 2 – Type B).

The present value can be determined using the following keystrokes on an HP-10BII calculator:
[SHIFT], C ALL (clears the calculator)
20000, +/-, PV (enters -$20,000 as the cost of college in today's dollars)
13, N (enters 13 as number of years until college begins)
5, I/YR (enters 5% as inflation rate; no need to enter this as a percentage, just enter the whole number)
FV (displays the solution to the question)

The future value equals $37,713.

132. C is correct. (Obj 2 – Type B).

The tuition can be calculated in two ways:
Method 1:
$FV = PV * (1 + i)^n$
$FV = \$15,000 * (1 + .06)^8$
FV = $15,000 * (1.593848)
FV = $23,908

Method 2: using a financial calculator, enter the following (make sure the calculator is set to annual payments):
PV = $15,000
N = 8
I = 6
Solving for FV, the solution is $23,908.

133. A is correct. (Obj 3 – Type A).

B is incorrect. The FAFSA can be used to obtain federal, state, or university financial aid.
C is incorrect. The FAFSA requires the reporting of both taxed and untaxed income.
D is incorrect. Families must repeat the FAFSA application process each year the student is enrolled in a qualified postsecondary program.

134. D is correct. (Obj 3 – Type A).

A is incorrect. FAFSA includes income from both the student and the parents.
B is incorrect. The opposite is true. FAFSA weighs the student's assets more heavily than the parents' assets.
C is incorrect. FAFSA is the initial step in the process of obtaining financial aid.

135. D is correct. (Obj 3 – Type A).

A is incorrect. The EFC formula weighs the student's assets up to six times more heavily than the parents' assets.
B is incorrect. The federal EFC formula determines a student's eligibility for government-backed grants and loans.
C is incorrect. The EFC formula excludes several items, including cash value life insurance policies.

136. B is correct. (Obj 3 – Type A).

The EFC formula excludes several items, including assets and income of noncustodial parents.

137. C is correct. (Obj 3 – Type A).

The EFC formula excludes several items, including equity in a principal residence.

138. B is correct. (Obj 3 – Type A).

A is incorrect. Retirement assets are not counted in the Expected Family Contribution formula. Therefore, spending down retirement assets will not lower the Expected Family Contribution. Liquid assets and savings would be more appropriate assets to spend down.
C is incorrect. Most assets count in the Expected Family Contribution formula. Therefore, to reduce the Expected Family Contribution, an individual might want to minimize savings levels.
D is incorrect. Assets of the student are weighted more heavily in the Expected Family Contribution formula than the assets of the parents. Therefore, the assets of the parents should be used first.

139. A is correct. (Obj 3 – Type A).

B is incorrect. Pell grants are not available to students who have already earned a bachelor's degree or other professional degree.
C is incorrect. Pell grants are not based on grades.
D is incorrect. Pell grants are not loans, and therefore do not need to be repaid.

140. D is correct. (Obj 3 – Type A).

A is incorrect. Pell grants are available (in lesser amounts) to part-time students.
B is incorrect. Stafford loans must be repaid within 10 years.
C is incorrect. Stafford loans are the major source of education borrowing.

141. A is correct. (Obj 3 – Type A).

Unsubsidized Stafford Loans are not need based loans.

142. B is correct. (Obj 3 – Type A).

A is incorrect. Perkins loans are serviced by outside lenders. They are repaid directly to the school.
C is incorrect. Subsidized Stafford loans typically have a lower interest rate than unsubsidized loans.
D is incorrect. Loans offered under the Federal Direct Loan Program are fixed-rate loans.

143. B is correct. (Obj 3 – Type A).

The following income and assets are excluded from the Expected Family Contribution formula:
-Primary residence.
-Qualified retirement plans.
-Income and assets of noncustodial parents.

144. D is correct. (Obj 3 – Type B).

A is incorrect. Municipal bonds are includable in determining the Expected Family Contribution.
B is incorrect. Although the gifts of cash to the daughter would help the daughter pay for college, it will not increase the Expected Family Contribution because assets in the name of the student are counted more heavily than assets of the parents.
C is incorrect. Equity securities are counted in the Expected Family Contribution formula.

145. A is correct. (Obj 4 – Type A).

There are two types of 529 plans: college savings plans and prepaid tuition plans.

146. B is correct. (Obj 4 – Type A).

A is incorrect. There is no maximum contribution limit for an UTMA or UGMA account.
C is incorrect. These accounts are less expensive than formal trusts.
D is incorrect. Funds can be used for the minor's postsecondary education, but the funds cannot be used for basic needs of the minor, such as housing or clothing.

147. C is correct. (Obj 4 – Type A).

A is incorrect. UTMA accounts are irrevocable, and the beneficiary cannot be changed.
B is incorrect. Almost any type of asset can be transferred to an UTMA account, including real estate.
D is incorrect. UTMA accounts are considered assets of the student.

148. A is correct. (Obj 4 – Type A).

B is incorrect. The ability to contribute to a Coverdell Education Savings Account is phased out for higher-income individuals.
C is incorrect. The maximum contribution to a Coverdell Education Savings Account is $2,000 per year.
D is incorrect. The account is considered an asset of the parent for purposes of the EFC formula.

149. C is correct. (Obj 4 – Type A).

A is incorrect. Anyone, including a grandparent or unrelated party, can establish a Coverdell Education Savings Account for a student.
B is incorrect. Contributions to the account are not deductible for federal income tax purposes.
D is incorrect. The account must be distributed within 30 days of the student's attainment of age 30 to avoid taxes and a penalty.

150. B is correct. (Obj 4 – Type A).

A is incorrect. Contributions to a 529 plan are not deductible for federal income tax purposes. However, some states do allow a deduction for state income tax purposes.
C is incorrect. Most 529 Savings plans are open to residents of any state. For example, a person living in Texas can contribute to the Nebraska Section 529 plan.
D is incorrect. The rate of return on a prepaid tuition plan is tied to tuition inflation rates. However, the rate of return on a SAVINGS plan is based upon the investments selected by the account owner. These investments can include various mutual funds that would have a rate of return based upon the fund's underlying investments.

151. B is correct. (Obj 4 – Type A).

State prepaid tuition plans are portable.

A is incorrect. Prepaid college plans are most attractive to conservative investors since the plan guarantees to pay for their student's tuition.
C is incorrect. These plans do not guarantee actual admission to the college. The student will have to meet the requirements of the school to gain admission.
D is incorrect. If the student chooses not to go to college, or receives a scholarship, the prepaid tuition plan will provide a refund of contributions. Some plans even pay a small amount of interest.

152. B is correct. (Obj 4 – Type A).

When a Section 529 plan beneficiary is changed, there will be gift tax consequences when the new beneficiary is at least one generation below the old beneficiary. However, when the new beneficiary is in the same generation, there is no resulting gift.

A is incorrect. The earnings portion of money withdrawn from a 529 plan that is not spent on eligible college expenses will be subject to income tax, an additional 10% federal tax penalty, and the possibility of a recapture of any state tax deductions or credits taken. The early withdrawal penalty will be waived in certain situations, but not when the account owner attains age 59 ½.
C is incorrect. Section 529 plans do not permit investments in individual stocks or bonds.
D is incorrect. Contributions made to the plan are NOT deductible in arriving at the donor's federal taxable income. However, there may be some state tax benefits for the donor.

153. D is correct. (Obj 4 – Type A).

A is incorrect. If a Series EE bond is purchased and held by the parents, the bond is considered an asset of the parent.
B is incorrect. Series EE bonds pay a relatively low rate of return.
C is incorrect. The maximum allowable purchase for an individual is $10,000 per year.

154. B is correct. (Obj 4 – Type B).

A Section 529 plan would be the best strategy, if the type of plan chosen is a Section 529 prepaid tuition plan. A Section 529 prepaid tuition plan provides a hedge against the rising cost of tuition, because it allows the saver to pay a specific school's tuition based on current tuition rates.

155. D is correct. (Obj 4 – Type B).

A Uniform Transfer to Minors Act account on behalf of their son would be considered the son's asset for purposes of obtaining financial aid. This would be the LEAST appropriate strategy. All of the other options would be considered assets of the parents, which would be more appropriate.

156. B is correct. (Obj 4 – Type B).

A Section 529 plan allows her to contribute the desired amount each year and allows Agnes to retain control over the account.

A is incorrect. A Coverdell Education Savings Account only permits a maximum contribution of $2,000 per year.
C is incorrect. An annual gifting program to the grandchildren is irrevocable, and therefore the amounts given cannot be reclaimed by Agnes.
D is incorrect. A Uniform Transfer to Minors Act (UTMA) account is an irrevocable gift that cannot be reclaimed by Agnes.

157. C is correct. (Obj 4 – Type B).

The brokerage account will allow Angie to have maximum investment control and would allow her to reclaim any assets not used for college. In addition, tuition payments made directly to an educational institution are not considered a gift for gift tax purposes.

MODULE 6

158. B is correct. (Obj 1 – Type A).

The steps of the retirement planning process, in order, are:
-Determining retirement goals
-Analyzing financial needs
-Arranging financing and control techniques
-Monitoring and revising the plan as necessary

159. A is correct. (Obj 1 – Type A).

B is incorrect. A retirement plan should generally be monitored annually or sooner if a significant event occurs.
C is incorrect. Financial needs analysis translates an individual's retirement goals into an accumulation goal that must be met.
D is incorrect. Only a minority of individuals modify their inflation or return assumptions and increase their risk.

160. C is correct. (Obj 1 – Type A).

A is incorrect. A nonqualified annuity is a tax-deferred funding vehicle but is not a tax-deductible funding vehicle.
B is incorrect. A municipal bond is a tax-free funding vehicle but is not a tax-deductible funding vehicle.
D is incorrect. A money market mutual fund is a currently taxable funding vehicle.

161. C is correct. (Obj 1 – Type A).

A is incorrect. A nonqualified annuity is a tax-deferred funding vehicle but is not a tax-deductible funding vehicle.
B is incorrect. A Roth IRA is a tax-free funding vehicle but is not a tax-deductible funding vehicle.
D is incorrect. A certificate of deposit is a currently taxable funding vehicle.

162. B is correct. (Obj 1 – Type A).

A is incorrect. A municipal bond is not subject to contribution limits and is not subject to required minimum distributions.
C is incorrect. A nonqualified annuity is not subject to contribution limits and is not subject to required minimum distributions.
D is incorrect. A Roth IRA is subject to contribution limits but is not subject to required minimum distributions.

163. D is correct. (Obj 1 – Type A).

A Section 401(k) plan is generally subject to a 10% penalty if withdrawals are made prior to age 59½.

164. A is correct. (Obj 1 – Type A).

B is incorrect. Access to certain accounts, such as Section 401(k) plans, may be prohibited before retirement or termination of employment. However, access to tax-free funding vehicles, such as municipal bonds, is not restricted.
C is incorrect. Minimum distribution rules do not apply to tax-free accounts, such as Roth IRAs.
D is incorrect. The early withdrawal penalty generally does not apply to tax-free funding vehicles.

165. B is correct. (Obj 1 – Type B).

When annual contributions to a retirement vehicle are tax deductible, the effect on an individual's spendable income are reduced, resulting in more current spendable income.

166. C is correct. (Obj 1 – Type B).

A is incorrect. A nonqualified annuity does not feature tax-deductible contributions.
B is incorrect. A Roth IRA does not feature tax-deductible contributions. In addition, the Roth IRA contribution limits will prevent Rob from contributing $800 per month.
D is incorrect. A savings account does not feature tax-deductible contributions. In addition, a savings account does not offer tax-deferral.

167. B is correct. (Obj 1 – Type B).

A is incorrect. A nonqualified annuity does not feature tax-free distributions.
C is incorrect. A Section 401(k) plan does not feature tax-free distributions.
D is incorrect. A traditional IRA does not feature tax-free distributions.

168. B is correct. (Obj 2 – Type A).

The following expenses typically decrease during retirement:
-Taxes.
-Home ownership expenses.
-Work-related expenses.
-Contributions to retirement plans.
-Support for dependent children.

169. D is correct. (Obj 2 – Type A).

A is incorrect. The income replacement ratio method usually uses an income replacement ratio of 60%-80%.
B is incorrect. The expense method for estimating retirement income needs is especially appropriate for individuals approaching retirement age.
C is incorrect. Taxes typically decrease during retirement.

170. B is correct. (Obj 2 – Type A).

A is incorrect. Taxes typically decline during retirement.
C is incorrect. Retirement contributions generally end once the individual stops working.
D is incorrect. Home-ownership expenses typically decrease during retirement, because the retiree usually pays off the mortgage.

171. C is correct. (Obj 2 – Type A).

A is incorrect. Work-related expenses typically end when an individual retires.
B is incorrect. Support for dependent children has usually ended by the time an individual retires.
D is incorrect. General expenses typically decrease during retirement, because the retiree often becomes less active.

172. D is correct. (Obj 2 – Type A).

A fund will discontinue distributions if the assets in the fund are exhausted, while an annuity guarantees payments for life.

173. B is correct. (Obj 2 – Type A).

A is incorrect. The retirement payout from a defined contribution plan is affected by the length of time the plan is funded, the rate of return on investments, and the age of retirement. It is not affected by Social Security benefits.
C is incorrect. Retirement savings amounts should be reviewed periodically, potentially on an annual basis.
D is incorrect. Income needs are determined first, by subtracting out pension and Social Security benefits. The annual savings requirement can then be determined.

174. A is correct. (Obj 2 – Type B).

In each subsequent year, the annual withdrawal must be increase by inflation. Since the withdrawal in the first year was $20,000, the second-year withdrawal will be $20,400, calculated as follows:
Second Year Withdrawal = First Year Withdrawal x (1 + Inflation Rate)
Second Year Withdrawal = $20,000 x (1 + .02)
Second Year Withdrawal = $20,400

175. B is correct. (Obj 3 – Type A).

A is incorrect. Contributions to a defined benefit plan are generally inflexible.
C is incorrect. In-service withdrawals are generally not permitted with a defined benefit plan.
D is incorrect. Communication of benefits to employees is generally difficult.

176. D is correct. (Obj 3 – Type A).

A is incorrect. A years-of-service cap should be used if the employer desires a more rapid turnover of older employees.
B is incorrect. The unit-benefit formula is the most frequently used benefit formula in a defined benefit plan.
C is incorrect. Employers typically provide an income-replacement ratio of approximately 40-60% of an employee's final average salary.

177. D is correct. (Obj 3 – Type A).

A cash balance plan is a type of defined benefit plan with a benefit that is defined more like a defined contribution plan. A cash balance plan defines benefits in terms of a specified account balance.

178. A is correct. (Obj 3 – Type A).

B is incorrect. A profit sharing plan permits in-service withdrawals, typically after two years of participation or in hardship situations.
C is incorrect. A profit sharing plan can conceivably invest up to 100% of the plan's assets in employer stock.
D is incorrect. Profit sharing plans cannot provide for past service.

179. A is correct. (Obj 3 – Type A).

B is incorrect. Contribution limits apply to 401(k) plans.
C is incorrect. Section 403(b) plans can only be established by tax exempt organizations.
D is incorrect. Future benefits of defined benefit plans can be accurately estimated.

180. B is correct. (Obj 3 – Type A).

A is incorrect. The maximum contribution is the lesser of 25% of compensation or the defined contribution limit.
C is incorrect. A SEP is technically not a qualified plan. However, it is similar in some ways to a defined contribution plan.
D is incorrect. SEPs are funded exclusively by the employer.

181. B is correct. (Obj 3 – Type A).

A is incorrect. SIMPLE IRAs are subject to a lower maximum contribution limit than 401(k) plans.
C is incorrect. SIMPLE IRAs do not allow loans.
D is incorrect. To sponsor a SIMPLE, an employer has to have 100 or fewer employees.

182. D is correct. (Obj 3 – Type A).

Deferred compensation plans are not taxed to the executive until the benefit is received.

A is incorrect. Nonqualified plans can be funded or unfunded.
B is incorrect. Nonqualified plans cannot be rolled over into tax advantaged plans.
C is incorrect. Deferred compensation plans do not provide an income tax deduction to the employer until the employee is taxed.

183. B is correct. (Obj 3 – Type A).

A is incorrect. SERPs are nonqualified plans, whereas profit sharing plans are qualified plans.
C is incorrect. SERPs are encouraged to discriminate in favor of highly compensated employees.
D is incorrect. SERPs are funded by employer contributions.

184. A is correct. (Obj 3 – Type A).

B is incorrect. A SERP is a type of salary continuation (not reduction) plan.
C is incorrect. A defined contribution is a qualified plan.
D is incorrect. A death benefit only (DBO) plan is a nonqualified plan designed to provide a survivor benefit at the participant's death.

185. D is correct. (Obj 4 – Type A).

Roth IRA contributions are not deductible.

A is incorrect. Taxpayers with AGI exceeding certain levels cannot contribute to a Roth IRA.
B is incorrect. The total contribution allowed for the year can be allocated between a Roth and traditional IRA, but an individual cannot contribute the maximum contribution to BOTH.
C is incorrect. A taxpayer must have earned income to contribute to a Roth IRA.

186. C is correct. (Obj 4 – Type A).

Contributions to a Roth IRA are never deductible. However, depending on the taxpayer's adjusted gross income, contributions to a traditional IRA may be deductible.

187. C is correct. (Obj 4 – Type B).

The entire $70,000 will be subject to income tax, because her initial contributions to the traditional IRA were made with pre-tax dollars. Therefore, she has no basis in the traditional IRA, resulting in the entire $70,000 being subject to taxation. Conversions from traditional IRAs to Roth IRAs are never subject to a penalty.

188. C is correct. (Obj 4 – Type B).

Although Sandra does not have compensation, she can attribute her husband's compensation to herself, and establish a spousal IRA.

A is incorrect. An individual can only contribute to an IRA to the extent they have compensation. Dividend income is not considered compensation income.
B is incorrect. An individual can only contribute to an IRA to the extent they have compensation. Since she only earns $3,500 from her part-time job, she will not be eligible to make a full contribution to the traditional IRA.
D is incorrect. An individual can only contribute to an IRA to the extent they have compensation. Rental income is not considered compensation income.

189. A is correct. (Obj 5 – Type A).

B is incorrect. Both the maximum Social Security benefit and the age at which a retiree can receive full Social Security benefits are increasing.
C is incorrect. The principal employer-sponsored plans in which employees are investing are 401(k) plans and 403(b) plans.
D is incorrect. Recent reports indicate that savings in 401(k) plans contain less than 25% of assets needed to maintain retirees' standard of living during retirement.

190. D is correct. (Obj 5 – Type A).

To maximize tax benefits, assets should be liquidated in the following order:
-Investments that have lost money, to take advantage of capital loss deductions.
-Cash available.
-Long-term capital gain assets, since there are favorable rates.
-Short-term capital gain assets.
-Tax-deferred assets, such as 401(k) plans.

191. B is correct. (Obj 5 – Type A).

If an individual has a Social Security full retirement age of 66, and he begins taking benefits at age 62, the reduction in benefits received will be 25%.

192. D is correct. (Obj 5 – Type B).

All of the vehicles listed are excellent vehicles for accumulating a retirement fund. However, Jamie should first consider putting money into her Section 401(k) plan. Not only are the contributions made on a pre-tax basis, she will be able to take advantage of the employer matching contribution.

193. B is correct. (Obj 5 – Type B).

When a couple is in a high-income tax bracket, they would normally withdraw funds from either a currently taxable account, or a Roth IRA. The currently taxable account will usually result in taxes paid at favorable capital gains rates. However, because their goal is to minimize income taxes, they should withdraw the funds from the Roth IRA since the withdrawal will be income tax-free.

MODULE 7

194. A is correct. (Obj 1 – Type A).

Probate costs include costs incurred to distribute the estate and costs incurred to defend against challenges to a Will.

195. B is correct. (Obj 1 – Type A).

An individual's estate is the total amount owned at the individual's death. The estate includes cash, investments, personal property, and business interests.

196. A is correct. (Obj 1 – Type A).

Estate shrinkage is the decrease in the size of an estate due to the payment of probate costs, estate taxes, and claims of creditors.

197. C is correct. (Obj 1 – Type A).

A is incorrect. All individuals who own property or has accumulated even a small amount of wealth should establish an estate plan.
B is incorrect. Few financial advisors have appropriate expertise to generate a complex estate plan for a client.
D is incorrect. A major goal of estate planning is to create the needed liquidity to ensure an estate can pay claims after the individual dies.

198. B is correct. (Obj 1 – Type A).

Estate planning goals include:
-Distributing property according to the decedent's wishes.
-Minimizing income taxes.
-Minimizing estate taxes.
-Minimizing probate costs.
-Ensuring adequate liquidity.

A is incorrect. All individuals, regardless of the size of their estate, should have a valid Will.
C is incorrect. A goal of estate planning is to create needed liquidity.
D is incorrect. Probate can be time consuming and costly. Therefore, a goal of estate planning is to minimize probate costs.

199. D is correct. (Obj 1 – Type A).

A is incorrect. Estate tax is a tax imposed on the transfer of property.
B is incorrect. Income tax is a tax on an individual's income.
C is incorrect. GSTT is a tax imposed on the transfer of property to a grandchild.

200. B is correct. (Obj 2 – Type A).

An executor is a party named in a decedent's Will to administer the estate. An administrator is named by the court to administer an estate if the decedent fails to name an executor in the Will.

201. C is correct. (Obj 2 – Type A).

The final step of the estate plan, "execute and monitor the new estate plan," is where additional life insurance may be purchased. In addition, gifts may be made, and new or revised legal documents may be created.

202. B is correct. (Obj 2 – Type A).

The following are the steps in the estate planning process (in order):
-Gather facts.
-Evaluate the existing estate plan.
-Formulate and test a new estate plan.
-Execute and monitor the new estate plan.

203. A is correct. (Obj 2 – Type A).

B is incorrect. Classifying the estate property to determine if it will be included in the probate estate is accomplished during the "evaluate the existing estate plan" step of the estate planning process.
C is incorrect. Estate shrinkage should be estimated and minimized during the "formulate and test a new estate plan" step of the estate planning process.
D is incorrect. Legal documents should be created and revised during the "execute and monitor the new estate plan" step of the estate planning process.

204. B is correct. (Obj 2 – Type A).

Classifying the estate property to determine if it will be included in the probate estate is accomplished during the "evaluate the existing estate plan" step of the estate planning process.
A is incorrect. Determining the estate owner's intentions for transferring property at death is accomplished during the "gather facts" step of the estate planning process.
C is incorrect. Estate shrinkage should be estimated and minimized during the "formulate and test a new estate plan" step of the estate planning process.
D is incorrect. Legal documents should be created and revised during the "execute and monitor the new estate plan" step of the estate planning process.

205. B is correct. (Obj 2 – Type A).

A is incorrect. An estate plan should be reviewed more frequently than once every 10 years. It may be appropriate to review the estate plan annually.
C is incorrect. Estate shrinkage should be estimated under several assumptions, including both spouses dying simultaneously.
D is incorrect. The estate plan should be designed to avoid involuntary liquidation of estate assets.

206. C is correct. (Obj 2 – Type A).

Merely having the right to pay the policy premiums does not constitute incidents of ownership.

207. D is correct. (Obj 2 – Type B).

Assets passed to heirs through the use of a Will are included in the probate estate.

A is incorrect. Property owned as JTWROS avoids probate because it automatically passes to the surviving tenants by operation of law after the death of a tenant.
B is incorrect. Life insurance death benefits will pass by contract to the named beneficiary upon the insured's death, thus avoiding probate.
C is incorrect. A revocable trust has a named beneficiary. The assets in the trust will pass by contract upon the grantor's death, thus avoiding probate.

208. B is correct. (Obj 3 – Type A).

A is incorrect. The donor of the property is responsible for any gift tax due.
C is incorrect. The gift tax rate is a graduated rate. In addition, the gift can be reduced by the annual exclusion and applicable credit amount before any tax is due.
D is incorrect. The estate tax is imposed on the individual's last gift.

209. C is correct. (Obj 3 – Type A).

In determining the gross estate for federal estate tax purposes, the valuation date is either the decedent's date of death or the alternate valuation date. The alternate valuation date is 6 months after the decedent's death.

210. C is correct. (Obj 3 – Type A).

The following are allowable deductions from the gross estate in arriving at the taxable estate:
-Administrative costs of the estate (including executor's fees and probate costs).
-Funeral expenses.
-Marital deduction.
-Charitable deduction.
-Debts of the estate.

211. B is correct. (Obj 3 – Type A).

A and C are incorrect. The sponge (or pickup) tax is a state estate tax equal to the amount prescribed in a table.
D is incorrect. The state estate tax is imposed on the right to transfer property to an heir. It is imposed on the estate.

212. A is correct. (Obj 3 – Type A).

The portability feature allows any unused portion of the exemption to pass to a surviving spouse at the time of the first spouse's death. This helps prevent a decedent from inadvertently wasting his or her exclusion amount at the time of death.

213. B is correct. (Obj 3 – Type A).

A is incorrect. States impose death taxes at different rates. Some states do not impose a state death tax.
C is incorrect. While all states impose the state death tax differently, in most states, transfers to surviving spouses are not subject to state death tax.
D is incorrect. There are two types of state death tax – state estate tax and state inheritance tax.

214. A is correct. (Obj 3 – Type B).

The medical bills and tuition payments are not considered gifts, as they are considered qualified transfers under the law. The apartment rent and the new car would be considered gifts.

The taxable gift is calculated as follows:
Taxable Gift = Apartment Rent + New Car – Annual Exclusion
Taxable Gift = $24,000 + $40,000 – $15,000
Taxable Gift = $49,000

215. D is correct. (Obj 3 – Type B).

A is incorrect. The gift can be reduced by the annual exclusion and gift-splitting in arriving at the amount of the taxable gift.
B is incorrect. Gifts received are not subject to income taxes.
C is incorrect. Gifts given are not deductible for income tax purposes.

216. C is correct. (Obj 3 – Type B).

A is incorrect. A gift made to a charitable organization is eligible for the gift tax charitable deduction, and therefore is not considered a taxable gift.
B is incorrect. A gift made to a spouse is eligible for the gift tax marital deduction, and therefore is not considered a taxable gift.
D is incorrect. Gifts below the annual exclusion amount are not considered taxable gifts for gift tax purposes.

217. D is correct. (Obj 3 – Type B).

The land will be included in Stephen's gross estate based on the consideration furnished rule. Since Stephen contributed the entire purchase price of the land, the entire value of the land will be included in his gross estate at the time of death.

218. C is correct. (Obj 3 – Type B).

Under the fractional interest rule, 50% of the date of death value of the property will be included in the gross estate of the first spouse to die. This is irrespective of which spouse paid for the property.

219. B is correct. (Obj 4 – Type A).

A is incorrect. A Will can accomplish goals unrelated to estate tax minimization.
C is incorrect. A Will is a part of a comprehensive estate plan but does not replace it.
D is incorrect. Revocable trusts must be established during an individual's lifetime. Therefore, a Will cannot be used to establish a revocable trust.

220. C is correct. (Obj 4 – Type A).

A is incorrect. Revocable trusts can only be established during a lifetime.
B is incorrect. For trust assets to be excluded from the grantor's gross estate, the trust must be irrevocable. Assets in a revocable trust are included in the grantor's gross estate at death.
D is incorrect. Even though the trust is revocable, the trust must have a trustee.

221. C is correct. (Obj 4 – Type A).

A sprinkle provision can provide flexibility in a trust by permitting a trustee to distribute income to the beneficiaries as needed.

222. B is correct. (Obj 4 – Type B).

Since there is a named beneficiary, the policy will avoid probate.

A is incorrect. The policy will be included in Tito's gross estate because he owned the policy at his death.
C and D are incorrect. The life insurance proceeds will be received income tax-free by Jerome.

MODULE 8

223. D is correct. (Obj 1 – Type A).

There are generally two primary objectives related to income tax planning:
-Minimizing an individual's overall income tax liability.
-Satisfying the individual's goals and objectives with minimal income tax consequences.

224. D is correct. (Obj 1 – Type A).

A is incorrect. "Above-the-line" deductions are available regardless of whether a taxpayer itemizes his or her deductions.
B is incorrect. Most "above-the-line" deductions are business related deductions, whereas most "below-the-line" deductions are deductions of a personal nature.
C is incorrect. "Below-the-line" deductions are itemized deductions. Deductions in arriving at adjusted gross income are sometimes referred to as "above-the-line" deductions.

225. B is correct. (Obj 1 – Type A).

Charitable contributions are deductible by the taxpayer as an itemized deduction.

A is incorrect. Deductible contributions to a traditional IRA are deducted "above-the-line" as a deduction in arriving at adjusted gross income.
C is incorrect. Business expenses are deducted "above-the-line" as a deduction in arriving at adjusted gross income.
D is incorrect. Alimony paid to a former spouse, if deductible, is deducted "above-the-line" as a deduction in arriving at adjusted gross income.

226. B is correct. (Obj 1 – Type A).

A is incorrect. Charitable contribution limits are determined based on an individual's adjusted gross income.
C is incorrect. Qualified dividends are taxed at long-term capital gains rates.
D is incorrect. A "below-the-line" deduction is a deduction from adjusted gross income to determine taxable income.

227. C is correct. (Obj 1 – Type A).

A is incorrect. Capital assets held more than one year will be considered long-term.
B is incorrect. The determination of whether a capital gain is short-term or long-term is determined exclusively by the period of time the asset is held.
D is incorrect. Under current tax law, long-term capital gains are subject to more favorable income tax rates than short-term capital gains.

228. A is correct. (Obj 1 – Type A).

B is incorrect. Although unreimbursed medical expenses are deductible within limits, a credit is not available.
C is incorrect. Although 50% of self-employment taxes paid are deductible as an "above-the-line" deduction, a credit is not available.
D is incorrect. Although casualty losses are deductible within limits, a credit is not available.

229. B is correct. (Obj 1 – Type A).

A is incorrect. Penalties actually increase the amount of tax due.
C is incorrect. Deductions reduce gross income in arriving at taxable income.
D is incorrect. Exclusions, such as tax-exempt interest income, reduce the amount of gross income.

230. B is correct. (Obj 1 – Type B).

Tax avoidance is the legal strategy of reducing or eliminating income taxation.

231. D is correct. (Obj 2 – Type A).

Withdrawals from a life insurance policy are usually taxed FIFO basis recovery (basis first).

A is incorrect. The cost basis of a life insurance policy is equal to the total premiums paid.
B is incorrect. The death benefit received from a life insurance policy is generally tax free to the recipient.
C is incorrect. If the policy is a MEC, loans and withdrawals are subject to LIFO basis recovery, meaning the loan or withdrawal will be partially or fully taxable.

232. A is correct. (Obj 2 – Type A).

The death benefit of a life insurance policy is typically 100% income tax-free to the beneficiary.

233. B is correct. (Obj 2 – Type B).

A is incorrect. The 10% early withdrawal penalty will not apply because she is older than age 59½.
C is incorrect. The annuity will be taxed at ordinary income tax rates.
D is incorrect. Contracts entered into after August 13, 1982 are taxed based on the LIFO basis recovery rule.

234. A is correct. (Obj 2 – Type B).

Delores has a total basis in her annuity of $170,000. Since her life expectancy is 16 years, she can recover $10,625 ($170,000 / 16) of her basis per year. Consequently, she will be able to recover $885 ($10,625 / 12) of her basis for each monthly payment received.

Her monthly annuity payment is $1,400, of which $515 ($1,400 total payment received less $885 basis) will be taxable to her.

235. C is correct. (Obj 2 – Type B).

The tax-free portion of an annuity payment is determined by calculating the exclusion ratio.
The exclusion ratio is determined using the following formula:
Exclusion ratio = Investment in the Contract / Expected Return Under the Contract
Exclusion ratio = $200,000 / $500,000
Exclusion ratio = 40%

Therefore, the tax-free portion of the annuity payment is $8,000 ($20,000 annuity payment x 40% exclusion ratio).

A is incorrect. Since Tommy's life expectancy is 25 years, and he will receive $20,000 per year, the expected return under the contract is $500,000 ($20,000 annual payment x 25 years). Tommy's INVESTMENT in the contract is $200,000.
B is incorrect. The exclusion ratio is 40%.
D is incorrect. The taxable portion of the annuity payment is $12,000 ($20,000 annuity payment less $8,000 tax-free portion).

236. D is correct. (Obj 2 – Type B).

Cash value withdrawals and contract loans taken under a nonqualified annuity contract during the accumulation period are considered distributions. These distributions are taxed under the last-in, first-out (LIFO) basis recovery method, meaning earnings are considered distributed first. Stacy currently has $25,000 ($75,000 cash value - $50,000 basis) of earnings in the contract.

Since her distribution was $9,000, the entire amount of the distribution will be taxable in the current year.

237. B is correct. (Obj 3 – Type A).

A is incorrect. Contributions to a Section 529 plan are subject to gift taxes. However, a large contribution is allowed to these plans before any gift tax is actually due.
C is incorrect. Distributions from a qualified tuition program that are used to pay for room and board are tax-free.
D is incorrect. The maximum permitted contribution to a Coverdell Education Savings Account is $2,000 per year.

238. B is correct. (Obj 3 – Type A).

A is incorrect. Contributions to a Section 529 plan are not deductible for federal income tax purposes.
C is incorrect. Most 529 Savings plans are open to residents of any state. For example, a person living in Texas can contribute to the Nebraska Section 529 plan.
D is incorrect. Section 529 plans have much larger contribution limits.

239. C is correct. (Obj 3 – Type A).

There is no such rule.

Note: the exclusion is only meant for those taxpayers with moderate income, as there is an AGI phase-out of the exclusion.

240. D is correct. (Obj 3 – Type A).

A is incorrect. The credit is equal to 20% of up to $10,000 of eligible expenses, resulting in a maximum possible credit of $2,000.
B is incorrect. The lifetime learning credit is not limited to the first two years of education.
C is incorrect. Unlike the American Opportunity Tax Credit, the lifetime learning credit applies on a per-taxpayer basis.

241. C is correct. (Obj 3 – Type A).

A is incorrect. Both the American Opportunity Tax Credit and the Lifetime Learning Credit are not permitted in the same year for the same student.
B is incorrect. The American Opportunity Tax Credit is only available for expenses incurred for the first four years of the student's post-secondary education.
D is incorrect. Up to 40% of the credit is available to taxpayers who do not have an income tax liability.

242. A is correct. (Obj 3 – Type A).

B is incorrect. The corpus of the account is transferred to the beneficiary upon attainment of the state age of majority.
C is incorrect. The account can contain different types of investments, including equities and fixed income investments.
D is incorrect. Gifts made to the UTMA are irrevocable.

243. B is correct. (Obj 3 – Type B).

For purposes of tax-free scholarships, qualified education expenses include: tuition, books, fees, equipment, and supplies.

244. B is correct. (Obj 4 – Type A).

A is incorrect. A fair market rate of interest must be charged.
C is incorrect. Loans must be repaid within five years unless the loan is used to acquire a principal residence.
D is incorrect. A loan will be income tax-free unless defaulted.

245. D is correct. (Obj 4 – Type A).

A is incorrect. The employee is not taxed on employer contributions to a qualified retirement plan at the time the contribution is made. Instead, the employee is taxed at the time amounts are withdrawn from the plan.
B is incorrect. Employer contributions made to the plan are deductible by the employer at the time they are made.
C is incorrect. When earnings are distributed from a qualified plan, the earnings are taxable to the recipient.

246. C is correct. (Obj 4 – Type A).

A is incorrect. The required beginning date for a retired participant is April 1 of the year following the year in which the participant attains age 72.
B is incorrect. There is no such rule.
D is incorrect. Roth IRAs are not subject to the minimum distribution rules as long as the owner is alive.

247. A is correct. (Obj 4 – Type A).

B is incorrect. If an individual is an active participant in a retirement plan, the ability to deduct traditional IRA contributions is phased out based on AGI. The contribution would not be deductible with an AGI of $300,000.
C is incorrect. Contributions to an annuity are not deductible, and therefore would not reduce the individual's current tax liability.
D is incorrect. Contributions to a Roth IRA are not deductible, and therefore would not reduce the individual's current tax liability.

248. D is correct. (Obj 4 – Type A).

A is incorrect. Assets in an irrevocable trust are excluded from the grantor's gross estate for estate tax purposes.
B is incorrect. Once assets are transferred into an irrevocable trust, the grantor can no longer take back the assets.
C is incorrect. Assets inside an irrevocable trust are generally subject to federal income taxation.

249. B is correct. (Obj 4 – Type B).

When a traditional IRA is converted to a Roth IRA, the account owner will be taxed on the earnings accumulated inside the traditional IRA. Andy had accumulated earnings in the traditional IRA of $95,000 ($110,000 value less $15,000 basis). The $95,000 will be included in his gross income. Roth IRA conversions are not subject to a penalty.

250. C is correct. (Obj 4 – Type B).

Brooke has a basis in her traditional IRA of $10,000, which represents the total after-tax contributions to the account. When a distribution is taken from a traditional IRA, the basis is considered distributed pro-rata from the account, based on the following formula:
Basis Distributed = (Total Basis / Total Account Value) * Distribution Taken
Basis Distributed = ($10,000 / $40,000) * $20,000
Basis Distributed = .25 * $20,000
Basis Distributed = $5,000

Therefore, the taxable distribution is $15,000 ($20,000 total distribution less $5,000 basis recovery). The early withdrawal penalty only applies to the portion of the distribution that is included in gross income. Since Brooke is only 42 years old, she will be subject to the early withdrawal penalty on the $15,000 distribution that is included in her gross income.

251. D is correct. (Obj 4 – Type B).

Since Marissa's contributions to the plan were made pre-tax, she does not have a basis in the 401(k) plan. Therefore, the entire plan balance will be taxable when converted to a Roth IRA.

252. D is correct. (Obj 4 – Type B).

Since Jay's contributions were tax deductible, he has no basis in his traditional IRA. Therefore, the entire distribution will be subject to income tax. Since Jay is over age 59½, there is no early withdrawal penalty.

253. C is correct. (Obj 5 – Type A).

A is incorrect. Income in respect of a decedent is included in the decedent's gross estate. However, since it does not receive a step up in basis, the IRD will also be subject to income tax to the recipient.
B is incorrect. IRD includes wages, retirement plans, IRAs, and annuities.
D is incorrect. IRD can result in both estate and income tax on the same income.

254. D is correct. (Obj 5 – Type A).

Income earned but not received as of the date of death is income in respect of a decedent.

A is incorrect. Interest earned by the estate after the death is not considered IRD.
B is incorrect. Capital gain realized after the decedent's death is not considered IRD.
C is incorrect. Wrongful death suits can only arise after the decedent's death, and therefore the proceeds will not be considered IRD.

255. B is correct. (Obj 5 – Type A).

If the fair market value of the property exceeds the donor's basis on the date of the gift (appreciated property), the recipient's basis is the sum of 1) the donor's basis in the property and 2) A portion of any gift tax paid by the donor.

256. C is correct. (Obj 5 – Type A).

A is incorrect. Income from a grantor trust is taxed to the grantor.
B is incorrect. Amounts distributed from a trust retain their character for tax purposes. Therefore, if capital gains are distributed from the trust, they are taxed to the beneficiaries as capital gains.
D is incorrect. Trust income retained by the trust is taxable to the trust at trust income tax rates.

257. C is correct. (Obj 5 – Type A).

Trust income from an irrevocable trust that is accumulated in the trust is generally taxed to the trust. Trust income from an irrevocable trust that is distributed to a beneficiary is generally taxed to the beneficiary.

258. B is correct. (Obj 5 – Type B).

When a done receives a gift of property from a donor, the donee's basis in the gifted property is equal to the donor's adjusted basis (carryover basis). Tara's basis in the stock was $20,000, which was the purchase price of the stock. The basis of $20,000 carried over to Jessica on the date of the gift.

259. C is correct. (Obj 5 – Type B).

If the death benefit is not from life insurance proceeds, the death benefit is fully taxable after being reduced by the decedent's cost basis.

260. B is correct. (Obj 5 – Type B).

The double-basis rule applies to gifts of loss property. Since the double-basis rule applies, the son would use the gain basis of $2,000,000 to calculate gain. Therefore, his gain is $200,000. The gift tax paid is irrelevant because gift tax is only allocated to the recipient's basis if the property given is appreciated property.

261. A is correct. (Obj 5 – Type B).

$30,000 of income will be taxed to Marion. This is a grantor trust, and therefore all of the trust income will be taxed to Marion (the grantor).

Module 10

Practice Exam

TYPE A QUESTIONS

1. Which one of the following statements is correct regarding the renewability feature of a term policy?
   A. This feature allows the insured to renew the policy for a period of time without providing evidence of insurability.
   B. Renewable term insurance is satisfactory for an individual and the insurance company when coverage extends into higher ages.
   C. The premiums will not increase if this feature is used to renew the policy.
   D. The chief function of this feature is to protect the insurance company from adverse selection.

2. Which one of the following represents a common trigger that determines eligibility for benefits under a long-term care policy?
   A. Substantial decline in standard of living due to excessive medical expenses.
   B. Inability to perform two or more activities of daily living.
   C. Inability to engage in any substantial gainful activity for at least one year.
   D. Attainment of age 65, and completion of 10-years of work experience.

3. Which one of the following statements is correct regarding structured settlements?
   A. Because of a structured settlement, an injured party is more likely to become a ward of the state.
   B. Courts cannot influence the method by which the structured settlement payment will be made.
   C. The settlement places the claimant at risk because the payments are typically discontinued after 10-15 years have elapsed.
   D. The settlement may need to be approved by the Centers for Medicare and Medicaid Services (CMS).

4. Which one of the following is the main difference between a traditional IRA and a Roth IRA?
   A. Eligible investment options.
   B. Dollar amount of allowed contributions.
   C. Accumulation of investment income.
   D. Tax treatment of contributions and distributions.

5. Which one of the following actions occurs during the fourth step of the estate planning process (Execute and Monitor the New Estate Plan)?
   A. Estate shrinkage is estimated.
   B. A determination is made if property is included in the probate estate.
   C. Legal documents are drawn up.
   D. The estate owner's intentions are stated.

6. Edward has a 3-year-old daughter that he hopes will attend college at the age of 18. When constructing an investment portfolio for the accumulated education savings, Edward would be wise to:
   A. Invest the portfolio in equity investments, and over time move some of the investments to short-term bonds and cash.
   B. Purchase a single premium deferred annuity and begin taking distributions when the daughter starts college.
   C. Buy a laddered portfolio of Treasury securities.
   D. Invest the portfolio in cash and short-term bonds because education savings should always be invested conservatively.

7. Janet converted her traditional IRA to a Roth IRA. Which one of the following statements is correct regarding the income tax treatment of this conversion?
   A. The conversion will be tax-free and penalty-free.
   B. The conversion will be subject to income tax but will be penalty-free.
   C. The conversion will be tax-free but will be subject to a penalty.
   D. The conversion will be subject to income tax and a penalty.

8. Although many expenses decline during retirement, certain types of expenses may increase. Which one of the following expenses is most likely to increase during retirement?
   A. Taxes.
   B. Work-related expenses.
   C. Medical expenses.
   D. Home ownership expenses.

9. Which one of the following is generally an eligibility requirement for Medicare?
   A. Must work at least 10 years in Medicare-covered employment.
   B. Must have paid Medicare premiums for at least 6 quarters in the 13 quarters before applying for benefits.
   C. Must be age 62 or older.
   D. Must be a U.S. citizen.

10. Dollar cost averaging represents what type of personal financial planning strategy?
   A. Savings and investment planning.
   B. Tax planning.
   C. Retirement planning.
   D. Risk management planning.

11. Many postsecondary education institutions use only the Expected Family Contribution (EFC) formula, while others use the formula in conjunction with the College Scholarship Service (CSS) profile to determine a student's eligibility for private institutional financial aid. Which of the following represents a major difference between EFC and CSS?
   A. CSS factors the student's grades into the analysis.
   B. CSS considers all assets owned by the child.
   C. CSS gives special consideration to the age of the parents.
   D. CSS incorporates the equity in the family home.

12. Stan (age 46) and Jan (age 42), a married couple, file a joint income tax return. Stan earns $50,000 working for a local bottling plant, and Jan earns $4,000 working part-time at a local law firm. Stan participates in the plant's 401(k) plan. How much can Jan contribute to a traditional IRA this year?
   A. $0.
   B. $4,000.
   C. $5,000.
   D. $6,000.

13. Financial risk is uncertainty about the future investment returns of a given asset because of:
    A. Changes in the level of interest rates.
    B. The amount of debt of the organization on which the investment is based.
    C. The lack of liquid assets owned by an organization.
    D. Changes in demand for the company's product or services.

14. Stock issued by a company with a stock price that is less than $1 is referred to as:
    A. Value stock.
    B. Illiquid stock.
    C. Defensive stock.
    D. Penny stock.

15. Which one of the following represents the first step in the financial planning process?
    A. Establishing and prioritizing goals.
    B. Analyzing the current situation.
    C. Developing a plan.
    D. Gathering information.

16. Which one of the following retirement vehicles is subject to both contribution limits and required minimum distributions?
    A. Municipal bond.
    B. Traditional IRA.
    C. Nonqualified annuity.
    D. Roth IRA.

17. The main reason a financial plan must be monitored and revised is because:
    A. Financial circumstances change and priorities shift.
    B. Financial planners require maintenance fees to ensure their practice remains viable.
    C. Federal law requires financial documents to be revised as needed.
    D. Continuing education requirements indicate that financial plans are fluid.

18. Probate costs must be considered when formulating an estate plan for an individual. Probate costs include:
    A. Costs to distribute the estate.
    B. Inheritance taxes.
    C. Estate taxes.
    D. Expenses associated with drafting a valid Will.

19. The waiver of premium provision in a disability income insurance policy:
    A. Enables an insured to purchase additional amounts of insurance without providing evidence of insurability.
    B. Excuses a disabled insured from making premium payments during a period of covered disability.
    C. Allows an insured to increase the benefit as their income increases, based on documented income increases.
    D. Provides additional benefits to the insured when Social Security disability benefits do not apply.

20. Which one of the following is a health insurance plan that allows patients to choose their own healthcare provider and reimburses the patient or provider at a certain percentage for services provided?
    A. Point-of-service plan.
    B. Preferred provider organization.
    C. Health maintenance organization.
    D. Indemnity plan.

21. Which one of the following statements is correct regarding a Coverdell Education Savings Account?
    A. The account is considered an asset of the student in the Expected Family Contribution formula.
    B. The maximum annual contribution is $2,000 per student.
    C. Once initially selected, the beneficiary cannot be changed without incurring taxes and a penalty.
    D. Contributions to the account are deductible for federal income tax purposes.

22. Which one of the following represents a tax-free funding vehicle?
    A. Nonqualified annuity.
    B. Money market account.
    C. Section 401(k) plan.
    D. Municipal bonds.

23. Which one of the following statements is correct regarding the comparison of life insurance and annuities?
    A. The main difference between life insurance and annuities is that there is no pooling of the funds from each annuity contract purchaser.
    B. Life insurance provides a financial hedge against dying too soon, while an annuity provides a hedge against living too long.
    C. The primary function of an annuity is to create an estate or a principal sum, while the primary function of life insurance is to liquidate a principal sum.
    D. An insurance company uses the same mortality table for both life insurance policies and annuities.

24. Which one of the following represents an advantage of a Roth IRA?
    A. An individual can contribute to a Roth IRA, regardless of their adjusted gross income.
    B. No minimum distributions are required to be taken during the account owner's lifetime.
    C. Amounts can be converted from a traditional IRA to a Roth IRA tax-free.
    D. Contributions to the account are deductible for federal income tax purposes.

25. Terri, age 60, purchased a nonqualified flexible premium deferred annuity several years ago. She has paid premiums totaling $20,000 over the years. The annuity was worth $25,000 yesterday. Today, Terri took a $3,000 loan from the annuity to purchase a car. How much of the loan will be subject to federal income taxation?
    A. $0.
    B. $600.
    C. $2,400.
    D. $3,000.

26. An advantage of a defined benefit plan is that:
    A. Contributions are flexible for the employer.
    B. In-service withdrawals are available once the employee attains age 50.
    C. Future benefits can be accurately estimated.
    D. Administrative costs are generally lower than other types of qualified plans.

27. An investor wanting to purchase an investment that focuses on capital appreciation with some investment income should purchase:
    A. Silver.
    B. Common stock.
    C. Government bond.
    D. Fine art.

28. If an irrevocable trust pays income to the trust beneficiary, the income is typically taxed to the:
    A. Beneficiary.
    B. Grantor.
    C. Trustee.
    D. Trust.

29. Which one of the following statements is correct regarding level term life insurance?
    A. If a convertibility provision is available, the policy can be converted to permanent insurance upon proof of insurability.
    B. It offers a cash value from which a policyowner can make withdrawals or take a loan.
    C. The annual premium charged initially is higher for longer term rate guarantee periods than for shorter rate guarantee periods.
    D. The death benefit under the policy decreases by a level amount over the term of the policy.

30. If a financial planner is attempting to determine a client's appropriate emergency fund, the best resource to determine the amount of the emergency fund is a:
    A. Balance sheet.
    B. Credit card statement.
    C. Net worth statement.
    D. Income statement.

31. Which one of the following statements is correct regarding Medicare Part C plans?
    A. They are financed through payroll taxes.
    B. They allow a retiree to qualify for coverage prior to age 65.
    C. They may offer more coverage than Part A and Part B, such as dental coverage.
    D. They are typically less expensive than coverage under Part A and Part B combined.

32. Which one of the following statements is correct regarding the Expected Family Contribution formula?
    A. The formula weighs the parent's assets and student's assets equally.
    B. The formula weighs the parent's assets up to 3 times more heavily than the student's assets.
    C. The formula only incorporates assets owned by the student.
    D. The formula weighs a student's assets up to 6 times more heavily than the parent's assets.

33. Many postsecondary institutions use only the Expected Family Contribution (EFC) formula to determine financial need, while others use the formula in conjunction with the College Scholarship Service (CSS) profile to determine eligibility for financial aid. One difference between these two methodologies is that the CSS:
    A. Considers the grade point average of the student.
    B. Considers the equity in the family home and qualified retirement plans.
    C. Ignores the assets and income of the student.
    D. Only considers applications for financial aid to attend private universities.

34. Which one of the following statements is correct regarding the taxation of annuity death benefits?
    A. The death benefit is fully taxed to the beneficiary, regardless of the decedent's cost basis in the annuity.
    B. The death benefit is received by the beneficiary income tax-free due to a step-up in basis at the time of death.
    C. The death benefit is taxed to the beneficiary only to the extent they exceed the decedent's cost basis in the annuity.
    D. The death benefit is not subject to income tax but is subject to a 10% penalty at the time of death.

35. Which one of the following statements is correct regarding the differences between a qualified and nonqualified annuity?
    A. Qualified annuities can only be purchased by individuals age 55 and older, while nonqualified annuities can be purchased by individuals at any age.
    B. Premiums for a nonqualified annuity may or may not be deductible, while premiums for a qualified annuity are always deductible.
    C. Individuals who sell qualified annuities must register with the SEC, while individuals selling nonqualified annuities need not register.
    D. Qualified annuities are typically subject to the required minimum distribution rules, while nonqualified annuities are not.

36. Which one of the following represents a social insurance program that must be incorporated into a risk management plan?
    A. Life insurance.
    B. Annuities.
    C. Health insurance.
    D. Medicaid.

37. Which one of the following is required information when estimating the cost of a four-year college education?
    A. Rate of increase in the Consumer Price Index.
    B. Number of years until enrollment.
    C. Marginal income tax rate of the parents.
    D. Rate of return on investments.

38. Which one of the following statements is correct regarding education funding vehicles?
   A. Contributions to a Section 529 plan are not subject to gift taxes.
   B. Room and board expenses are not eligible expenses for purposes of the Series EE bond interest exclusion.
   C. Distributions from a qualified tuition program that are used to pay for room and board are taxable.
   D. The maximum permitted contribution to a Coverdell Education Savings Account is $5,000 per year.

39. A 20-year certain annuity will provide:
   A. A guaranteed rate of return for a period of up to 20 years.
   B. Payments to the annuitant's beneficiary for five years if the annuitant dies 15 years after the annuity start date.
   C. Payments to the annuitant that will last no longer than 20 years.
   D. Lifetime payments to the annuitant beginning 20 years after the annuity purchase.

40. If an employee elects to defer a portion of their salary into a Roth 401(k) plan, the employee contributions are:
   A. Tax deductible and the subsequent distributions during retirement are taxable.
   B. Non-deductible and the subsequent distributions during retirement are taxable.
   C. Tax deductible and the subsequent distributions during retirement are tax free.
   D. Non-deductible and the subsequent distributions during retirement are tax free.

41. Which one of the following statements is correct regarding lawsuit judgments paid in either the form of a lump sum or a structured settlement annuity?
   A. While lump sum payments are tax free for federal income tax purposes, structured settlements in the form of an annuity are taxable as ordinary income.
   B. Structured settlement annuities typically present high risk to the annuitant because they are issued by negligent parties who often do not have the means to satisfy the required payments.
   C. One of the advantages of using annuities in a structured settlement is that there is a lower probability the annuitant will become a burden on society.
   D. Courts in most states are no longer permitted to require a structured settlement, as the risk of default by the negligent party is too great.

42. For a young, unmarried individual with no debt and no dependents, which one of the following represents the best reason to purchase permanent life insurance?
   A. The premiums are tax deductible.
   B. The policy will help the individual focus on maintaining a healthy lifestyle.
   C. The cash value can be used as part of a successful retirement plan.
   D. The policy can provide income replacement in the event of disability.

43. Which one of the following investments is insured by the Federal Deposit Insurance Corporation?
   A. Fixed annuity.
   B. Bank certificate of deposit.
   C. Municipal bond.
   D. Series EE savings bonds.

44. Which one of the following statements is correct regarding the tax treatment of disability income insurance benefits?
    A. When premiums are paid with pre-tax dollars, the benefits are tax free.
    B. When premiums are paid with after-tax dollars, the benefits are tax free.
    C. When premiums are paid with after-tax dollars, the benefits are taxable at ordinary income tax rates.
    D. When premiums are paid with pre-tax dollars, the benefits are taxable at capital gain rates.

45. Some types of investments are subject to inflation risk. Which one of the following statements about inflation risk is most accurate?
    A. Assets that emphasize capital appreciation are less susceptible to inflation risk than fixed rate investments.
    B. Investors should be primarily concerned with historical rates of inflation when determining inflation risk.
    C. The more stable the rate of inflation, the higher the inflation risk for any particular investment.
    D. The rate of inflation is typically measured by the growth of the S&P 500 stock index.

46. Which one of the following statements is correct regarding planning for the funding needs to meet postsecondary education goals?
    A. The rate of inflation associated with education costs has been lower than the general rate of inflation over the last few decades.
    B. The average cost of attending a vocational trade school is higher than the average cost of attending a university.
    C. The lower the investment rate of return earned on education savings, the more that will need to be saved to meet a future funding goal.
    D. Online schools typically offer a significant tuition savings over brick-and-mortar schools.

47. When determining an individual's income tax liability, which one of the following would usually be the largest amount?
    A. Adjusted gross income.
    B. Itemized deductions.
    C. Gross income.
    D. Interest income.

48. For a young, newly married couple with no children, which one of the following typically represents the primary focus of personal financial planning?
    A. Long-term care costs.
    B. Saving for retirement.
    C. Saving for a major purchase.
    D. Implementing estate planning techniques.

49. When determining the annual savings needed to successfully fund a retirement, which of the following would be subtracted from the targeted income amount in arriving at the retirement income shortfall?
    A. Current fair market value of home.
    B. Pension and Social Security income.
    C. Anticipated medical expenses.
    D. Traditional IRA balance.

50. If an individual elects to defer Social Security benefits beyond their full retirement age, their benefits will increase by:
    A. 4% for each year they are deferred.
    B. 8% for each year they are deferred.
    C. 10% for each year they are deferred.
    D. 12% for each year they are deferred.

51. When determining life insurance needs, which one of the following is considered a final expense when an insured dies?
    A. Paying off a mortgage balance.
    B. Funding education of children.
    C. Paying funeral expenses.
    D. Creating an emergency fund.

52. A certificate of deposit is an example of a:
    A. Tax-deductible, tax-deferred funding vehicle.
    B. Currently taxable funding vehicle.
    C. Tax-deferred funding vehicle.
    D. Tax-free funding vehicle.

53. If a policy continuation provision of a disability income insurance policy indicates the insurer is required to renew the policy at each anniversary, but may change the premiums, this represents a policy that is:
    A. Guaranteed renewable.
    B. Noncancelable.
    C. Conditionally renewable.
    D. Renewable without prejudice.

54. The maximum annual purchase limit for Series EE savings bonds per individual is:
    A. $2,000.
    B. $5,000.
    C. $8,000.
    D. $10,000.

55. Which one of the following statements is correct regarding unemployment risk?
    A. Unemployment risk is a potentially catastrophic risk that can affect multiple areas of a financial plan.
    B. Most individuals manage unemployment risk through the purchase of private insurance.
    C. All state government unemployment programs are uniform.
    D. Most unemployment benefits last for two or more years.

TYPE B QUESTIONS

56. Tom contributed the maximum allowable pre-tax amount to his 401(k) plan in the current year to lower his current tax liability. Tom has implemented the tax planning strategy of:
   A. Tax deferral.
   B. Tax avoidance.
   C. Tax evasion.
   D. Tax development.

57. Five years ago, Sara purchased stock in a publicly traded company for $50,000. The stock has paid a dividend to Sara of $2,000 over the years. Today, she sold the stock for $45,000. Sara has a:
   A. Realized capital loss of $5,000.
   B. Realized capital loss of $3,000.
   C. Unrealized capital gain of $5,000.
   D. Unrealized capital loss of $3,000.

58. Jennifer and her brother, Harris, purchased real estate together for $300,000. Jennifer paid $200,000 for the property, and Harris paid $100,000, and each can prove their contribution. Jennifer died when the property was worth $900,000. What is the value of the real estate that will be included in Jennifer's gross estate for estate tax purposes?
   A. $200,000.
   B. $300,000.
   C. $600,000.
   D. $900,000.

59. Lori is considering an investment in a common stock. She is considering the following stocks:

Name	Share Price	Beta	Return
Stock A	$13.50	1.2	12%
Stock B	$25.00	1.0	9%
Stock C	$22.36	0.9	14%
Stock D	$20.25	1.3	11%

If Lori's goal is to invest in a stock with the lowest systematic risk, what would be the best option?
   A. Stock A.
   B. Stock B.
   C. Stock C.
   D. Stock D.

60. Mack and his wife Sally have four children. They have decided to give $200,000 of cash to each of the four children this year. Assuming an annual exclusion of $15,000, what is the total amount of the gift that is subject to gift tax?
   A. $0.
   B. $680,000.
   C. $748,000.
   D. $800,000.

61. Stan and Cindi, a married couple, retired several years ago. They fund their annual expenses with a combination of Social Security benefits, employer-sponsored retirement plan benefits, and an annuity. They want to take an expensive vacation and are wondering which account to withdraw the money. Their goal is to minimize the income taxes associated with the withdrawal, since they are currently in a high income tax bracket. From which of the following accounts should they take the needed funds?
    A. Currently taxable account.
    B. Roth IRA.
    C. Annuity.
    D. 401(k) plan.

62. Jamie, age 25, is interested in saving for her retirement. She currently earns a salary of $50,000 and is willing to set aside $5,000 per year to fund her retirement. Her employer offers a Section 401(k) plan, with a dollar-for-dollar match up to 5% of compensation. Which of the following retirement savings vehicles should Jamie first consider when saving for her retirement?
    A. Traditional IRA.
    B. Nonqualified deferred annuity.
    C. Roth IRA.
    D. 401(k) plan.

63. ABC Corporation wants to establish a retirement plan that closely resembles an IRA. The company would like to make all the contributions to the plan and would like to make higher annual contributions each year than those permitted under a traditional IRA or Roth IRA. Which of the following would be the most appropriate plan for ABC Corporation?
    A. 401(k) plan.
    B. Simplified employee pension plan.
    C. 403(b) plan.
    D. Employee stock ownership plan.

64. At the time of his death, Stan bequeathed shares of ExTell stock worth $500,000 to his daughter Susan via his Will. Assuming this was the only bequest to Susan from her father, what is Susan's primary concern?
    A. Making sure she has sufficient cash to pay capital gain taxes if the stock were sold immediately.
    B. Depositing the stock into a traditional IRA or Roth IRA within 60 days of receipt.
    C. Diversifying her concentrated portfolio.
    D. Transferring the stock to an irrevocable trust to provide creditor protection.

65. Which one of the following individuals would be eligible to make a $5,000 contribution to a traditional IRA?
    A. John, an unmarried 40-year-old individual, whose only income is $60,000 of dividends.
    B. Kristen, a college student who earns $3,500 from a part-time job.
    C. Sandra, an unemployed homemaker, whose husband earns a $100,000 salary.
    D. Bob, an unmarried 55-year-old individual, who only income is $100,000 of rental income.

66. Sonny, age 60, is retired and he uses his pension income to fund his current living expenses. He would like to upgrade his home theatre, which will cost $25,000. Assuming his main priority is to minimize his tax consequences, which one of the following accounts should he use to obtain the $25,000?
   A. 401(k) plan.
   B. Traditional IRA.
   C. Roth IRA.
   D. Taxable brokerage account.

67. The parents of a five-year-old girl are determining the amount that needs to be saved for a college education. One year of tuition costs $20,000 in today's dollars, and the girl will begin college in 13 years. Assuming an education inflation rate of 5%, what will be the future value cost of her freshman year in college?
   A. $25,525.
   B. $28,421.
   C. $37,713.
   D. $48,132.

68. Janice received an inheritance from her recently deceased father. She would like to purchase an annuity with the inheritance. Her objectives are:
- Leave a lump sum inheritance to her children at her death.
- Prevent the insurance company from receiving a sizeable profit in the event she dies in the near future.
- Avoid investment risk.

The most appropriate type of annuity for her to purchase is a:
   A. Variable annuity.
   B. Single life annuity.
   C. Refund annuity.
   D. Joint annuity.

69. A retired individual has the following assets:
- Cash - $10,000
- Traditional IRA - $20,000
- 401(k) plan - $500, 000
- ABC Company stock (held long-term) - $30,000

If the individual needs $20,000 to repair his home, what would be the best withdrawal strategy if the goal is to minimize income taxes?
   A. Withdraw $10,000 from the cash account and $10,000 from the ABC Company stock holdings.
   B. Withdraw $20,000 from the traditional IRA.
   C. Withdraw $20,000 from the 401(k) plan.
   D. Withdraw $10,000 from the 401(k) plan and $10,000 from the ABC Company stock holdings.

70. A financial planning professional was approached by Tom, a 70-year-old individual who is terminally ill. Tom asked the professional to evaluate his existing estate plan. Which one of the following actions would be an important part of the evaluation of the existing estate plan?
    A. Determine if all estate taxes have been paid.
    B. Create an irrevocable trust to hold Tom's life insurance policies.
    C. Elect the appropriate date to value Tom's assets for estate tax purposes.
    D. Categorize Tom's property as probate property or non-probate property.

71. Ken purchased a long-term care insurance policy that contains a 30-day elimination period. The policy pays Ken $200 per day for covered treatment. During the current year, Ken experienced the following events:
    - February-March – spent 60 days in a drug addiction treatment facility.
    - July-October – spent 110 days in a nursing home because of injuries sustained in a boating accident.

What amount would be covered under the policy?
    A. $12,000.
    B. $16,000.
    C. $28,000.
    D. $34,000.

72. Dennis has $30,000 that he plans to set aside as an emergency fund. He is willing to take on some investment risk in order to earn a higher rate of return on these funds, but he has decided to limit his choices to highly liquid investments with relatively little risk to the principal. Which one of the following types of investments would be most likely to generate the highest rate of return for his emergency fund investment?
    A. Checking account.
    B. Certificate of deposit.
    C. Money market mutual fund.
    D. Short-term bond mutual fund.

73. Johnny, age 31, has $60,000 he wants to invest in tax-advantaged securities that emphasize income over capital appreciation. He currently makes the maximum allowable contribution to his 401(k) plan sponsored by his employer. Which one of the following securities would allow him to receive a relatively stable level of income while at the same time minimizing his current year tax liability?
    A. High-yield bond mutual fund.
    B. Series EE savings bonds.
    C. Municipal bonds.
    D. U.S. Treasury bills.

74. Stuart and Joanna, both aged 33, are considering appropriate funding vehicles for their three-year-old daughter Carla's college education expenses. They would like to purchase life insurance that could be used to meet both their premature death loss exposure goals and their education expense funding goals. Stuart and Joanna have a long-term planning horizon and are risk tolerant. Which one of the following types of life insurance would be most appropriate based on their objectives?
    A. Variable universal insurance.
    B. Decreasing term insurance.
    C. Whole life insurance.
    D. Annual renewable term insurance.

75. A manufacturing company announced that it was laying off 5,000 workers because of a fire that occurred in its main production facility. The company's common stock price immediately declined by 10% per share. The decline in share price is an example of:
    A. Purchasing power risk.
    B. Business risk.
    C. Credit risk.
    D. Reinvestment rate risk.

TYPE A QUESTIONS

1. A is correct. (Module 2 – Obj 1).

The main function of a renewability feature of a life contract is to ensure that the insured may renew without a medical exam or evidence of insurability as long as the renewal is within the periods outlined in the contract, and there has been no lapse in payment of premiums.

B is incorrect. Insurance companies typically do not allow renewals beyond a certain age.
C is incorrect. If a term policy is renewed, the premiums will most likely increase upon renewal.
D is incorrect. The chief function of the renewability provision is to protect the insurability of the named insured.

2. B is correct. (Module 3 – Obj 4).

Many long-term care policies have one or both of the following coverage triggers:
-Inability to perform two or more activities of daily living.
-Cognitive impairment.

3. D is correct. (Module 2 – Obj 5).

A is incorrect. Because of a structured settlement, an injured party is less likely to become a ward of the state.
B is incorrect. In cases involving minors, courts can require a structured settlement to guarantee income, rather than a lump sum award.
C is incorrect. Structured settlements are often paid in the form of an immediate annuity that lasts for the claimant's lifetime.

4. D is correct. (Module 6 – Obj 4).

Roth IRA contributions are always nondeductible, while a traditional IRA has contributions that may be deductible. Distributions from a Roth IRA are tax-free if certain conditions are satisfied, while distributions of earnings from a traditional IRA are always taxable.

5. C is correct. (Module 7 – Obj 2).

A is incorrect. Estate shrinkage is estimated during the "Formulate and Test a New Estate Plan" phase.
B is incorrect. A determination is made if property is included in the probate estate under the "Evaluate the Existing Estate Plan" phase.
D is incorrect. The estate owner's intentions are stated during the "Gather Facts" phase.

6. A is correct. (Module 5 – Obj 1).

The further the saver is to the funding need, the more aggressively the portfolio allocations should be.

7. B is correct. (Module 8 – Obj 4).

When a traditional IRA is converted to a Roth IRA, previously untaxed contributions are subject to income taxation in the year of conversion. No premature distribution penalty applies.

8. C is correct. (Module 6 – Obj 2).

Expenses for healthcare (medical), travel and entertainment, and hobbies often increase during retirement.

9. A is correct. (Module 3 – Obj 4).

B is incorrect. There is no such requirement.
C is incorrect. Medicare is generally available to individuals upon attainment of age 65, not age 62.
D is incorrect. In order to be eligible for Medicare, an individual can be either a U.S. citizen, or a non-citizen who is a permanent resident of the U.S.

10. A is correct. (Module 1 – Obj 2).

Dollar cost averaging represents a savings and investment planning strategy. It involves the systematic purchase of the same dollar amount of a security on a periodic basis.

11. D is correct. (Module 5 – Obj 3).

CSS incorporates the equity in the family home, the value of qualified retirement plans, and the income and assets of noncustodial parents.

12. D is correct. (Module 6 – Obj 4).

Traditional IRA contributions are typically limited to the amount of earned income, up to $6,000. However, a spousal IRA does not require the IRA owner to have any earned income. Since Jan is married to Stan, her earned income includes Stan's earned income. Therefore, Jan is eligible to make a full $6,000 contribution to her traditional IRA.

13. B is correct. (Module 4 – Obj 2).

A is incorrect. Interest rate risk is uncertainty about the future investment returns of a given asset because of changes in the level of interest rates.
C is incorrect. Liquidity risk is uncertainty about the future investment returns of a given asset because of the lack of liquid assets owned by an organization.
D is incorrect. Business risk is uncertainty about the future investment returns of a given asset because of changes in demand for the company's product or services.

14. D is correct. (Module 4 – Obj 4).

Penny stock is stock trading for a price less than $1. These stocks are generally illiquid and are very risky.

15. A is correct. (Module 1 – Obj 4).

The personal financial planning process begins by establishing and prioritizing goals.

16. B is correct. (Module 6 – Obj 1).

A is incorrect. A municipal bond is not subject to contribution limits and is not subject to required minimum distributions.
C is incorrect. A nonqualified annuity is not subject to contribution limits and is not subject to required minimum distributions.
D is incorrect. A Roth IRA is subject to contribution limits but is not subject to required minimum distributions.

17. A is correct. (Module 1 – Obj 4).

The main reason a financial plan must be monitored and revised is because financial circumstances change and priorities shift.

18. A is correct. (Module 7 – Obj 1).

Probate costs include costs to distribute the estate and costs to defend against challenges to the Will.

19. B is correct. (Module 3 – Obj 1).

A is incorrect. A guaranteed insurability provision enables an insured to purchase additional amounts of insurance without providing evidence of insurability.
C is incorrect. A future increase option allows an insured to increase the benefit as their income increases, based on documented income increases.
D is incorrect. A Social Security Supplemental Coverage provision provides additional benefits to the insured when Social Security disability benefits do not apply.

20. D is correct. (Module 4 – Obj 2).

An indemnity plan is a health insurance plan that allows patients to choose their own healthcare provider and reimburses the patient or provider at a certain percentage for services provided.

21. B is correct. (Module 5 – Obj 4).

A is incorrect. The account is considered an asset of the parent in the Expected Family Contribution formula.
C is incorrect. If the beneficiary is an eligible family member, the beneficiary can be changed without incurring taxes or a penalty.
D is incorrect. Contributions to a Coverdell Education Savings Account are not deductible for federal income tax purposes.

22. D is correct. (Module 6 – Obj 2).

A is incorrect. A nonqualified annuity is a tax-deferred funding vehicle.
B is incorrect. A money market account is a currently taxable funding vehicle.
C is incorrect. A Section 401(k) plan is a tax-deductible, tax-deferred funding vehicle.

23. B is correct. (Module 2 – Obj 5).

A is incorrect. Annuity contracts and life insurance contracts both rely on a pooling of funds arrangement to provide benefits.
C is incorrect. The primary function of an annuity is to liquidate a principal sum regardless of how it was created. The primary function of life insurance is to create an estate.
D is incorrect. Different mortality tables are used for life insurance and annuity calculations.

24. B is correct. (Module 6 – Obj 4).

A is incorrect. Unlike a traditional IRA which permits contributions for individuals regardless of adjusted gross income, the ability to contribute to a Roth IRA is phased out based on the individual's adjusted gross income.
C is incorrect. Roth IRA conversions are taxable.
D is incorrect. Contributions to a Roth IRA are never deductible.

25. D is correct. (Module 8 – Obj 2).

When a loan or withdrawal is taken from an annuity during the accumulation phase, all taxable gain is deemed distributed on an interest-first basis before any tax-free cost basis is distributed (LIFO basis recovery).

The amount of interest earned in the annuity was $5,000 ($25,000 value less $20,000 basis). Therefore, the first $5,000 withdrawn or borrowed by Terri is fully taxable as ordinary income. Since Terri borrowed $3,000, the entire amount is taxable as ordinary income.

26. C is correct. (Module 6 – Obj 3).

A is incorrect. A disadvantage of a defined benefit plan is that employer contributions are inflexible.
B is incorrect. In-service withdrawals are typically not permitted with a defined benefit plan.
D is incorrect. Maintenance costs of a defined benefit plan are typically higher than other qualified plans because a defined benefit plan requires an actuary and PBGC insurance.

27.B is correct. (Module 4 – Obj 1).

A is incorrect. Silver offers capital appreciation but does not offer any investment income.
C is incorrect. Government bonds offer investment income with some potential for capital appreciation.
D is incorrect. Fine art offers capital appreciation but does not offer any investment income.

28.A is correct. (Module 8 – Obj 5).

Unless the trust is a grantor trust, the income from the trust is taxed either to the trust or to the beneficiary. If the income is retained by the trust, it is taxed to the trust. If the income is paid to the beneficiary, it is taxed to the beneficiary.

29.C is correct. (Module 2 – Obj 1).

A is incorrect. Evidence of insurability is not required to convert a term to a permanent insurance policy, if a convertibility provision exists in the policy.
B is incorrect. Term policies are temporary policies, and therefore do not offer a cash value.
D is incorrect. The death benefit remains constant with a level term life insurance policy.

30.D is correct. (Module 1 – Obj 1).

An emergency fund is typically based upon 3-6 months of expenses, depending on the client. The income statement would reflect a client's expenses and can be used to estimate an appropriate amount for an emergency fund.

31.C is correct. (Module 3 – Obj 3).

A is incorrect. Medicare Part C plans are financed in part by premiums paid by the insured.
B is incorrect. Medicare Part C plans are generally available upon attainment of age 65.
D is incorrect. An individual enrolling in Part C must pay Medicare Part B premiums and generally must pay an additional premium for added services offered under Part C.

32.D is correct. (Module 5 – Obj 3).

The Expected Family Contribution formula weighs a student's assets up to 6 times more heavily than the parent's assets.

33.B is correct. (Module 5 – Obj 3).

The CSS profile considers:
-Equity in the family home
-Qualified retirement plans
-Income and assets of noncustodial parents
-Taxed and untaxed income for the two previous years

34. C is correct. (Module 8 – Obj 2).

Any payment a beneficiary receives on the annuity that exceeds the decedent's cost basis is taxable to the beneficiary. An annuity does not receive a step-up in basis at the time of death.

35. D is correct. (Module 2 – Obj 4).

A is incorrect. Both types of annuities can be purchased at any age.
B is incorrect. Premiums for a nonqualified annuity are never deductible, while premiums for a qualified annuity may or may not be deductible.
C is incorrect. Regardless of whether an annuity is qualified or nonqualified, only a variable annuity requires registration.

36. D is correct. (Module 1 – Obj 3).

The following types of social insurance programs must be incorporated into a risk management plan:
-Social Security.
-Medicare and Medicaid.
-Unemployment insurance.

A is incorrect. Life insurance is a type of private insurance product.
B is incorrect. Annuities are a type of private insurance product.
C is incorrect. Health insurance is a type of private insurance product.

37. B is correct. (Module 5 – Obj 1).

A is incorrect. The education inflation rate, not the rate of increase in the Consumer Price Index, is needed when determining the cost of funding a college education.
C is incorrect. Although it may be helpful when determining the appropriate education savings vehicles to implement, it is not necessary to know a client's current income tax bracket when determining the costs of a college education.
D is incorrect. Although the rate of return on investments is important in determining the amount needed to FUND a college education, this information is not required in determining the actual cost of the education itself.

38. B is correct. (Module 8 – Obj 3).

A is incorrect. Contributions to a Section 529 plan are subject to gift taxes. However, a large contribution is allowed to these plans before any gift tax is actually due.
C is incorrect. Distributions from a qualified tuition program that are used to pay for room and board are tax-free.
D is incorrect. The maximum permitted contribution to a Coverdell Education Savings Account is $2,000 per year.

39.B is correct. (Module 2 – Obj 4).

An annuity certain guarantees that payments will last for a minimum of the number of years in the guarantee. Therefore, if the annuitant dies 15 years after beginning the annuity, and the annuity is a 20-year certain annuity, the annuitant's beneficiary will continue to receive payments for another 5 years. If the annuitant lives beyond the 20-year guarantee, payments will continue for the remainder of the annuitant's life.

40.D is correct. (Module 6 – Obj 3).

Contributions to a Roth 401(k) plan are non-deductible. These contributions are included in the employee's income and taxed immediately. However, subsequent distributions from the Roth 401(k) plan (for example, distributions received during retirement) are tax free when received.

41.C is correct. (Module 2 – Obj 4).

A is incorrect. Both lump sum and structured settlements in compensation for personal physical injury or illness are not taxable. However, the interest income on a lump sum payment is taxable.
B is incorrect. Structured settlement annuities typically present low risk to the annuitant because they are issued by insurance companies.
D is incorrect. Courts can and often do require a structured settlement to guarantee regular income to the victim.

42.C is correct. (Module 1 – Obj 3).

For an individual that has no dependents and no debt, life insurance is not necessarily needed for income replacement. However, permanent life insurance could be used to build up a cash value that could be accessed during retirement.

43.B is correct. (Module 5 – Obj 4).

Bank accounts, including checking, savings, and CDs, are all insured by the FDIC.

44.B is correct. (Module 3 – Obj 1).

When disability insurance premiums are paid with after-tax dollars, any benefits received under the policy are income tax free. When disability insurance premiums are paid with pre-tax dollars, any benefits received are taxed at ordinary income tax rates.

45.A is correct. (Module 4 – Obj 2).

B is incorrect. What should matter most to investors is what inflation will be over the life of the investment, not the historical inflation rate.
C is incorrect. The more stable the rate of inflation, the lower the inflation risk for any particular investment.
D is incorrect. Inflation is typically measured by the consumer price index (CPI).

46.C is correct. (Module 5 – Obj 1).

A is incorrect. The education inflation rate has been higher on average than the general rate of inflation applicable to other goods and services.
B is incorrect. A university is more costly than a vocational trade school.
D is incorrect. Online schools do not offer much tuition savings over brick-and-mortar schools.

47.C is correct. (Module 8 – Obj 1).

Gross income is the starting point for federal income tax. It represents all income from whatever source derived.

A is incorrect. Adjusted gross income represents gross income REDUCED by various deductions. Therefore, gross income would be higher than adjusted gross income.
B is incorrect. Itemized deductions include deductions such as charitable contributions and real estate taxes. Although it is theoretically possible that itemized deductions could exceed gross income, this is extremely rare.
D is incorrect. Gross income includes interest income, so the gross income amount would be larger than interest income.

48.C is correct. (Module 1 – Obj 1).

Typically, a primary focus for a young, married couple with no children is saving enough money for a major purchase, such as a home.

49.B is correct. (Module 6 – Obj 2).

When determining the annual savings needed to successfully fund a retirement, the income target is first determined by multiplying the current earned income by a replacement percentage. The income target is then reduced by anticipated pension and Social Security benefits to arrive at the retirement income shortfall amount.

50.B is correct. (Module 6 – Obj 5).

If an individual elects to defer Social Security benefits beyond their full retirement age, their benefits will increase by 8% for each year they are deferred. Therefore, if an individual's full retirement age is 67, and they defer their Social Security benefits until age 70, their benefit will be increased by 24% (8% x 3 years).

51.C is correct. (Module 2 – Obj 2).

The following are considered final expenses:
-paying estate taxes and estate settlement expenses.
-paying funeral expenses and final medical bills.
-provide income to surviving family members.
-making charitable and noncharitable bequests.

52.B is correct. (Module 6 – Obj 1).

Currently taxable funding vehicles are purchased with after-tax dollars. The earnings are taxable in the year in which they are credited.

Examples of currently taxable vehicles include:
-certificates of deposit.
-savings accounts.
-money market accounts.

53.A is correct. (Module 3 – Obj 1).

B is incorrect. With a noncancelable policy, the insurer cannot change the premium and is required to renew the policy at each anniversary.
C is incorrect. With a conditionally renewable policy, the insurer can increase the premium and change the policy terms at renewal. In addition, the insurer may cancel the contract if the conditions for renewal are not met.
D is incorrect. Renewable without prejudice is not a type of policy continuation provision.

54.is correct. (Module 5 – Obj 4).

The maximum annual purchase amount for Series EE savings bonds is $10,000.

55.A is correct. (Module 1 – Obj 3).

B is incorrect. Unemployment risk is managed through state unemployment compensation programs.
C is incorrect. States differ with respect to coverage and benefits.
D is incorrect. Although states differ, benefits are typically limited in duration to one year or less.

TYPE B QUESTIONS

56.A is correct. (Module 8 – Obj 1).

Tax deferral represents the delay of income taxation until a later date. By contributing to the 401(k) plan, Tom will lower his current tax liability. However, when Tom takes a distribution from his 401(k) plan in the future, he will pay income tax at that time.

57.A is correct. (Module 4 – Obj 1).

Sara sold the stock, and as a result has a realized gain or loss. Since she sold the stock for $45,000, and purchased the stock for $50,000, she has a realized loss of $5,000. The dividends received by Sara were taxed to Sara when she received them, and since she retained the cash (as opposed to reinvesting the cash), the dividends will not affect her gain or loss.

58.C is correct. (Module 7 – Obj 3).

Under the consideration furnished rule, the property is included in the decedent's gross estate based on the consideration furnished for the property.

Jennifer contributed $200,000 towards the purchase of the property, which represents 2/3 of the purchase price. Therefore, 2/3 of the date of death value will be included in Jennifer's gross estate.

Inclusion = ($200,000/$300,000) x $900,000 = $600,000

59.C is correct. (Module 4 – Obj 4).

Beta is a statistic that measures only systematic risk. The stock with the lowest beta has the lowest systematic risk.

60.B is correct. (Module 7 – Obj 3).

Since Mack and Sally are married, they can each take advantage of the annual exclusion. Therefore, the annual exclusion that can be used for each gift is $30,000 ($15,000 x 2).

The portion of each gift that is subject to gift tax is $170,000 ($200,000 gift less $30,000 annual exclusion).

Since four gifts were given, the total amount is $680,000 ($170,000 x 4).

61.B is correct. (Module 8 – Obj 4).

When a couple is in a high income tax bracket, they would normally withdraw funds from either a currently taxable account, or a Roth IRA. The currently taxable account will usually result in taxes paid at favorable capital gains rates. However, since their goal is to minimize income taxes, they should withdraw the funds from the Roth IRA, since the withdrawal will be income tax-free.

62. D is correct. (Module 6 – Obj 1).

All of the vehicles listed are excellent vehicles for accumulating a retirement fund. However, Jamie should first consider putting money into her Section 401(k) plan. The contributions are made on a pre-tax basis and she will be able to take advantage of the employer matching contribution.

63. B is correct. (Module 6 – Obj 3).

A SEP is a retirement plan that is a type of IRA but permits contributions up to the greater of 25% of compensation or the dollar limit applicable to defined contribution plans.

64. C is correct. (Module 8 – Obj 5).

A is incorrect. When Stan died, his stock received a step-up in basis.
B is incorrect. Susan does not need to deposit the stock into an IRA. In addition, the IRA contribution limits are well below $500,000.
D is incorrect. If Susan transferred the stock to an irrevocable trust, this would be considered a completed gift and would be subject to gift tax. There is no indication that Susan desires to gift the stock.

65. C is correct. (Module 6 – Obj 4).

Although Sandra does not have compensation, she can attribute her husband's compensation to herself, and establish a spousal IRA.

A is incorrect. An individual can only contribute to an IRA to the extent they have compensation. Dividend income is not considered compensation income.
B is incorrect. An individual can only contribute to an IRA to the extent they have compensation. Since she only earns $3,500 from her part-time job, she will not be eligible to make a full contribution to the traditional IRA.
D is incorrect. An individual can only contribute to an IRA to the extent they have compensation. Rental income is not considered compensation income.

66. C is correct. (Module 6 – Obj 5).

A Roth IRA offers tax-free distributions. Distributions from a 401(k) plan or traditional IRA would be taxable. In addition, if assets in a taxable brokerage account were sold to generate the $25,000 needed, any gain on the sale would be taxable.

67. C is correct. (Module 5 – Obj 2).

The present value can be determined using the following keystrokes on an HP-10BII calculator:
[SHIFT], C ALL (clears the calculator)
20000, +/-, PV (enters -$20,000 as the cost of college in today's dollars)
13, N (enters 13 as number of years until college begins)
5, I/YR (enters 5% as inflation rate; no need to enter this as a percentage, just enter the whole number)
FV (displays the solution to the question)

The future value equals $37,713.

68.C is correct. (Module 2 – Obj 3).

A is incorrect. A variable annuity would subject Janice to investment risk.
B is incorrect. A single life annuity would end at the time of Janice's death. This would prevent her from being able to leave something to her children at the time of her death.
D is incorrect. Janice's goal is to leave an inheritance at the time of her death. A joint annuity would not accomplish this goal as it would leave a stream of payments to a survivor (not a lump sum).

69.A is correct. (Module 6 – Obj 5).

Withdrawals from the traditional IRA and 401(k) plan would be fully taxable as ordinary income. The cash account can be accessed without paying any taxes, and any gains associated with the sale of ABC Company stock would be taxed at favorable capital gain rates.

70.D is correct. (Module 7 – Obj 2).

A is incorrect. Estate taxes would not be payable until after Tom's death.
B is incorrect. An irrevocable trust may be an appropriate strategy, but this would not be an action that would be performed during the "Analyze the Existing Estate Plan" phase of the estate planning process.
C is incorrect. The valuation date of assets would not be determined until after Tom dies.

71.B is correct. (Module 3 – Obj 4).

Long-term care policies typically exclude coverage for services for alcoholism or drug addiction. The nursing home stay, however, would be covered under the policy.

Therefore, coverage would apply as follows:
Covered amount = (Covered Days – Elimination Period) x Daily Coverage Amount
Covered amount = (110 – 30) x $200
Covered amount = (80) x $200
Covered amount = $16,000

72.D is correct. (Module 1 – Obj 2).

The short-term bond mutual fund would likely pay a higher rate of return than the other choices because a short-term bond fund would be a riskier investment.

A is incorrect. A checking account is a type of cash equivalent. Cash equivalents generally offer a lower rate of return in comparison to fixed income investments.
B is incorrect. A certificate of deposit is a type of cash equivalent. Cash equivalents generally offer a lower rate of return in comparison to fixed income investments.
C is incorrect. A money market mutual fund is a type of cash equivalent. Cash equivalents generally offer a lower rate of return in comparison to fixed income investments.

73.C is correct. (Module 4 – Obj 4).

A is incorrect. A high-yield bond mutual fund would provide income, but not necessarily a stable income. In addition, the income received would be taxable.
B is incorrect. Series EE savings bonds would not provide a stable level of income.
D is incorrect. Treasury bills would provide income, but the income would be taxable.

74.A is correct. (Module 2 – Obj 3).

Variable universal insurance would provide flexibility in premiums and benefits (universal) and the ability to invest the cash value in equities and fixed income securities. Term insurance would be less appropriate given their long-term planning horizon.

75.B is correct. (Module 4 – Obj 2).

Business risk is the exposure a company has to factor(s) that will lower its profits or lead it to fail. Anything that threatens a company's ability to achieve its financial goals is considered a business risk. Business risk is a type of unsystematic risk.

This page intentionally left blank